UNEARTHING CANADA'S HIDDEN PAST

A Short History of Adult Education

Information on how to obtain copies of this book is available at:

Website:	http://www.thompsonbooks.com
E-mail:	publisher@thompsonbooks.com
Telephone:	(416) 766-2763
Fax:	(416) 766-0398

Library and Archives Canada Cataloguing in Publication

Welton, Michael Robert, 1942-

Unearthing Canada's hidden past: a short history of adult education / Michael Welton.

Includes bibliographical references.

ISBN 978-1-55077-228-9

      1. Adult education--Canada--History.   I. Title.

LC5254.W44 2012   374.971   C2012-906576-5

Production Editor:	Katy Bartlett
Cover Design:	Michelle Lynch
Copy Editor:	Gillian Buckley

Every reasonable effort has been made to acquire permission for copyrighted materials used in this book and to acknowledge such permissions accurately. Any errors called to the publisher's attention will be corrected in future printings.

We acknowledge the support of the Government of Canada through the Book Publishing Industry Development Program for our publishing activities. We also acknowledge the support of the Government of Ontario through the Ontario Media Development Corporation Book Initiative.

Printed in Canada.

1 2 3 4 5   18 17 16 15 14 13 12

UNEARTHING CANADA'S HIDDEN PAST

A Short History of Adult Education

Michael Welton

THOMPSON
PUBLISHING

TABLE OF CONTENTS

Preface: What a Journey This Has Been!, vii

Introduction, xiii

1. **Reclaiming Our Past: Memory, Tradition, Kindling Hope, 1**
    Memory, Tradition, Identity, 1
    Rendering the Invisible Visible, 5
    The Place of History in the Training of Adult Educators, 8

2. **Encounters in the New World (1492–1760), 11**
    First Encounters: New Worlds, Old Maps, 12
    Cunning Pedagogics: The Encounter Between the Jesuit Missionaries and the Amerindians of Seventeenth-Century New France, 17
    "A Country at the End of the World": Living and Learning in New France, 1608-1760, 20

3. **Adult Learning in the Age of Improvement (1760–1880), 29**
    "Extending the Circle of Conversation": Agricultural Education in Nova Scotia in the Eighteenth and Nineteenth Centuries, 34
    Mechanics' Institutes and the Opening up to Science and Technology, 36
    The Education of Public Opinion, 44
    Benign Improvement or Persistent Antagonism? First Nations Under Colonialism, 45
    Learning Traditions Among African Nova Scotians Under Bitter Conditions, 52

4. **Adult Learning in the Age of the "Great Transformation" (1880–1929), 59**
    The Education of the Working Man, 68
    Educating for a Brighter New Day: Women's Organizations as Learning Sites, 82
    Pioneers and Pedagogues: Carrying the University to the People, 95

5. **Adult Learning and the Crisis of Democracy (1929–1960), 115**
    On the Eve of a Great Mass Movement, 120
    An Authentic Instrument of the Democratic Process: Outward to the Nation with the Citizens' Forum, 129
    "Real Adult Education Springs from the Heart and Pains of the People:" The Antigonish Movement and the Impossible Dream, 136
    Adult Education and Union Education: Aspects of English-Canadian Cultural History in the Twentieth Century, 156
    Intimations of the Just Learning Society: Guy Henson and Watson Thomson's State-Supported Projects, 160

Adult Education in a Chilly Climate: The Cold War Era, 171

**6. Adult Learning Under Siege in a Disorded World
   (1960–2012), 183**
   Media with the People: Challenge for Change / Société Nouvelle, 190
   The Emergence of Academic Study of Adult Learning and Education, 196
   *In Defence of Civil Society: Canadian Adult Education in Neo-Liberal
       Times, 210*
   Pioneers of the Learning Age, 222
   Pedagogical Advice for Perilous Times, 227

What a Journey This Has Been!

This short history of Canadian adult learning and education has been brewing for a long time. It started in the early 1980s, while I was doing doctoral studies in educational history at the University of British Columbia. There I completed my research on the educational thought and practice of Watson Thomson in the 1930s and 1940s. Shocked at how dynamic (and even radical) Thomson and many of his comrades in the Canadian Association for Adult Education (CAAE) were, my thirty-year venture into trying to understand how one could conceptualize the field of study of adult education had begun. And what a journey this has been!

Only a small number of adult education theorists in Canada and round the world have actually been interested in adult educational history. E. A. ("Ned") Corbett, the first director of the Canadian Association for Adult Education in 1935, must be acknowledged for his interest in Canadian adult educational history. He wrote articles—one raised the pertinent question of "But, is it adult education?"—thus signalling the difficulty of conceptualizing "adult learning." Corbett (1992; see Rouillard [1952]) also did profiles of some of our now mostly forgotten pioneers of adult learning. George Boyle also wrote popular texts on the co-operative movement; his biography of *Father Jimmy Tompkins of Nova Scotia* (1953) is lively and speaks in the vernacular of its day. Corbett and Boyle's works were inspirational in nature. J. Roby Kidd, who assumed directorship of the CAAE officially in 1951, followed in his mentor's footsteps. While the head of OISE's Department of Adult Education from the late 1960s until the early 1980s, Kidd encouraged doctoral work in such areas as Mechanics' Institutes, University Extension, and the origins of the CAAE. I have tried to make use of these theses and dissertations now buried dustily in the archives.

By the end of the 1970s, the historiographic winds had blown much dust from the fusty discipline of history. The old history—basically histories of the evolution of the nation state and how great men had led Canada from colony to nation—was unsettled as new questions and methods were introduced. The rebellions of the 1960s, with young intellectuals re-discovering Marx and the Frankfurt School as well as gaining energy from various anti-colonial movements, began to write "history from below." This meant—for labour or feminist historians—that they had to rediscover those without voice or prestige. I began historical studies at the age of thirty-seven in 1979 after two years of theological study, a stint with CUSO in Nigeria, teaching at Seneca Community College, and working with an innovative program for Natives and Metis at Brandon University in Manitoba.

E. P. Thompson's *The making of the English working class* (1963) was the keystone text for many young historians (like Bryan Palmer and Greg Kealey). They rejected the idea that men and women were mere victims, and they explored the culture of the working class in order to see the full and complex range of the lives of ordinary people. Feminist history was also born in this era. Early works revealed the lives of working women and themes such as the "feminization of teaching" became popular. From this point onward, social history has explored every nook and cranny of Canadian lives. This, in turn, has led to problems of fragmentation and over specialization, leading to the loss of a coherent understanding of Canadian history. This has been rectified to some extent by Ian McKay's offering of the "Liberal Order Framework" as organizing paradigm for writing Canadian history (from the mid-nineteenth century onward). I write as a social and intellectual historian; I have benefitted from McKay's notion of the Liberal Order. I have also quite consciously given my own shape to writing the history of adult learning and education in Canada. I am interested in burrowing in our past in order to ferret out our emancipatory tradition and struggles that mobilized the people to seek enlightenment and take action to make the world more just.

I had the good fortune while teaching at Dalhousie University to publish *Knowledge for the People* in 1987, which offered nine case studies (from 1828-1973). It was my first venture into structuring ways of seeing the unfolding of adult education. In 1992, I edited *Educating for a Brighter New Day: Women's Associations as Learning Sites* to integrate women's experience, movements and learning into a previously patriarchal construction. Teaching graduate seminars in the history of Canadian adult education also forced me to think holistically—what were the central components of the field of adult educational history? I also pursued studies in critical learning theory, drawing primarily on Jurgen Habermas' scholarly work (1984 and 1987) to fashion a new way of seeing adult learning in social and historical context. Habermas' core concepts— system and lifeworld, instrumental and communicative learning, active citizenship and public spheres—are evident in this book. Habermas' recasting of historical materialism as an evolutionary social learning theory has led me into seeing historical unfolding and contemporary dynamics—be they pathologies, problems, accomplishments—through his optic. In *In Defense of the Lifeworld: Critical Perspectives on Adult Learning* (1995), I argued that the central task in our time is to defend the lifeworld from its colonization and damaging from "the System" by which Habermas means the economic and administrative systems that are governed by an instrumental logic. The system concept enables adult learning theorists to gain conceptual clarity on the early Canadian society as we observe the particular way the fur trade penetrated into indigenous lifeworlds, disrupting their balance and throwing all relationships askew. For Habermas, the lifeworld is the reservoir of culturally transmitted and linguistically organized meaning patterns where cultures learn to make sense of the world, acquire the knowledge and skills to be competent persons, and learn the norms and values of the given society.

Participants in the lifeworld take for granted the language and way things just are. What is crucial for Habermas, however, is that the lifeworld is governed by communicative forms of action. People determine the norms and values they live by, unlike the logic of administrative or economic systems which operate behind our backs. As societies modernize, the relationship of worker and citizen to the system worlds becomes more opaque. There people learn the myths and narratives that give depth to their lives. The lifeworld can also be rationalized. By this, Habermas means that a critical inquiry can lead men and women to question their norms and values, and change their ways of being and doing (Welton, 2005, pp. 180-209).

Another Habermas-inspired theme that is central to the history of adult learning and education is the struggle for recognition. Opened up recently by Axel Honneth (1995), this theme enables us to capture central learning motivations in many of our great social movements, from the "great awakening" of women in the early twentieth century to the struggles of First Nations peoples throughout our history. It is also foundational to human well-being: with self-confidence as bedrock, and self-respect flowing from a society that respects individual and collective rights and self-esteem.

While at Mount St. Vincent University, I wrote a course on historical perspectives on Canadian adult education for our new, distance-based graduate program in 1996. This gave me further opportunity for synthesis and conceptual work. During the late 1990s, I was researching and writing books on Father Jimmy Tompkins (*Father Jimmy: Life and Times of Jimmy Tompkins* [1997]) and Moses Coady of the Antigonish Movement

(*Little Mosie from the Margaree: A Biography of Michael Moses Coady* [2001]); and was certainly aware that most of the time our general histories stop at around 1828—the birth of Mechanics' Institutes in Canada. They also exclude women, First Nations, and other ethnic groups (such as African Canadians), and Quebec is often in the far distance. Alas, this forced me to set out to think through how I could re-imagine the movement of Euro-Christians (explorers, missionaries, settlers, governing agents, habitants) into the new world of Canada in the early sixteenth century as a pedagogical encounter, as a communicative venture between two very different learning systems. I had known that missionaries have been some of our most courageous adult educators (though in a post-Christendom and post-colonial era they were looked at somewhat askance). I thought that it might be fruitful to dig into the sources and analyze the Jesuits as adult educators in seventeenth century New France. I also became convinced that the colonial Canadian state can best be understood as a pedagogue in its own right. Through its various agents and projects, the Canadian state sought to regulate and discipline the minds and bodies of the First Nations peoples (as well as others). To paraphrase Marx, we never learn under circumstances of our own choosing.

I knew that as an Anglo-Canadian historian that I had not written much on New France or Quebec. By writing a case study of New France from 1608 to 1760, I could learn to think about a learning society that did not use any discourse of adult education, or even have anything that to us might look an adult education institution. I felt confident in proceeding because I knew that human beings, wherever they were in time and space, had to live their lives in some form of community and express themselves. I admit that it is not easy to write about learning that occurs informally or that is woven into the activities of life itself. One has to extrapolate to what extent and how the learning to be a voyageur or canal worker or farmhand or ballet dancer occurred. These studies on European encounters with the new world and learning in New France served, then, as preparatory studies for this book. They gave me enough confidence to think that I might be able to write a history from colonialism to the information age.

Two intersecting disciplines—history and critical social theory—have enabled me to think about the learning dynamics of feudal and industrializing societies. When the opportunity to write an undergraduate history course on Canadian adult education for Athabasca University arose in 2009, I took the opportunity to see if I could, with all the problems that such a work entails, craft an intelligible framework and a compelling story. This book is the result of those efforts; the vexing nature of this task is good reason why it has not been attempted before. It reflects my way of seeing our adult learning and education tradition. It is not a comprehensive history: that would require many researchers and many volumes, but this is a beginning.

It could also not have been written without the love of my wife, Carmen. My close friend Bruce Spencer also encouraged me, mostly gently, to do this crazy project. My former colleague and long-time friend, Donovan Plumb, has been a consistent dialogue companion for twenty years. I am grateful to Delvina Bernard, an African-Nova Scotian, who assisted me with understanding Black history. Budd Hall, Deb Bartlette, Patti Gouthro, and Tom Nesbit, good friends and colleagues, have also encouraged me and fed me some meaty insights (and teasing). Leona English sent me two of her recent essays on Newfoundland adult education history just as I was finishing the book. I am thankful to her. I also acknowledge the support of Keith Thompson, who is a great friend of adult education in Canada. I also consider him my good friend.

References

Boyle, G. (1953). *Father Jimmy Tompkins of Nova Scotia.* New York: P.J. Kenedy and Sons.

Corbett, E. A. (1992). *Henry Marshall Tory: A biography.* Edmonton (AB): University of Alberta Press.

Habermas, J. (1984). *The theory of communicative action. Volume 1: Reason and the rationalization of society.* Boston: Beacon Press.

Habermas, J. (1987). *The theory of communicative action. Volume 2: Lifeworld and a system: A critique of functionalist reason.* Boston: Beacon Press.

Honneth, A. (1995). *The struggle for recognition: The moral grammar of social conflict.* Oxford: Polity Press.

Lotz, J. & Welton, M. (1999). *Father Jimmy: Life and times of Jimmy Tompkins.* Sydney (NS): Breton Books.

Rouillard, H. (1952). *Pioneers of adult education.* Toronto: Nelson and Sons.

Thompson, E.P. (1963). *The making of the English working class.* New York: Vintage.

Welton, M. (Ed.). (1995). *In defense of the lifeworld: Critical perspectives on adult learning.* Albany (NY): State University of New York Press.

Welton, M. (2001). *Little Mosie from the Margaree: A biography of Michael Moses Coady.* Toronto: Thompson Educational Publishing.

Welton, M. (2005). *Designing the just learning society: A critical inquiry.* Leicester (UK): NIACE Publishers.

Introduction

Canada has one of the most illustrious, experimental, and innovative traditions of adult education in the world. Our experiments and projects are viewed as exemplary by international observers. Ironically, Canadians know very little about these struggles to create a vibrant and dynamic learning society. Today we speak easily of living in the learning age, a knowledge society and an information age. We celebrate learning that is lifelong, life-wide, and learner-centred. But we are unaware of how a vision has evolved into its present complex and intricate system. Indeed, global elites contend that adult learning holds the key to the twenty-first century.

This "short history" will provide an overview of adult learning and education from the sixteenth century to the twentieth. We will learn about "uncommon schools," and be encouraged to think about how men, women, and children learned in different times and places. We will learn to break out of our own "schooled imaginations" as we consider how our foremothers and forefathers learned to make a living, live their lives, and express themselves, often in difficult and taxing circumstances.

In this book we do not limit our attention to formal adult education projects. Rather, we start from the premise that all societies, from primeval times to the present, are evolved learning systems. Learning both precedes schooling and cannot be contained in its professionalized boxes. The well-known typology of formal, non-formal and informal learning signals this expansive mode of thinking. It opens the way to see what might be hidden if we were simply searching for the "seeds of the present in the garden of the past." Our net is cast wide, and our challenge is to invent new ways of understanding how adults learned before and during the age of formalized schooling.

One must be careful not to think of adults too abstractly. As children and adults, as men and women, we are always situated in worlds where inequities abound. From its beginnings as a white settler colony, Canada has been a class-based, patriarchal, and racialized society ruled and dominated by economic, political, and cultural elites. The forms of knowledge—whether of governance, of the sacred, of the natural world, or of how we ought to relate to each other in our differences—have often been monopolized by the few at the expense of the many. Elites have

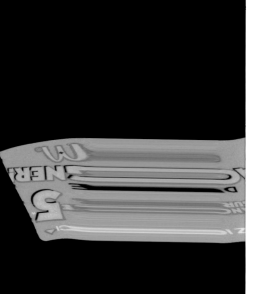

sought to exercise hegemony over those below through controlling what their subordinates learn about a world that might, to them, appear rather indifferent to their needs and interests.

Throughout Canadian history there has been a fundamental contest over what counts as knowledge and who ought to know in the first place. Thus there is a "great debate" at the heart of our collective existence. We can speak of a struggle weaving its way as a red thread through the past five hundred years of our history. This struggle has been essentially about people's huge efforts to create and sustain pedagogical social and learning space that would enable them to gain some mastery over their life situations. Elites have always sought to maintain tight control over the "circle of learning" in order to maintain their power over others. Those below and those on the outside have fought hard to widen the societal circle of conversation. Class control of pedagogical space is a primary form of conflict that pervades our history. Historians also maintain that we ought to be attentive to two other threads, pink and multicoloured, that also weave through our history: gender and ethnic relations. Women have had to struggle incessantly to achieve their full potential as human beings with the right to all forms of knowledge and vocational mastery. And those of non-European origins, First Nations and many others, have found themselves outside the halls of power, circles of conversation, wealth, knowledge, good work, and recognition.

This critical historical analysis of Canadian adult learning and education enables us to speak of discordant and outcast pedagogies. Discordant pedagogies arise in the tense interplay between dominant elites and those below. Those below contest and challenge the hegemony exercised over them. Outcast pedagogies, while having some oppositional traits, are more oriented to survival and adaption to really difficult circumstances (when most of a community's learning energies and resources are mobilized to stay alive and afloat). These discordant and outcast pedagogies arise in the tense interplay between dominant elite control of knowledge and learning processes and the forms of knowledge of those who are the objects of control or domination.

In Canadian history we will have many opportunities to examine this essential learning dialectic. In fact, the modern country of Canada arises out of the pedagogical encounter between Europeans and people of the First Nations. Beginning many thousands of years ago, people of the First Nations created an intricate learning system to create and sustain their existence: a tribal wilderness learning system. These indigenous knowledge forms consisted of rich myths and stories, rituals, ceremonies, and ways of being with the earth. This pedagogical encounter between European and First Nations was not an equal exchange. The learning history of Canada is born in coercive pedagogies and the corollary pedagogies and spiritualities of resistance (as well as fusion of various kinds).

The learning dynamics of Canadian society cannot be fully grasped without understanding the conflictual nature of our history. The great splits in human existence—class, gender, and race—appear to play themselves out in the way Canadians have sought to organize various forms of pedagogical space. Wherever one looks along our historical landscape—Cartier's perception of the Indians he met, the Jesuit missionary enterprise in seventeenth century New France, the initiatives in agricultural education in the late eighteenth century, the heroic role of the Black Church, the rise of the Mechanics' Institutes everywhere in Canada, the emergence of workers' education, leftist socialist parties and Frontier College, the uprising of women's voluntary associations, the agrarian radical movements, the great extension initiatives at the universities of Saskatchewan and Alberta, the community-based folk schools, the remarkable emergence of the Antigonish Movement in eastern Nova Scotia, and the contemporary scene of complex ecological and other social movements (such as land claim projects)—one cannot escape the fact of struggle at the heart of our society.

In fact, the learning dialectic of Canadian society suggests that the common people have had to work hard to create, along with visionary leaders, the learning infrastructure that meets their need to participate in the making of the world. The liberal democratic, multicultural society we inhabit at the beginning of the twenty-first century did not drop out of heaven. Anglo-Canadian elites have been reluctant to open the doors of learning and wisdom to those of differing ethnicity. The rights and equalities we currently enjoy were fought for, often bitterly. Mainstream historians often miss the "learning matrix" out of which social welfare policies and justice projects have grown.

Historians try to identify salient features of a particular time. It is rather common, for example, to highlight the fundamental nature of the economy as a way of delineating one period from another. We can speak of early industrial society, or of a colonial mercantile economy, and, more recently, of a new form of capitalism, the knowledge-based society. Each of these forms of society has to organize its learning system to produce men and women who are capable of making a living, living their lives well, and expressing themselves. The nature of the learning and the form of the organization of pedagogical space itself is shaped by the state of the evolution of our cognitive understanding of nature and social organization. We cannot imagine a project such as an agricultural society without presupposing the emergence of the science of chemistry and its application to understanding and managing soils and plants. We cannot understand our contemporary commitment to the rights of the individual apart from the Enlightenment's secularization of the core Judeo-Christian vision that humans were made in "God's image." The great axial events of Western history—the Protestant Reformation, the Scientific Revolution, and the Enlightenment—have shaped the contours and outlook of Canadians.

For example, we cannot imagine Mechanics' Institutes without understanding the new ethos of improvement that swept through nineteenth century England and its colonies. Both of these initiatives—agricultural societies and Mechanics' Institutes—were projects of a democratic impulse to expand the circle of learning. They were important, but contested, learning sites. One can construct a configuration (for the mid-nineteenth century) that would link Mechanics' Institutes with the appearance of scientific institutes, museums, exhibitions, fairs, literary societies, and churches. These configurations, then, are interrelated and did provide some of the learning resources that some men and women drew upon to live in their worlds. Adults were sliding out from under the gaze of elites and organizing their own forms of mutual instruction, or struggling to open space for themselves within existing associations. Moreover, these configurations remain specific to distinct parts of the country; Halifax or Montreal in the mid-nineteenth century was rather far removed from the dark forest tribal communities of the Pacific Northwest.

Reading this book, the reader will move inside the process whereby Canadians, high and low learned in their everyday lives—in spaces and places they created to learn something new as well as in the formally authorized sites that gradually emerged in Canadian society (universities, technical institutes, and so on). This book begins with Europe's first encounters with new land and peoples in the early sixteenth century, then travels and winds its way into the present. Along the way we will meet many different kinds of adult educators with a rather amazingly diverse set of purposes and intentions. Many are voices now silent or forgotten. The historian's task is to remember them. Given the scope of this survey—from the world of Columbus and Cartier to Steve Jobs and Facebook—one must face the troublesome issue of inclusion and exclusion. Stories of African Canadians, Chinese immigrants, and First Nations are woven into this history. But the learning and action projects of many of our ethnic groups and voluntary associations are not highlighted. The ethnic groups in Canada have many resources to help understand how their learning networks and institutions intersected with mainstream ones. I have attempted, within the range of my time, resources, and scope of this short history, to redress somewhat the criticism that much of Canadian adult education history has been largely the story of visionary white men (like Moses Coady or Alfred Fitzpatrick). Hopefully readers might be encouraged to dig into their own communities and backgrounds to uncover the richness of learning resources and experiences.

I hope to persuade readers that adult learning is not marginal to our understanding of the evolution of Canadian society. We need to "deschool" our imaginations in order to grasp the subtleties and nuances of adult learning—in informal, non-formal, and formal modes. This book also celebrates our learning capacities as human beings. There is much dynamite in adult education, and some of it is here. The reader ought to know, as well, that I have used many of my previously published and unpublished writings to create the fabric of this text. The sources are all listed in the bibliographies at the end of each chapter.

1
Reclaiming Our Past: Memory, Tradition, Kindling Hope

Can history provide a vantage point from which we can understand present trends and practices? Does the past speak to the present? If so, how? Does historical consciousness provide us with essential insight and deep understanding of how to act morally and ethically in our own time? Renowned British social historian Eric Hobsbawm (1994) said that the "destruction of the past is one of the most characteristic and eerie phenomena of the late twentieth century. Most young men and women at the century's end grow up in a sort of permanent present, lacking any organic relation to the public past of the times they live in. This makes historians, whose business it is to remember what others forget, more essential at the end of the second millennium than ever before" (p. 3). Canadians often know little about their own history, and even less, perhaps nothing much at all, about adult educational history.

History is about who we are, our identity, our connection to time and space. Historians are, first and foremost, storytellers. In this book, we explore the bewildering theme that the richness of our adult educational heritage has remained relatively un-mined. We will learn that Canadians have been bold inventors of new kinds of teaching practices, and imaginative adaptors of what they have learned from others. Finally, we examine the usability of the past for our present roles as educators and citizens. The fundamental sensibility required of us is openness to enter the worlds of those in the past to see how they responded to the learning challenges of their time. What did they know that we may have forgotten?

Memory, Tradition, Identity

The world we currently inhabit is convulsive, unpredictable, and rather dangerous. We appear to be living in wild, screaming, apocalyptic times. Very few secure anchor points exist any longer. The teachings of ancient sages about impermanence and insecurity and widespread suffering seem apt for our day. Karl Marx's famous mid-nineteenth century aphorism—"All that is solid, melts into the air"—is truer now than perhaps ever before. We are living and learning our way through a time of great global troubles and dangers. Yet we also see signs throughout the world of a deep, hopeful yearning for dignity, mutual respect, and the right to full participation in society. We have seen tyrants toppled in the Middle East, and the Occupation movement break out in the chaotic streets of many countries of the world. Old certitudes and taken-for-granted assumptions about the future—whether pertaining to the future configuration of the geopolitical world order, our precarious jobs, future opportunities for our children, or the fate of the earth itself—are eroding. New forms of social movements erupt, fusing social media and street meetings.

In his important book, *The Past in Ruins: Tradition and the Critique of Modernity,* David Gross (1992) writes of the forces at work in the West that attempt to erase our memories of anything other than what is present to us. But tradition has always been central to human life. It has helped provide the beliefs and guidelines for conduct that link generation to generation. It has helped meld us as persons into deeply bonded communities. Tradition reminds us of the kind of questions our forebears asked about the collective meaning of their lives. It is really only in recent times that one hears that tradition itself is evaporating and can no longer prevent the social fabric from disintegrating. To be sure, some celebrate the "end of tradition" because it appears to free us from the cages of archaic ways of thinking and being in the world. Yet one can easily exaggerate the demise of tradition, or fail to recognize its presence, or perceive its shadows across intellectual and built landscapes.

Glance around a modern city like Halifax. See the towering spire of the Roman Catholic Cathedral on Barrington Street. Its architecture reminds us of ancient texts and truths. Notice the graveyard next to the cathedral where some have lain for centuries, several of them victims of the sinking of the *Titanic.* As you stroll along the ocean front, you round the point and notice cast iron cannons pointing out to the harbour's entrance. Our memories drift to a bygone era. The gleaming grey steel naval ships in the harbour meld into the wooden ships filling the harbour centuries ago. Walk further along the path and notice the War Memorial. It reminds us of the deaths of men and women in the "great wars." Fading wreaths, placed lovingly at the monument's base, keep our memories of sacrifice and heroism alive. Think, too, of the museums, statues, festivals, music, and art where the different cultures represent the stories of their lives and experience. A film like *Margaret's Museum* keeps alive our memories of suffering and struggle for love and justice in the coal mines of Cape Breton. The presence of indigenous people's drumming at their contemporary ceremonies creates echoes of the ancient past by linking them with ancestral spirits and us with them in their humanity and longing. African Heritage month speaks of the centuries-old presence of African-Canadians in our midst. Their stories of pain and triumph add to the rainbow of Nova Scotian (and Canadian) peoples.

It is easy for the Western anthropologist to think that we, in the modern West, are rather narratively thin. Northwest Coast Aboriginal cultures, including peoples such the Haida, Kwakiutl, and Tsimshian (I am using the old orthographic spelling), invented marvellous stories about where they came from, who they were, and what it meant to live on earth among killer whales and a plenitude of sea life. Many of their stories were about the origins of things and intricate tales of that uncanny trickster, the Raven, who taught the people lessons about the subtleties of power and moral intention. These stories were embodied in the awesome totem poles, fabulous creatures piled one on another, each deeply meaningful for the people of that place and time. Many of European ancestry sensed they were in the presence of something sacred when they first sighted these poles standing over villages tucked into isolated bays along the rugged northwest coast forests. Aboriginal peoples have their storytellers, but where are ours? It is obvious that we, too, are surrounded by our stories. We fill our children's lives with storybooks. Even if we didn't, the popular culture (television, film, video games) would do it for us. Scripts are everywhere, teaching many conflicting things. The colossal impact of *Star Wars* (and now *Lord of the Rings*) and the stunning success of the Harry Potter series of books and films certainly lends support to Joseph Campbell's claim that human beings cannot live without myths. Deep down, we all love the romantic narrative (where the hero triumphs in the end, the antagonist is vanquished, and the world is made right). But the romantic narrative or plot structure is only one of several choices facing the historian (the others are comedy, tragedy, irony, and satire). The technical term historians use for the choice of narrative is "emplotment" (White, 1973).

Those living in post-traditional societies distinguish fabulous tales and legends (like ghost stories) from stories about people and events that actually happened (history). We know that myths contain truths (kernels in husks), but we do separate myth and history. Even when we move on the ground of stories about what actually happened, contemporary historians inform us that there is usually "something added" to the "objective events." History can be poetic, and the facts in themselves do not magically tell the "one best story." The historian is also a fabricator, one who uses language at hand, with its vast stock of historical devices, tropes, and tricks, to craft an appealing and persuasive narrative. But history, unlike myth or legend, keeps scraping to find the facts of the situation. How many died at the battle of the Somme or Gallipoli? How many people participated in the study clubs? Did so-and-so actually say that?

Our goal as historians is to tell the truth about events and people, but we know that, finally, we can never get it right (truthfulness about history always places the historical narrative in dialogical tension with myths— or outright lies—about the past). The struggle over the meanings of history is particularly poignant in conflict situations in different parts of the world, now and in times past. Power and interest tend to creep into narrative construction. Although it is difficult to establish the rightness of any version of any story, be it of one's own life or that of others, three criteria can help us in this task: coherence, believability, and empirical adequacy. New data that surfaces from the archives can always wreck someone's story, if that story has been censored for one reason or another. Thus, we can also see that storytelling is a political act. Those with power, who triumph over others, may get to have their stories prevail, but that only means other stories have gone underground.

During the past three decades, the notion that one could construct a grand, unifying narrative of Canada's political evolution as a nation-state literally crumbled. Silenced groups (workers, women, minorities) sought to recover their buried, forgotten, or repressed pasts and position themselves in the dominant narrative. Each group had (potentially) its own history; history from the bottom up speaks to us with eloquent fierceness and anger about oppression, suffering, and exclusion. Many excluded voices are clamouring to be included in the stories being told about inhabiting this place called Canada. When oppositional histories first appeared in the 1960s and 1970s, historians sought to include the contributions of women, workers, or minorities. Margaret MacMillan's eloquent exploration of the "history wars" in *The Uses and Abuses of History* (2008) captures the constructed nature of narrative beautifully.

This "contributionist approach" was often allied with perceptions of the excluded other as victim. But if women, First Nations, Blacks, or any colonized people simply occupy the victim position, how would it have been possible for them to resist? Thus, recently feminist, Black, and Native historians have shifted their focus to more complex analyses of human beings as agents. For example, contemporary scholarship on land-claim disputes and the sorrowful history of residential schools indicates that natives made their own arguments, understood what their children needed, and sought to resist various political manoeuvres to steal their land and refashion their children (see C. Harris, *Making Native Space: Colonialism, Resistance, and Reserves in British Columbia* [2002]). We are being pressed, perhaps in the deepest spiritual sense, to re-story our lives, nations, traditions. The unfinished tapestry of late-modern global society is in the process of being re-woven and re-coloured. New strands are being added and old ones re-twisted. This is true of Canadian history in general and it is true of the history of adult learning and education in particular.

In the last decade or so, the field of Canadian history has been fragmented. The Canadian professional historian community is grappling with how to best narrate our past, now that so many different monographs have been written in social and cultural history. This has led Ian McKay to offer the "Liberal Order Framework" as a potential unifying narrative structure (see Constant and Ducharme, 2009). For adult education historians, this new synthesis (one of many possibilities) recognizes that civil society is a learning space. There is a virtual treasure trove of material still un-mined in the history of Canadian adult education. There are many archives of material to be discovered, and the fact that so little of this history has been written is bewildering.

Rendering the Invisible Visible

If the world is going to be changed, it is not the children who will do it. Moses Coady and other Canadian visionary adult educators discovered this truth deep in their bones when they faced head-on the intertwined economic and social crises of their societies in the agonizing 1930s. This idea that children cannot be society's redeemers is more pertinent now than ever. Lifelong learning is the hallmark of our society. We live longer, and our learning capacities as human beings stretches well beyond our early schooling and encompasses the life-wide dimensions of living well. Adult learning is central to the way society reproduces itself over time and to the way it changes or responds to various crises within the system (the realm of economy and polity) and the lifeworld (the realm of family, voluntary associations, public spheres, social movements, and sacral institutions).

It is not a simple matter to figure out what "adult education history" ought to be about. The easiest route, and one that is followed by many historians of adult education, is to begin in the present and look to the past to identify institutional precursors to the modern practice. This is called "whig history": the past is dimly lit, and history is a tale of the progressive unfolding of an enlightened world. Some historians of schooling are interested only in those institutions in the past that seem to be similar to what we have in the present. Yet, this approach presents serious problems if you want to know how and what and where children learned in the seventeenth and eighteenth centuries. Children, in fact, did not attend schools for most of human history. Likewise, adult educational historians face the problem that though adults have always been learning, the idea of "adult education" as a conscious, intentional practice (and professional field of study) is a relatively new idea. The professionalization of adult education (its entry into the university as a field of study) did not occur until the mid-1950s. They named this upstart new discipline "andragogy" to demarcate it from "pedagogy" (Welton, 2010).

The peculiar problem of adult educational historians is that their object of study, unlike those who study schools, does not remain consistent through time. Thus, it should not be a surprise that we find adult education historians squabbling over definitions of the field, or arguing about what forms of adult education should be included within the field's boundary. For example, those adult educators who see adult education as a professionalized field of practice are inclined to omit certain forms—such as workers' education or social movements—from their master narrative of adult education. Only those institutions that are intimations of professionalized things to come are worthy of analysis. One can see, too, how one's values will influence what one sees in the past as an important learning site. As E. H. Carr (1961) reminds us a half century ago, "we can view the past, and achieve our understanding of the past, only through the eyes of the present" (p. 28). The historian's job is always to make sense of people's thoughts and actions in context. We have to recognize that all of us inhabit a specific time and space; we are thrown into the world already constituted and alive with ways of seeing. We are captive to the prejudices and limitations of our own time. Knowing this makes us, at least potentially, more compassionate towards our forebears. Carried too far, the historian who sees in the past only in terms of things present will not understand the past on its own terms.

The American educational historian, Lawrence Cremin (1977), writes that "history is always the history of something in particular, and the explanatory categories the historian uses in writing about that something in particular are almost invariably drawn from other domains—from politics or philosophy …" (p. 162). He defines education as the "deliberate, systematic, and sustained effort to transmit, evoke, or acquire knowledge, skills, values, or sensibilities, as well as any outcomes of that effort" (1976, p. 29). This broad definition projects us beyond colleges and schools to

Family members, factories, blogs, study groups, newspapers and volunteer associations are just a few of the people, places, and experiences that make up the broad spectrum of adult education today.

the "multiplicity of individuals and institutions that educate" (p. 29). Parents, peers, siblings, libraries, museums, camps, voluntary associations, churches, fairs, settlement houses, factories, social movements, radio stations, study circles, television, newspapers, blogs—all these can be understood as educative, forming and shaping the outlook and character and actions of adult learners.

We should think of adult learning broadly and imaginatively. What were the most important learning sites for adults in different times and places? Where and how did adults acquire knowledge and skills about how to work in the world? Where and how did adults learn about the values and norms that ought to govern their interactions with others in a constantly changing, often vulnerable, world? Where and how did adults learn about why some people suffered or were exploited by others? Who (and what) have been the teachers of adults in times past?

These questions presuppose that adult learning can be informal (woven into everyday activities), non-formal (intentionally organized to achieve various ends), and formal (the historically emerging formal institutions of education for professional and humanistic training). This well-known typology is easy to say; it is enormously difficult to weave these elements into a coherent social learning theory. Adult learning, then, is much broader and deeper than adult education, if by the latter we mean participation in a course for credit. Indeed, this form of learning (say, an ESL class) is one small spark in the kaleidoscopic array of adult learning projects, ranging from self-initiated projects to learning in the midst of action in a social movement. Adult learning is about how we make sense of our world and give meaning to our lives, and how we acquire the knowledge and skills to live well on the earth. This will be a repeated refrain throughout this book.

The Place of History in the Training of Adult Educators

Historians are storytellers who select events, make stories out of mere chronicles, and arrange materials into a narrative structure. Therefore, historians are faced with several interrelated tasks. They must choose the kind of story to tell (romance, comedy, tragedy, satire, irony). They must try to interpret the narrative they discover, and different possibilities are open as they do so. For instance, they can try to use a cause-effect social science framework or, like many historians, create a thickly described context for the events and ideas being examined. And they may affirm certain values and not others in the course of constructing the narrative. For example, the story of the Antigonish Movement has often been told as a romance: the heroic Moses Coady rose like a giant in the land of oppression to lead his people out to the promised co-operative land. But Marxist social historians have offered us an ironic narrative: the movement imagined it was transforming Nova Scotian society, but played right into the hands of the capitalist state.

The past is usable in at least four different ways. First, the past provides a critical vantage point on the present. History helps us to determine what is new; it helps to filter peripheral from perennial issues; it adds important players to contemporary discourse. Without historical understanding, we will not be able to penetrate to the heart of our society's central problems and concerns. For example, the question "Has adult education always been preoccupied with preparing adults for the job market?" cannot be answered adequately apart from historical knowledge and understanding.

Second, we can study the past to discover "liberatory moments" within our past. We might imagine ourselves as divers who descend into the murk, hoping to ascend to offer a pearl to the present. There are problems with this way of thinking—it seems quite arbitrary—but the historian can retrieve those moments that illuminate our darkness or troubles. The retrieval of liberatory moments from our past—an "affirming flame" (W. H. Auden)—fill us with hope. If adult educators in times past could dream such dreams, so can we. If they could launch bold and courageous projects in the midst of vast poverty and apathy, so can we. One can criticize aspects of Alfred Fitzpatrick's work with the "men of the camps" in his great Frontier College initiative, but one can also identify with his compassion for the neglected adult learners working in places remote from the seminar rooms of McGill and the University of Toronto. What, or who, are we forgetting that our foremothers and forefathers remembered? What are we confronting that they did not?

Third, historical studies may be a useful way of generating theorems about the many themes and issues having to do with how and where and why adults learn. A multiplicity of possibilities is available to us. For instance, in the exploration of adult learning in New France, 1608-1760, because of the theoretical work done by many philosophers and political scientists on the historical origin and meaning of the public sphere, we are able to consider the axial question of how citizens would learn by assembling together to address matters of concern to the community. In the encounter between the Jesuits and Amerindians in seventeenth century New France, we can draw upon contemporary understandings of adult education pedagogy in order to make sense of how Jesuit missionaries taught. (Indeed, they were surprisingly modern and innovative.) Opening to their pedagogical strategies and tactics can also permit us to see our own practices afresh. We are also able to think more deeply about the pedagogical encounter between the two ways of seeing and being once we have been alerted to the salient themes within the discourse of colonialism. Historical studies are a good way to test hypotheses because of the contextual nature of the investigation.

Fourth, historical understanding of adult education can play a modestly important role in shaping our identity as adult educators. As we learn about Canadian traditions of adult education, we may come to locate ourselves within a particular stream. This latter statement recognizes that adult learning can be harnessed to different and often conflicting purposes. Those educators with a critical sensibility, whose core values foster social justice, will find a warm stream to keep faith with.

Does Canada have a "great tradition" of adult education? I think so, but we will only find out at the end of journey.

References

Carr, E. H. (1961). *What is history?* London: Penguin Books.

Constant, J.F. and Ducharme, M. (Eds.). (2009). *Liberalism and hegemony: Debating the Canadian liberal revolution.* Toronto: University of Toronto Press.

Cremin, L. (1976). *Public education.* New York: Basic Books.

Cremin, L. (1977). *Traditions of American education.* New York: Basic Books.

Gross, D. (1992). *The past in ruins: Tradition and the critique of modernity.* Amherst (MA): The University of Massachusetts Press.

Harris, C. (2002). *Making native spaces: Colonialism, resistance, and reserves in British Columbia.* Vancouver: UBC Press.

Hobsbawm, E. (1994). *Age of extremes: The short twentieth century. 1914–1991.* London: Abacus Books.

MacMillan, M. (2008). History wars. In *The uses and abuses of history* (pp. 111–38). Toronto: Viking Canada.

Welton, M. (2004). Surrounded by our stories: Learning lessons from history. In G. Foley. (Ed.). *Dimensions of adult learning: Adult education and training in a global era.* (pp. 122–126) Crows Nest, Australia: Unwin and Allen.

Welton, M. (2010). Histories of adult education: Constructing the past. In C. Kasworm, A. Rose & J. Ross-Gordon. (Eds.). *Handbook of adult and continuing education* (pp. 83–91). Los Angeles: Sage Publishers.

White, H. (1973). *Metahistory: The historical imagination in nineteenth-century Europe.* Baltimore: The Johns Hopkins University Press.

Photo Credits

2

Encounters in the New World
(1492-1760)

New forms of learning emerged on the cusp of the scientific revolution in Europe which enabled the early explorers, such as Christopher Columbus and Jacques Cartier, to sail across the seas. This new learning released considerable energy to empirically investigate the natural world. The Christian community also fractured, which itself released fierce moral and spiritual powers upon the world. This chapter examines how the explorers filtered their perceptions and learning through their inherited cosmography when they encountered the indescribable and the unfamiliar. Attention is also given specifically to the voyages of Jacques Cartier in order to detect pedagogical elements in his mission to plant the cross and claim land for France. The Jesuit missionaries who came to New France in the seventeenth century can be understood as adult educators who desired to execute a profound transformation within the Amerindian's inner and outer life experience. We can view this pedagogical encounter as an integral of the colonial imagination—that believes that the objects of instruction have everything to learn and nothing of value to teach. Under siege, the tribal wilderness learning systems faced intense pressure to abandon their own lifeworld resources and meaning systems.

The emergence of New France between 1608 and 1760 provides opportunity to sketch out the contours of this feudal learning society. The prevalent notion that our contemporary society can be marked off from all previous societal forms by naming it as a "learning society" is subverted. Here we focus on how men and women in New France learned to make a living in difficult circumstances, live their lives in a tightly managed hierarchical world, and express themselves before the idea of "autonomous subjectivity" was in full bloom. The historical scholarship on the gradual emergence of a public sphere in both Europe and Canada serves as an interpretive cue to search New France for evidence of citizens assembling and engaging in conversational learning. This proves to be a valuable hermeneutical move.

This chapter, then, probes the origins of Canada as a white settler colony and focuses attention on Europe's movement into the new world as a pedagogical encounter between peoples with different ways of seeing and acting within the world. To accomplish this task, the historian must map out the cosmography of Europe's and First Nations' mentality in early modernity, and examine the learning challenges faced by Europeans of high and lower class, and their reluctant hosts, the First Nations peoples. These learning challenges are presented to us by our very nature as human beings on the move: we must learn to use nature to survive, we must learn to establish the norms and values by which we will interact with others and find ways of making sense of our world as we are experiencing it.

First Encounters: New Worlds, Old Maps

Our species is endlessly restless and curious. Perhaps we do bear the "mark of Cain," condemned to wander without a secure intellectual or earthly habitat in search of truth, always fearful of those who might destroy us. This has always been so—the ancient Genesis narrative teaches this deep truth—but curiosity to learn about the plenitude of nature, ourselves, and others and to map their contours, breaks out in all directions during the great Renaissance age of exploration. During the Renaissance, men unveiled the world previously hidden behind a theological curtain. The ancient teachings of Holy Writ and the sturdy philosophy of Aristotle contained most of the truths needed to make one's way in the world. But David Woodward (cited in Boorstin) observes that a "new way of looking at the earth was coming into being. In place of the legendary and theological maps which had placed Jerusalem at the centre, the earth was being measured and mapmakers were offering new aid to navigators" (p. 16).

Once men and women began to adopt an empirical attitude to the world, carefully observing its workings and character—"vast areas of ignorance" were "so suddenly unveiled." The entire earth appeared to be there to be "mastered and mapped, winds and ocean currents to be harnessed …" (Boorstin, 1991, p. 16). It was all there for our understanding, and some European members of the human species were willing to set out on amazing journeys of discovery into the terrifying and the unknown. The Romantic poet, John Keats, captured the spirit of awe before the unfamiliar in his poem of 1816, "On first looking into Chapman's Homer." After immersing himself all night in Chapman's fresh translation of Homer, Keats thought that the emotional intensity of the experience must have been like that of "stout Cortez when with eagle eyes/he stared at the Pacific—and all his men/Look'd at each other with wild surmise—/Silent upon a peak in Darian." The juxtaposition of "wild" with "surmise" suggests a wrenching free of the imagination and mind from calm reflection in the face of something never before seen.

When Christopher Columbus sailed into his imaginary Indies on a "sea of learning and scholarship" (Watson, 2005, p. 424), he really was more of a medieval man than a modern one. He drew on the navigational triumphs of earlier geographers, but their work had been a strange mix of the scientific and the exotic. They didn't really know what to expect. From annotations on old maps, they expected to see various monstrous creatures. From stories and legends, they thought they would find a promised "land of gold." As their cherished maps of knowledge, hybrid concoctions that they were, met empirical reality, they found it hard to give up old ideas. Gradually, though, new ideas were bound into books and the recently invented printing press spread these new ideas into the learned culture. One result of the new printing press was the sense of the fluidity of knowledge. Another was the ability to conduct spiritual and intellectual warfare through the battle of books, strikingly illustrated in the ferocity of struggle in the Protestant Reformation between Trinitarians and non-Trinitarians (Grayling, 2007, pp. 17-57; MacCulloch, 2003).

The medieval *mappemundi* emphasized the spiritual meaning of God's creation and Christ's redemption. They divided the world into four parts, placing the walled garden of Eden distant from the countries known around the Mediterranean. But the rediscovery of Ptolemy's second-century work on measuring space led to a new, abstract way of conceiving of spatial relations. One can observe this discovery of proportionality and geometric sensibility in the peerless works of Leonardo Da Vinci, Michelangelo, and Hieronymus Bosch. A radically new sense of spatial organization on canvas and ideals of proportionality are effusive in their magnificent works. The flat planes of the late medieval period, beautiful and solemn, gold and red, give way to the depth and beauty of Renaissance painting and sculpture. And the maps saturated with Christian imagery were replaced by rational techniques of ordering space.

Maps, as Jill Lepore, author of *Encounters in the New World: A History of Documents* (2000), states, "In the broadest sense … are windows into whole systems of knowledge and belief: through them one can chart the evolution of navigational, geographical, and cartographic knowledge and trace the history of religious, political, and cultural ideas" (p. 17). Unlike the maps of indigenous peoples, Europeans' maps documented possession, their lines, essentially, separating property. Instead, the Indian maps depicted relationships between groups (see Chamberlin, 2003, for an illuminating account of aboriginal mapmaking). However, we can also think of maps as cognitive, as intellectual ways of perceiving the world. We never see the world "as it is"; our modes of interpretation are intimately bound up with cultural categories that provide us with lenses to see the natural and the human worlds (and imagine the supernatural presence of various beings). The new realistic painting style that gradually emerged out of the late medieval period of European history tried to get close to things as they are. But the gap between eye and object always remained; one can never quite get to what is there. With the outbreak of the scientific revolution in the sixteenth century, philosophers and astronomers sought to reduce the gap through penetrating beneath the appearance to get at the mathematical essence resting with certainty underneath the transitory object.

The first explorers found the Indians they encountered startling and bizarre. They were shockingly naked and reddish of skin. But the Indians were equally shocked. The Aztecs of Mexico described the Spaniards this way. "Their bodies were everywhere covered, only their faces appeared. They were very white; they had chalky faces; they had yellow hair; though the hair of some was black. Long were their beards; they were also yellow." The Iroquois of the St. Lawrence Valley also reacted to the white men's beards and rejected pictorial representations of Jesus wearing a beard as offensive to their sensibility. The encounter was deeply disturbing for both parties. European Christendom's cultural conventions led the European conquerors, missionaries, and explorers to see the other as different and inferior (the indigenous peoples were "savage" (fierce and unsettled), "heathen" (un-Christian), and "barbaric" (spoke strange languages)). For their part, indigenous peoples' cultural maps forced them to name the Europeans as strangers, and therefore, as gods. Their cultural imaginaries differed, with grave consequences for both parties to this fraught learning adventure (Lepore, 2000, pp. 33-34).

Europe entered into momentous learning challenges in the sixteenth and seventeenth centuries. Perhaps the greatest of all these challenges lay with the unsettling of the authority of the sacred text, the Holy Bible. As the new empirical attitude gained momentum, the new discoveries—such as Copernicus's shattering text, *De Revolutionibus* of 1534—directly confronted ancient Christian teachings of an earth standing still in the cosmos. But the direct experiential learning of explorers and missionaries introduced a new kind of text into the world of scholarship: what our eyes have observed, what we have touched and duly recorded in our notebooks. Columbus floated to the West Indies on this sea of adult learning. There are many dimensions to this learning—wonderfully explored by many scholars. It is worth noting that Renaissance humanism highly valued universality and the interconnectedness of knowledge. Now the whole earth could be imagined and humankind could get on with the monumental task of discovery, classification, and scientific sense-making. But when Columbus ventured out in 1492, and Cartier in 1534, natural history and ethnology were in their infant stages. They lacked adequate classification schemes and vocabularies (Thomas,1983).

Thus it comes as no surprise to us half a millennium down the road that when the Europeans encountered new species of flora, fauna, and living creatures that they tried to fit them into their pre-existing cognitive maps. But they didn't fit—pumas were not lions—and later, when Europeans encountered the kangaroo in Australia, they were flummoxed, depicting it in their art works as something between the kangaroo as we know it now and the deer. Those meeting the new, in Anthony Pagden's resilient phrase, struggled with their own "helplessness before the indescribable" (Pagden, 1982, p. 12). They had to finally realize that the egg was not the chestnut. But, rather than giving up, Europeans in the sixteenth and seventeenth centuries (and thereafter) began collecting curiosities and assembling them in cabinets and museums. This collecting mania was one trajectory that adult learning in the late Renaissance and in early modern Europe travelled along. The assemblage of objects, where similarities and differences can be observed, is an early form of the scientific sensibility.

The Renaissance and early modern European perception of Amerindians was shaped by both their Imperial Christian beliefs in "one world under Christ's rule" and teachings inherited from Aristotle. The latter's ideas were synthesized into a coherent Christian system by St. Thomas Aquinas in the thirteenth century. From that tributary, they flowed into the stream of Western thought. Christian Europe classified all of humankind into Christian/non-Christian and, from Aristotle, inferred that non-Christians who did not inhabit the city-state were beast-like in their thoughts and actions. But the Greeks were not racists; through instruction, they believed, *les sauvages* could become fully human and civilized. The label *barbarian* was affixed to those deemed to be living "close to nature." Father Le Jeune, a Jesuit priest in seventeenth-century New France, exclaimed: "Let these barbarians remain always nomads, then their sick will die in the woods, and their children will never enter the seminary. Render them sedentary, and you will fill these three institutions." Barbarians were pagans: those of strange tongues, incomprehensive beliefs, and wandering lifestyle.

The imagination of the High Middle Ages and Renaissance was peopled with strange creatures that were "half-man/half-beast." These creatures dwelt on the border between human and animal, introducing a profound ambivalence into both the ethnological reflections of intellectuals and the missionary-civilizing work of Europeans. The wild man was not-quite-man. Yet Aristotle's ethnographic scheme also contained a strange and contradictory category of the "natural slave." This "person" lacked reason and control of his passions and was fit by nature for subservience. This slippery category of the natural slave justified, one might argue, the enslavement of Amerindians. It also precipitated furious theological debate regarding the Spanish treatment of Indians on their *encomienda*. But the core adult education philosophy of the missionaries (that won the day) assumed that barbarians could be educated. They could learn. They could be objects of pedagogical transformation. They could be incorporated into the universal kingdom of Christ. This powerful idea may well be our first early modern philosophy of adult education.

Jacques Cartier is one of Canada's historical icons. He is a romantic figure of high adventure along with the gallant *coureurs des bois,* noble Indians, and courageous priests who ended up being burnt at the stake. Cartier is very much a man of the High Renaissance. He embodies the themes and explorations of our opening chapter. Arriving in the Gaspé on July 24, 1534, Cartier immediately erected a cross on Canadian land. This act was, perhaps, Canada's first instructional object lesson. He and John Cabot and the other explorers were on a sacred mission to conquer and possess. Cartier naturally assumed that Catholic Christendom ought to be extended to the entire world. He had no doubts, in Ramsay Cook's words, that the "line between France and Canada, between civilization and savagery, was sharply drawn and that civilization was on the march" (Cook, 1993, p. xv). Later, in the ironic and skeptical writings of Michel de Montaigne, we see the tables being turned on Europe's self-confident assertion of superiority.

In twentieth century terms, Cartier was no post-colonial relativist. He thought of the Indians in terms of his own cultural codes. There were no permanent settlements that he could easily identify; they were not overdressed the way the French were; they were impoverished materially; and their commodities were of little value. They were only potentially full humans. Cartier, then, could not imagine that native people had any real religion or rights to their habitation.

Cunning Pedagogics: The Encounter Between the Jesuit Missionaries and the Amerindians of Seventeenth-Century New France

This section focuses our attention on the learning dynamics of the encounter between Jesuit missionaries and the Amerindians of New France in the seventeenth century. France only began to take a serious interest in a permanent settlement in the late sixteenth and the early to middle seventeenth centuries. Imperialism now depended on discovery, conquest, and settlement. Unless one settled land and defended it with armaments and skilful management of indigenous populations, papal or royal proclamations meant little. In 1603, Henry IV, the Huguenot turned Catholic, appointed Pierre Gua Sieur de Monts, a prominent merchant, to procure settlers for New France. He ordered Samuel de Champlain to increase these numbers. This was to be accomplished through evangelization and assimilation of native peoples into French culture. Thus, France's fur trade interests could be protected, and the census would be able to report more French habitants than English residents. These purposes were encased within the dream of fulfilling the dictates of the papal encyclicals to bring the knowledge of God, the Catholic Church, and religion to the native peoples. The story of Champlain has been told most recently in David Hackett Fischer's *Champlain's Dream* (2008).

Another way of telling the story of the unfolding of the Canadian learning society would be to begin with the tribal wilderness learning systems of indigenous peoples. Here, one would do one's best to construct the nature of the indigenous learning systems as they adapted to changing circumstances over time and then responded to the invasion of germs and foreigners. Recently, John Ralston Saul has challenged Canadian historians in a controversial new book, *A Fair Country: Telling Truths About Canada* (2007), to reimagine the way Native cultures have actually created contemporary Canada. This idea is radical and controversial, and neither assimilated nor fully understood by Canadians (or historians). In this section, however, we have a more modest goal of highlighting the pedagogics of the unequal encounter between Jesuit missionaries and Amerindians. Both actors are agents in an asymmetrical dialogue.

Essentially, the pedagogical encounter between the Jesuits and the Amerindians of Canada highlights the way one society's learning system can disrupt, often in radical ways, that of the other. Traditional Amerindian world orientations had to cope with changes to their way of symbolically ordering the world and learning systems during many centuries. But Amerindian modes of subsistence and production came under relentless assault. It began inconspicuously in the late fifteenth century and continued inexorably into the sixteenth and through to the eighteenth century as the fur trade penetrated the St. Lawrence Valley and onward to the west. Between 1632 and 1670, approximately one hundred Jesuit missionaries went to New France, made possible by the French occupation of the St. Lawrence Valley in 1632. The pioneering, cunning, resourceful Jesuits got to know their learners, tried to displace indigenous adult educational leaders (they were the new shaman) and gradually produce Euro-Catholic subjectivities in their learners. Their pedagogical techniques were imaginative and surprisingly modern—all of this used to undermine the indigenous belief and action system and replace it with Euro-Catholic subjectivities.

We can identify the different dimensions of the tribal wilderness learning system (in our day, we speak of indigenous forms of knowledge). This learning system experienced severe strain as new problems and ideas were fed into it from external sources. The shaman—perhaps the most significant adult educator in Amerindian tribal society—had the role of maintaining the balance and order of the society. In unusual times of trouble or foreboding, the shaman was called upon to restore order and good times. He could teach his people what the new signs and dreams meant and allay collective anxiety. But the shaman, as guardian of the traditional lifeworld (its sources of meaning, social stability, and personal coherence), was in a precarious situation. If his techniques failed, he could be easily discredited and the traditional lifeworld as a legitimate fund of meaning would be undermined.

"Tension points" were introduced into the differing learning systems (European and Indian) that disenabled dialogue and mutual understanding. For example, the Amerindians had considerable trouble comprehending some of the basic Christian dogmas: sin, guilt, and hell. The Hurons could not grasp the idea of primordial fault. Although the Jesuits were not in New France to foster inter-religious or spiritual dialogue (to use contemporary language), they occupied common ground with Amerindian belief in the supernatural realm. Both believed in evil spirits. Both accepted the dualism of the body and soul. But the Jesuits could neither accept nor possibly even grasp the idea that a soul could leave the living body or that a shaman could kill, or injure, a faraway enemy. As Charles Taylor (2007) might argue everyone in the fifteenth and sixteenth centuries believed in some form of the supernatural. Taylor might also add that the Amerindians and the Europeans had different conceptions of the self; the former being more porous than the emergent buff-

In this painting by Frank Charles Hennessey, a Jesuit missionary is shown travelling through New France. (Credit: Library and Archives Canada, Acc. No. 1970-188-425 W.H. Coverdale Collection of Canadiana)

ered self of early moderns. In fact, doubt about the existence of God does not even become a viable option for people in the US and Canada until the late nineteenth century.

The Jesuits were in New France to convert the Indians to Catholic Christianity. They were highly intelligent and pedagogically innovative educators who used a wide array of techniques and even tricks to undermine the indigenous lifeworld. The Christian colonizers of the seventeenth century used popular theatrics, visualizations, and intense campfire debates to convince their foes to embrace their imaginary Christ. They used every opportunity to discredit the shaman; in fact, one might argue that they sought to substitute themselves as Christian shamans. The Jesuits believed that their Indian pupils learned best at moments of heightened emotion and melodrama. Believing that perspective transformation required shock treatment, Jesuit educators painted frightening verbal portraits of hell, the fiery underworld. Indian catechumens were encouraged to use the see-hear-taste-touch mode of pedagogy to instruct their novice Christians.

They also used pictures to instruct their adult pupils when they first landed in Acadia in 1611. Gradually, after some failures, they learned how to meet the visual preferences of their learners. Jesus had to be beardless and colourful (the Hurons' favourite was a picture of the child Jesus clutching the knees of the Virgin, regally crowned and holding a scepter in her right hand and the earth in her left). From reading

Jaroslav Pelikan's *Jesus Through the Centuries: His Place in the History of Culture* (1985) one is reminded that the "cultural matrix" of different ages produces different understandings of Jesus. The Indians preferred illuminated paintings to highlight the sacred mysteries. This is brilliant pedagogy. One can surmise that the Franco-Jesuits had more than a few surprises to their received wisdom.

The Jesuit encounter with the Amerindians of the St. Lawrence Valley in seventeenth-century New France provides us with insights into the inner workings of the colonial imagination. This brilliant marshalling of pedagogical energy was ultimately, however, in the service of a world view that divided humankind into (Christian) friends and (Satanic) enemies. The Jesuits had nothing important to learn and everything important to teach. The political context of pedagogical instruction in the early Jesuit era and our own are neglected at our peril. Their gutsy and dogged determination was captured powerfully in the dark Canadian film, *Black Robe.* For their part, First Nations peoples had to re-orient their own religious understandings as this new vision intruded and forced its way inside their symbolic ordering of the world. And they had to do so in a damaged world, which rendered them vulnerable and open to consider a new orientation to a world that was changing before their very eyes. In one sense, the Jesuits as ambassadors of a Christian Europe in its civilizing mode sets the stage for the long contestation between the Canadian state, government authorities, and missionaries to transform them into liberal and Christian subjects.

"A Country at the End of the World": Living and Learning in New France, 1608–1760

What might it have been to live and learn in New France between the early seventeenth and late eighteenth centuries? It is not easy to shed our cultural clothing of the early twenty-first century (or put down our cellphones for a minute or two), and travel through time to the beginnings of settlement in New France. Try to imagine the ghastly eight- or ten-week creaking and groaning journey across the Atlantic. What could possibly have occupied the minds and imaginations of many of these illiterate (or scarcely literate) men and women who were coming to this "country at the edge of the world"? Hope and fear probably ran together like ink in water in their hearts. Perhaps deep faith in their Catholic God and protective amulets somehow sustained them. We may never know.

The scholarship on New France is vast. We can only sketch the contours of New France as a learning society. The concept of "learning society"—drawn from contemporary vocabulary—can be used fruitfully as a lens to conduct a reconnaissance of a society in the past which did not use such language. All societies are learning societies. As human beings, we are fated to find ways to make a living, live our lives with others, and express ourselves. As German philosopher Jurgen Habermas (1972) has argued, our "knowledge-constitutive" interests are anchored in our species' relationship to nature, others, and self. He thinks that instrumental forms of knowing (how to master nature to serve efficient ends) and communicative knowledge (how we construct norms and values to order our community lives) can be distinguished. This duality echoes the well-established notion of humanness defined in terms of work and language.

It is true, however, that the idiom "express ourselves" does hint at a more modern conception of the individual. Some philosophers, for example, pinpoint the emergence of the expressive individual in the Romantic era of the nineteenth century. Be that as it may, I assume, without making all the elaborate arguments that human persons never merely play out socially prescribed roles. They are unique, each one, and some find ways to express this uniqueness through art, play, ritual, ceremony, and imaginative problem-solving.

It is an exacting task to understand how men and women in New France learned to make a living, live their lives, and express themselves. It is an exacting task, first, because most of the learning processes and pedagogical procedures were either non-formal or woven into life activities, and second, because we don't always have the records necessary to help us understand the instructional processes underpinning the work of constructing a new world society in the image of the old. Thus, one must imagine one's way into another world and extrapolate key ideas from historians who are neither focusing on nor having an interest in how people actually acquire the knowledge and skills to sustain themselves in their worlds, with the host of learning challenges that erupt in their presence as their worlds unfold, oftentimes with acute disruptions. In contemporary society, we need only think of the fortunes of the ill-fated people who have had to flee for their lives and live as refugees. For their part, those interested in adult education history—such as prominent Canadian adult educator J. Roby Kidd, formerly of OISE—begin their narrative in the nineteenth century, with a few touchdowns in the remote past.

The elites who governed New France recreated feudal conditions in the new world to ensure the flow of goods into the imperial centre. New

France was organized as a colonial outpost to ensure the continuing flow of the "brown gold" of the fur trade (in swing for a hundred years prior to settlement). By 1590, the fur trade had gained such momentum that the French Crown wanted to secure its control against its chief competitor, the English. The story of Samuel Champlain occupies considerable attention in the first decades of seventeenth-century New France. In fact, Quebec recently celebrated the 400th anniversary of his founding of Quebec City in 1608. The conflict between the French and their First Nations allies, and that of the English and theirs, is intricate and well documented. From our vantage point, the alliance between the French and First Nations, each forced into the other's arms, created our first fraught example of cross-cultural learning in Canadian history. Yet the intercultural exchange, if one may grant it this label, was asymmetrical, framed within the French project of imperial domination. Here, we might be reminded that Cartier took Indians hostage and transported them to France as curiosities. Historians of adult education like their counterparts working on different themes, have to work creatively with concepts such as power and hegemony. They must show how the learning process is distorted by those holding power over others and are trying to impose a particular form of rule. This latter assumption is integral to the new critical history.

What did those in the fur trade need to know, be, and do to perform their work? One can see, though, that the knowledge and skill of the Indian trappers was distorted by their integration into the global fur trade. Some scholars have even suggested that the Indians lost their moral footing as the imperial centre pressured them (and perhaps they pressured themselves, hungry for commodities) to capture more and more beaver. The *coureurs des bois* were drawn into their form of work because they couldn't sustain their families by working the land. Their work was dangerous and highly organized, demanding tough, strong bodies and disciplined minds. The work appears to have been a kin-related affair. Theirs was a pedagogy of daring and danger, learned experientially in the face of death, a world far removed from the relative safety and moral surveillance of the Catholic "garrison culture" emerging reluctantly in the Canadian wilderness.

The habitant was created by and for the feudal seigneurial system; immigrants were transformed into habitants. The famous strip farms of Quebec, now a part of our Canadian imagination, were imposed upon the geography and landscape of New France. Those who ended up clearing and gaining a living from these lands had some leeway, but were essentially bound to a legal system that extracted surplus from their labour (this is called the *corvée*). But the shift to agriculture away from the centrality of the fur trade—called for because of the early problems of getting settlers—only occurred in the latter seventeenth century. By mid-eighteenth century, with the Indian wars ended, agriculture was the main pursuit of almost all of the inhabitants of the area. A European rural society had emerged on this corner of the new world, and it was one whose life was centred on the self-sufficient peasant household.

Drawing from the work of cultural historians such as John Demos (*A Little Commonwealth,* 1970), we can postulate that the habitant family household was the pre-eminent learning site for men and women and their children (with the Roman Catholic Church watching warily over it). The habitants were hardly ignorant. To manage their farms, woven tightly into their lifeworld, they had to have a wide range of knowledge and skills at their disposal. Attuned to the rhythms of the seasons, the habitants had to know how to plow with a team of animals (much-loved horses, oxen, or a mixed team) They used the heavy wheeled plow; they made the beam, axle, and handle from wood, fitting them with two wheels, a chain, an iron coulter, and a small iron plowshare. In May, after plowing, they sowed grain and seed, covered by the passing of a harrow, a crude device made with wooden pegs mounted in a simple frame. Women had the responsibility for the tilling and planting of the kitchen garden. With the arrival of summer, the habitants erected fences around freshly planted grain fields. They whitewashed the house and got on with other chores, like digging ditches. If they didn't learn how to sharpen their scythes, the tons of hay would lie uncut. The time of the grain harvest in the early fall was busy and bustling. After the harvest, internal fences had to be removed to allow animals to roam over the entire farm (Greer, 1985). They were hardly ignorant and backward, resistant to change and superstitious. This derogatory labelling was read back into their experience by elites who were embracing the scientific forms of agriculture in the age of improvement in the late eighteenth and early nineteenth centuries.

Today we value critical thinking very highly; we are products of the Enlightenment Era whose philosophers fiercely believe that we have rights as individuals to question wrongful authority. We can, then, explore the question of just how much autonomy the peasants actually had in eighteenth century New France. There were some "thunder gusts of popular sentiment, but they did not bring any revolutionary storm" (Crowley, 1983, p. 144). Resistance to authority was mainly episodic.

Even the habitants' religious expression was not entirely autonomous. They were under surveillance and had to steal their own time. A magical sacred canopy enveloped them, giving cosmological meaning to the unpredictability of their lives, even though there is evidence of disrespectful attitudes to the church amongst habitants. Following Peter Moogk's (2000) seminal work on New France, we gain insights into what the habitants believed about the world. One might add this dimension to the triad of making a living, living our lives, and expressing ourselves. We must make sense of our lives and bind each one's discrete elements into something like a whole. Human beings long for transcendence and cannot live on the horizontal plane alone. The phrase sacred canopy is used to capture the idea of a canopy of meaning that makes sense of the whole (Berger, 1967).

The history of New France contains an unusual and remarkable number of women. Jeanne Mance, for example, is named as co-founder of Montreal in 1642. The redoubtable duo, Marie de l'Incarnation and Marguerite Bourgeoys established Canada's first reasonably accessible education system. These amazing women were working in an environment scarcely hospitable to women. But the nuns came and established hospitals and other institutions. No matter what their status, high or low, the situation of women in the colony was insecure. The famed *les filles du rois* are an amazing story in themselves. Between 1663 and 1673, 770 women, average age of twenty-four, left farms and orphanages to sail for an unknown country. It is hard to imagine the learning and spiritual challenges they faced. If the men they met and married in the new country turned out to be brutes, that was bad enough; they also faced disease, childbirth, backbreaking work, and war. But learn they did, and the life of Louise, born around 1645, provides a window on to the life of the peasant woman, one of the legendary *filles du roi*.

She had been placed in a poorhouse in France, where she learned the basics of religion, housekeeping, and knitting. That was her lifeworld curriculum. At age thirteen, she was sent out to do domestic service. She returned to the Hospital at age twenty-four, and a government agent arrived with an offer to pay her fare for New France. She arrived in Quebec City, where she stayed at a boarding house supervised by the sisters. There she met numerous suitors who would come calling. She chose one, and after travelling to Trois-Rivières she and her husband built a small cabin near the riverbank. Louise used her dowry to purchase a cow and some chickens. From her neighbours, Louise learned how to turn suet into candles and bake bread in an outdoor over. After the arrival of

A painting entitled "L'arrivée des Filles du Roi" which depicts Jean Talon (who orchestrated the "filles du roi" plan) and François de Laval (the first Roman Catholic Bishop of Quebec) welcoming women to New France in 1667. (Credit: Library and Archives Canada)

the first baby, her work grew more arduous. Like so many other pioneering women, she had to haul water, beat the wash, stoke the fires, turn the roast deer, mend clothes, tend to the cow, and care for the baby. After Louise lost her husband, she was entitled to run the family farm. The daunting work of managing the lifeworld inscribed itself on the bodies of these habitants, *filles du roi*. They wore out in the service of peopling the land of New France to establish France's imperial dominance in this land (Noel, 1998, pp. 16-18). The household, the grounding place of the lifeworld, needs to be taken seriously as a crucial learning site.

The craftsmen and their associations: how did they learn their work as shoemakers and stonemasons and carpenters and coopers, to name only a few crafts? Interestingly, we notice an incipient professionalization of work processes occurring with the appearance of textual representation. Architects, for instance, were the ones who knew what the authoritative texts on design were and referred to them in the construction process. But others also drew on texts, including teachers and merchants. Moreover, child rearing handbooks were around, but probably available only to the merchant class. One cannot understand the social organization of craft learning apart from understanding how the apprenticeship system in New France worked. Many fathers passed their craft skills on to their sons. It was not easy for any craftsperson to move out of his (or her) class location. The craft guilds were important learning sites for workers to learn about the wider meanings of their work and how it related to other sectors of life in New France (and beyond, too). Their "collective voice" was restricted; the first strike in the colony is dated at 1741. Clearly, the instincts of the colonial administration were repressive and colonial workers were less likely than recent Europeans to act collectively. Each of the crafts had their own patron saints and rituals. They were often rowdy affairs, prompting the priests to move in as their guides.

The idea of the public sphere has gained considerable prominence in contemporary philosophy and political and social science. The use of this important concept is often attributed to the seminal works of Jurgen Habermas (see *The Structural Transformation of the Public Sphere* [1989]). The public sphere emerges gradually in European historical development as a conversational space between the state and the economy. Using this concept as lens, we can scan the social and political landscape of New France for evidence of spaces where people could reason together about the basic rules governing the spheres of labour and commodity exchange as well as forms of governance (and, one might add, their general conditions of well-being). The historical evidence suggests that the New France ruling elites did not tolerate an "open space" between state and the people. New France in the seventeenth and eighteenth centuries was constituted as an aristocratic, patriarchal, agricultural, and Roman Catholic community. Unauthorized assemblies and public protest were perceived as serious offences. Nonetheless, one detects the presence of occasional consultative assemblies. But Frontenac ended any form of popular representation as early as 1677. If as Gramsci has claimed, "all of society is a vast school," then all of the institutions and legal formulations of New France were harnessed toward the end of creating a submissive, hard-working, dutiful, pious subject. Ritual and law, and not doctrine, bound the people together into an exclusive community.

But this authoritarian control over the people's minds didn't last for too long. Dictatorial systems are leaky, though they can survive for a time on terror and coercion. The liberal and radical currents of Enlightenment thought made their way into a post-conquest Quebec. The printers and newspapermen introduced perhaps the first "critical spirit" into an intellectually conservative culture. They challenged court decisions, railed against the abuses of the clergy, attacked the backwardness of the colleges, and advocated for a legislative assembly. This small, courageous "republic of letters" had a difficult time establishing a beachhead. One could say that the backrooms of their print shops were the first critical learning sites in Quebec history. The now forgotten and silent names of two of those radical printers, Fleury Mesplat (who founded the *Quebec*

Gazette in 1764) and the gallant Valentin Jautard, who edited *The Gazette of Montreal* in 1778, should be retrieved from history's dustbins.

References

Berger, P. (1967). *Sacred canopy: Elements of a sociological theory of religion.* Garden City, (NY): Doubleday.

Boorstin, D. (1991). The realms of pride and awe. In J. A. Levenson (Ed.). *Circa 1492: Art in the age of exploration* (pp. 19–22). New Haven: Yale University Press.

Chamberlin, J. E. (2003). *If this is your land, where are your stories?* Toronto: A. A. Knopf Canada.

Cook, R. (1993). Introduction. In *The voyages of Jacques Cartier.* Toronto: University of Toronto Press.

Crowley, T. (1983). Thunder gusts: Popular disturbances in early French Canada. In M. Cross & G. Kealey (Eds.), *Economy and society during the French regime, to 1759* (pp. 122–51). Toronto: McClelland and Stewart.

Demos, J. (1970). *A little commonwealth: Family life in Plymouth Colony.* New York: Oxford University Press.

Grayling, A.C. (2007). *Towards the light: The story of the struggles for liberty and rights that made the modern West.* London: Bloomsbury.

Greer, A. (1985). *Peasants, lord, and merchants: Rural society in three Quebec parishes, 1740–1840.* Ithaca (NY): Cornell University Press.

Habermas, J. (1972). *Knowledge and human interests.* London: Heinemann Books

Habermas, J. (1989). *The structural transformation of the public sphere.* Cambridge (MA): MIT Press.

Lepore, J. (2000). *Encounters in the new world: A history of documents.* NY/Oxford: Oxford University Press.

MacCulloch, D. (2003). *Reformation: Europe's house divided. 1490–1700.* London: Penguin Books.

Moogk, P. (2000). *La nouvelle France: The making of French-Canada: a critical history.* East Lansing (MI): Michigan State University Press.

Noel, J. (1998). *Book #59: Women in new France.* Ottawa: Canadian Historical Association.

Pagden, A. *The fall of natural man: The American Indian and the origins of comparative ethnicity.* Cambridge UK: Cambridge University Press, 1982.

Pelikan, J. (1985). *Jesus through the centuries: His place in the history of culture.* New Haven: Yale University Press.

Saul, J. R. (2007). *A fair country: Telling truths about Canada.* Toronto: Penguin Canada.

Taylor, C. (2007). *A secular age.* Cambridge (MA): Belknap Press of Harvard University.

Thomas, K. (1983). *Man and the natural world: Changing attitudes in England 1500–1800.* London: Allen Lane.

Watson, P. (2005). The mental horizon of Christopher Columbus. In *Ideas: A history from fire to Freud* .London: Weidenfeld and Nicolson.

Welton, M. (2005). Cunning pedagogics: The encounter between the Jesuit missionaries and Amerindians in seventeenth century New France. *Adult Education Quarterly,* 55(2), 101–115.

Welton, M. (2009). First encounters: New worlds and old maps. *The Canadian Journal for the Study of Adult Education,* 21(2), 66–79.

Welton, M. (2010). "A country at the end of the world": Living and learning in New France, 1608–1760. *The Canadian Journal for the Study of Adult Education,* 23(1), 55–71.

3

Adult Learning in the Age of Improvement (1760-1880)

Up until the mid-nineteenth century most Canadians lived in rural areas and engaged in agricultural activities. But by mid-century one could see something new appearing on the landscape: factory chimneys, Mechanics' Institutes, and common schools. These were the surface indices of something new emerging. Canada was in transition from a mercantile commercial economy to an early modern form of industrial society. The organization of work required that both employer and employee learn how to work under new and harsh conditions. Bodies and minds had to be transformed. Agriculture had its inescapable work rhythms attuned to seasonal changes. Factories knew neither night nor day. The old seasonal forms of work on land or sea were demanding enough, but did not require the same discipline and enslavement to the clock. In the 1840s, Karl Marx described the harsh and hardening factory work as a "school of labour." This was the only school many workers knew; the lessons they learned had to do with a new consciousness of what it meant to work and live in a capitalist (and enlightened) society.

The unskilled and rough Irish labourers, untutored in the ways of industrialism, who worked on the Welland or Lachine Canals in the early 1800s contributed much to Canada and learned severe lessons about the necessity of combining to keep their wages from falling below the level needed for personal and familial sustenance. The Irish children, often found wandering in the streets of the new urban areas, were perceived as "street Arabs" by the colonial educational elite. They needed to be in school to save the nervous British colony of Upper Canada from disorder and chaos. For their part, the skilled tradesmen knew that their knowledge and skill positioned them strongly in the productive process. They knew how the machines worked; they were mainly British up to the 1850s; they had a strong sense of occupational status. H. Clare Pentland (1981) observes that few blueprints existed in the 1850s, and the skilled workers held the crucial knowledge in their brains and inscribed into their muscles. The employers needed them; and had to both recognize their status and pay them reasonably decently. Clearly, then, both employer and employee had to learn different things. The skilled strata of the working class, like their employers, knew that seat of the pants common sense was inadequate before the new industrial processes. They needed scientific and technical formal instruction. Like their employers, they too were interested in the new scientific ethos permeating the cultural atmosphere. They would have visited zoos, public gardens, and exhibitions. They would have read journals and newspapers. They also knew that their children needed to go to school to prepare to be workers and citizens in this new world. The skilled craftsmen were the ones who attended Mechanics' Institutes; few of the rough Irish lads would have bothered.

The scientific revolution that had been brewing, bubbling, and developing in Europe since the sixteenth century turning of the world upside down came to maturity in the Enlightenment Age of the eighteenth. In 1784 German philosopher Immanuel Kant announced that humankind was emerging out of state of self-imposed immaturity—he insisted in his classic essay, "What is Enlightenment?," that humankind could use its own reason to understand the laws governing the world. They didn't need the tutoring of priests or bureaucrats. They could stand on their own two feet with confidence that the light of reason could deflect the darkness of superstition and outmoded forms of knowledge. Human beings could set their gaze on the horizontal plane, and discover the transcendent in their ethical actions. Kant separated "faith" from "knowledge," thus signalling for future generations the tension between believer and secular outlook. And in the nineteenth century, the "masters of suspicion" Marx and Darwin added to the unsettling erosion of faith in God's providential existence. The opening out to the world—to investigate and discover its rules—begun in the Renaissance period—now intensified with the industrialization of work and society. "All that is solid melts into the air"—Marx captured the relentless dynamism, driven by science and technology, in *The Communist Manifesto* of 1848. A new spirit had been loosed on the world: a spirit of inquiry, investigation, and transformation.

Thus, the spread of Mechanics' Institutes in both Britain and Canada were but one significant index of the new ethos of science that was gradually changing the outlook of men and women. Pentland (1981) saw the Mechanics' Institutes and explosion of inventions as signs of the "diffusion of belief in progress and of industrial ambition" (p. 182). But so were the agricultural societies established in the late eighteenth century in Nova Scotia. The colonial elites initiated them, and held to a paternalistic sense of responsibility for their subordinates; these societies nonetheless also signalled a democratic impulse to share knowledge with others. Indeed, some colonial elites in the early nineteenth century may have tried to discourage working class and poor children (and their parents) from learning to read and write because that might make them demanding and unruly. But this reactionary attitude could not sustain itself in this new emergent world. Nor would colonial elites such as the Upper Canadian Family Compact be able to debar ordinary citizens from having some say in governance (the "responsible government" movement manifest in the rebellions of 1837-8). It makes sense, then, to identify a configuration of institutions (agricultural societies, Mechanics' Institutes, literary and scientific societies, museums and libraries, public gardens, common schools, the education of public opinion, mutual aid and benevolent societies, churches) that were created to both understand and explore this new world, but also to equip men and women with a new, progressive, liberal outlook. This was, after all, the "Age of Improvement." And it required an early, industrial form of learning infrastructure: the rudiments of a civil society with open public spheres. The explosive expansion of civil society and public spheres would have to wait until the early twentieth century, when Canadians of all stripe responded to the next phase of capitalism's unfolding: the corporate form of capitalist organization.

The world "liberal" captures the nature of the society that the Canadian state was attempting to instantiate, beginning roughly in mid-nineteenth century. Historian Ian McKay (2009) has offered us a new paradigm for understanding Canadian history: the Liberal Order framework. This is very helpful: the British governing class wanted to create a society of liberal subjects: persons who would see themselves primarily as individuals with rights who would ascribe to notions of private property as well as British values (affirming our ties to the British monarchy) and norms (which were assumed to be Christian). The white governing elites, then, were set for a project of assimilating all immigrants into a British, mainly Protestant, liberal way of being and doing. The Canadian constitution is called the *British North American Act* (1867). During the period of British rule, so to speak, the British simply assumed that they were fit for rule, given the evidence of their power and savvy throughout the growing British Empire. They believed that all non-British (with the exception of Quebec perhaps) had to conform to the norm of the dominant ethnic class. Until well into the twentieth century, the Anglo-conformity model was in place. Indeed, even the most progressive-minded didn't think the Chinese or other Asians were assimilable to the British norm. Expressed in theoretical idiom, the discourse of most white Canadians until the 1960s was "racialized" (some might argue it still is [Kelly, 1998; 2006]).

The Liberal Order framework enables us to understand more fully how to tell the story of First Nations struggle for recognition and resistance to the "assimilation and Christianize" vision of the British governing class and missionaries who flooded into Canada in the late Victorian era (the highpoint of the missionary era for Protestants and Roman Catholics). Put simply, Anglo-conformity meant that the British governing class had to turn Natives into liberal subjects. To do this, they had to sever their ties to collectively held land and to their own indigenous traditions. And then they had to convince (or coerce) them into becoming enfranchised as atomized individuals who would eschew entitlement to collective land. We have already seen that Cartier had initiated the Christianizing process when he planted the cross on Native land in 1534. The Jesuits who came to New France in the early seventeenth century sought to undermine Native culture and transform them into Euro-Christian subjects only began a process that continued well into the twentieth century. But, alas, these very treaties (beginning with the *Royal Proclamation Act* of 1763), ironically enough, thwarted the state's efforts to create loyal, British, Christian, individualized subjects. Thus, the Canadian state can be understood as the primary pedagogue with Natives as often unwilling objects. This vision for the Natives required various projects: these included residential schools after the 1880s and the permitting of missionary work among First Nations peoples from coast to coast. But the historical evidence does not permit a superficial understanding of the adult education work of various missionaries. Missionaries often defended Native rights to their land and fended off those who would do them harm. William Duncan even tried to create a utopian community of Tsimshian natives living according to British ways of working and worshipping. And missionaries often railed against a government that never provided the resources to do the difficult educational work of forming Natives who could function in a new, industrial order. The resistance of Native peoples to the "assimilate and Christianize" vision gestures toward understanding the lifeworld sources of this resistance. Native peoples somehow found the strength and courage within their own cultural rituals, ceremonies, and world outlook to fend off various projects to unsettle them from land and culture. They fought furiously to enact the rituals that symbolized their identity and deep heritage (such as the Sun Dance on the plains or the Potlatch on the west coast). The struggle to maintain their identity, we can argue, was the primary social learning process at work in their history. For Native peoples, the age of improvement was neither inevitable nor benign. There is a dark side to the age of improvement. It is called racism, and left many Native people (and many other non-Anglo-Saxons) devastated and broken-spirited. The "pathologies of modernity" continue to this day (and account for much of the remedial forms of adult education offered in various communities).

The treatment of people of African descent in Canada also illustrates—unfortunately—the utter inability of the Canadian white settler society to accept Blacks as full human beings and citizens. Between 1500 and 1800 approximately eleven million Africans were moved by force into new worlds. Sir Phillip Sherlock and Hazel Bennett (1997) write of the immensity of the "physical suffering, anguish of spirit and unbearable cruelty" of their lot "from the time of … capture" (p. 122). Those 3,500 Blacks who first arrived in Nova Scotia in 1782-85 from New York were loyal to the British crown and fled from the new republic. Later, they were joined, for a brief time, by Trelawney Jamaicans (the Maroons), who soon left for Sierra Leone. In 1813, approximately two thousand Blacks arrived in Nova Scotia from the US (others made their way to Ontario). These new immigrants were not of the right colour to be assimilated easily into British colonial Canada. Europeans of the late eighteenth and into the early twentieth centuries simply took for granted the racial inferiority of Blacks. Hegel and Kant, great enlightenment philosophers, assumed this to be so. Cultural historian Edward Said in his influential *Culture and Imperialism* (1993) brilliantly argues that Jane Austen's famous novels set in great houses raised no questions about where the wealth came from. To be sure, the anti-slave trade movement, often led by Quakers, placed some whites on the Black side. Ironically, the burning cane field revolts in Jamaica were often led by men who turned biblical text into fiery denunciation of their own unequal and often murderous treatment. The Bible and the whip are, as Lawrence Cremin once said, effective instruments of a brutal pedagogy of subordination. But the Bible can be used against its oppressors and Jesus himself used a whip to drive out the money-changers. We do, then, see a social pedagogy of resistance to the inhumanity of plantation culture in the West Indies and the US. The Act of Emancipation was proclaimed in 1833. They came bearing the physical and psychological scars of the plantation culture. Itself a brutal learning system, the plantation fostered subordination and colonization of the spirit. Thus, in the age of improvement—which would improve both nature and people, turning the former into commodities and the latter into a homogenous citizenry—Black Canadians had little respect and less opportunity for work and viable community life. Their primary social learning vision entailed survival. They had to stay alive and maintain some sense of "Africanness." They were engaged in a long struggle for recognition. Even in the age of white unionization, Black workers were not allowed to join.

"Extending the Circle of Conversation:" Agricultural Education in Nova Scotia in the Eighteenth and Nineteenth Centuries

In our reflections on learning to make a living in New France in the seventeenth and eighteenth centuries, we considered briefly what men and women needed to know and be able to do in order to cultivate the land. The learning process and procedures were primarily experiential. Men and women had different tasks on the farm; the insights and knowledge gained in the difficult interplay between old ways of doing things and the challenges of the unfamiliar were transmitted orally to other habitants as they, too, made their way across the Atlantic and onto strips of farms running off the St. Lawrence River. Seigneurs may well have had access to more academic forms of knowledge. But agricultural societies with an educational intent (which was part of, and integral to, other goals) formed only in the post–Conquest era. When we examine some of the educational forms emerging in the late eighteenth and throughout the nineteenth century, we "cannot divorce Canadian history from its imperialist past" (Bannister, 2009, p. 101).

Our colonial past is all tangled up with events occurring across the Atlantic (and, in later years, the Pacific). This British imperial project made an uncertain peace with the French in Quebec and deported Acadians in the 1750s. The purpose of this deportation was simply to clear the way for a British liberal regime. This imperial project also clashed with Native peoples in Canada. This project—of instantiating a liberal form of rule anchored in a new conception of the individual (who had rights, liberty, and property)—was resisted by Native peoples who refused to accept liberal conceptions of property and the powerful idea that only individual persons had rights. Clearly, the highly controversial discussion of the consequences of residential schools in Canada cannot be understood apart from the Liberal Order Project.

The study of agricultural adult education is important because we see clearly how scientific knowledge was placed in the service of usefulness. Indeed, in late eighteenth-century England numerous texts appeared that began to advocate improvement in agriculture. The word "improvement" is the key to understanding the energy and desire released into the entire society. This ethos of improvement was fuelled by the scientific revolution that had been launched in the seventeenth century and the Enlightenment in eighteenth-century England and in France. Thus, the older fly-by-the-seat-of-your-pants modes of farming were now contested by proponents of "scientific agriculture." This tension is aptly captured in the words of one W. Marshall (1796), who reported on his travels in Devonshire in England in the late eighteenth century. He thought that the poor Devonshire farmers' knowledge restricted: "the 'spirit of improvement' deeply buried under an accumulation of custom and prejudice" (pp. 106–7).

The condition of the soil in Nova Scotia was discouraging and the travails of trying to establish an economy from 1740 to 1815, when wars between France and England reverberated through Nova Scotia and the American northeast, became even more taxing (Gwyn, 1998). In the late eighteenth century, responding to the plight of agriculture (and the larger economy), several agricultural societies appeared in Nova Scotia. These associations (in what we today call "civil society") were a new pedagogical form, organized, to be sure, by Nova Scotia elites in response to an acute problem of collective life. In 1818 John Young, the Scottish-born Nova Scotian, adopted the pen name of "Agricola" and began publishing letters in *The Acadian Recorder*. His thirty-eight letters, published in 1822 as *The Letters of Agricola*, may be Canada's first text on adult education. Using rather aggressive rhetoric, Young sought to drive a wedge between the dark past and an enlightened present. He lashed out at Nova Scotian farmers' lack of knowledge and skill at the science of farming.

Among other things, he accused them of not understanding the importance of manure for plant growth. The new scientific spirit was the foundation of Young's confident (and paternalistic) sense of pedagogical mission. He advocated strongly that the "circle of conversation" about agricultural matters be widened, and the agricultural societies be revived to serve as the appropriate pedagogical form. He wanted, simply, an "educated agriculture." He ardently believed that with the remarkable increase in agricultural knowledge, farmers would be spurred to emulate the successful and to demonstrate efficient enterprise. Like other liberal thinkers of the time, Young believed that only cultivated land could be identified as property. The wilderness had to be turned into lovely cultivated gardens. This refrain echoes throughout all white, colonial settler societies.

The trajectory of agricultural societies began in 1789, when governing elites created a Society for Promoting Agriculture in Nova Scotia. They had great hopes—never fully realized—but they created a rudimentary communicative learning network. Ideas were seeping out from behind closed doors; the gateway to a more inclusive social learning process was struggling into existence. Indeed, as one correspondent to the agricultural society office declared in November 1791: "The best modes of farming are becoming a topic of conversation." He went on to exhort farmers to reflect seriously upon how to make the most of their farms and how to direct their labours. Learning has always been inextricably bound to our species' interest in controlling nature to maintain our existence. Nonetheless, older more established settlers often continued in their habitual ways, though younger and more vigorous farmers seemed able to leap out of ruts and march down the improvement road.

How deep were these agricultural reforms? Pedagogical science in the early to mid-nineteenth century encouraged competition and rivalry among members to foster an interest in improved farming through exhibitions, fairs, and plowing matches. Heaman (1999) states that exhibitions were designed to incite the "noble passion" of emulation. The mind itself was like unto a field needing preparation for the "seeds—knowledge itself." Historians dispute how effective the reformers' intentions were. We can conclude that despite accusations of paternalism on the educators' part, the struggle for a rationally considered agricultural practice was one useful knowledge resource for farming practice. The opening up of forums for conversational learning on agricultural themes—even though these pedagogical spaces were often peopled with small groups—was no small accomplishment.

Mechanics' Institutes and the Opening up to Science and Technology

In the nineteenth century Canada awakened into its age of industry. The rhythms of everyday life were undergoing profound changes as a new educational configuration was put in place. The pre-industrial sense of space and time was replaced by regularized spatial organization and work life. The lives of children, previously woven into the household economy, were transformed as they were pressed into the "common schools" that were emerging through the worried initiatives of the "school promoters" (led by Egerton Ryerson in Upper Canada). The school and the factory appeared on the changing landscape almost simultaneously. The Methodist educational visionary, Ryerson, contested the limitation of education to the few, opening up the school to everyone. He imagined that the common school could nurture a British North American identity, provide a solution to the presence of disorderly street children, expunge ignorance and crime, harmonize a potentially class fractious society, and prepare children and youth for life in the industrial world (McDonald & Chaiton, 1978).

The intellectual and religious lives of Canadians also underwent significant changes in the nineteenth century. Cultural and intellectual historians have identified the conflict between science and religion as the fundamental conflict of the century. A. B. McKillop's *A Disciplined Intelligence: Critical Inquiry and Canadian Thought in the Victorian Era* (1979) provides an excellent guide to the intellectual and moral challenges of this age. The "higher criticism" and "historical methods" of German theologians unsettled those who defended the sacred authority of the Bible and the historicity of Jesus. The philosophical works of Kant, Hegel, and Marx disrupted the conventional providential understanding of God's purpose unfolding through history. Marx, in particular, cut right to the heart of Christendom, accusing the Christian religion (and all others) of providing mere solace for those suffering from class-based oppression. Once liberated and having cast off their chains, the proletariat would have no further need of its opium (Marx had said, famously, that religion is the opium of the people).

If this was not a full enough smorgasbord of despair, Charles Darwin wrote his earth- and complacency-shattering work, *The Origin of the Species* in 1859. If one follows the contemporary form of the ongoing conflict and dialogue between science and religion, Darwin is still not incorporated into many people's common sense understanding of who we are and where we have come from. McKillop shows how Canadian philosophers and theologians (some of whom were then famous, such as John Clark Murray and Jacob Schurman) generally sought two things: to find some balance between science and religion, and to articulate a "social gospel" which would provide dignity for the worker while securing the institution of private property. Philosopher Leslie Armour (1980) comments: "The philosopher as intellectual munitions maker was unknown." In his perceptive review of McKillop, Armour (1980) observes further: "The models our Victorians looked to could be applied both to nature and to society. Applied to nature, they tended to reconcile the transcendent and the immanent. Applied to society, they tended to insist on a structure ample enough so that everyone had a place which he could hold with dignity…" (p. 36). Nonetheless, the higher criticism, Marxian social critique, and the Darwinian revolution made it more difficult for intellectuals to believe in William Paley's (1802) clockmaker God and a providential understanding of history. Some think that Canadian society was undergoing a profound secularization as the "sea of faith" receded from our shores (see Marshall (1992) and Allen (2008)), the latter's view challenges Marshall). But one has to proceed carefully with such generalizations. As Canadian philosopher Charles Taylor (2007) has argued, secularization is used in different ways, and religious experience may not disappear as such, but take on new forms. Canadian religious history is a thriving and dynamic sub-field of study; religion has not vanished from our lives. In fact, it shapes our current geopolitical landscape of misery and violence.

Suzanne Zweller's major work, *Inventing Canada: Early Victorian Science and the Idea of a Transnational Nation* (1987), and her popular booklet, *Land of Promise, Promised Land: The Culture of Victorian Science in Canada* (1996), documents the growth of numerous natural history associations during the period from around 1830 to 1880. She demonstrates that a new "perceptual framework"—attributing "increasing importance to science, the rational study of nature" (1996, p. 1)—was put in place. But she argues that this new perceptual framework was harnessed to a utilitarian ethic driven by Canada's need to discover sources of coal and other metals to build its industrial base. One can see, then, that local natural history societies nurtured in their conversational learning processes the desire to create state-sponsored scientific projects. One such institutional creation, the Geological Survey of Canada, launched in 1841, was a particularly important exemplar of Victorian "inventory science" (we have identified the collecting mania with an earlier period of European history). The survey was believed to open the path to industrialization and transform the inhabitable wilderness of the northwest into a habitable space.

Three figures—Abraham Gesner, William Logan, and J. William Dawson—played significant roles in the surveying process. In 1838, Gesner was commissioned to find coal for Nova Scotia's development. Logan had the same task for the Canadas in 1841. For his part, Sir William Dawson, principal of McGill College for many years, believed that a "unified nation" could be found within Canada's "natural endowments." Dawson had an accomplished career as a geologist. He worked in the field and made close to two hundred fossil discoveries. His personal collection of Canadian rocks and fossils formed the basis of the holdings of the Peter Redpath Museum. In 1882 they were donated to McGill in his honour. Susan Sheets-Pyerson (1996), his biographer, claims that his scientific reputation rests on his research into paleobotany. He published *Geological History of Plants* in 1888. Dawson was no stranger to controversy as he became an ardent critic of Darwinism. One of his many honours was his successful lobbying for the creation of the Royal Society of Canada in 1882. Dawson was also a major lecturer at the Mechanics' Institutes and other literary and scientific societies. His adult education work involved the communication of scientific ideas and his vision of a transformed Canada to popular audiences.

Mechanics' Institutes embody the ethos of an age intent on the improvement of our minds and productive capacities. Whatever they might have been named, one senses that some sort of institution (or learning site) such as a Mechanics' Institute would have emerged in Canadian society as had its parent in Britain as the country transited from a pre-industrial, largely rural, society to a modern industrial form. This transition required, among other things, a place where people could gather to explore the new scientific inventions, discoveries, and ideas. However, it is important to recognize that while new forms of work requiring more complex cognitive and technical skills were emerging, most people remained in agricultural forms of work. In the pre-industrial period, in places like Nova Scotia and Upper Canada, merchant elites both governed the colonies and sought to control the sources and flow of knowledge. Essentially, three strata existed: a merchant elite, an entrepreneurial elite, and the working class (which consisted of skilled artisans, unskilled labourers, and agricultural workers). These strata were not like the Indian caste system, bound and fixed, with no movement from one caste to the other permitted. They were fluid. This meant that artisans could share a commitment to improvement and progress along with their elite counterparts. Artisans could and did move through apprenticeship ranks to own their own businesses. This fluidity is the main reason for the ambivalence of various scholarly interpretations of Mechanics' Institutes. For example, in New Brunswick and Nova Scotia, elements of the merchant elite actually resisted the formation of Mechanics' Institutes. They wanted to maintain their control over the distribution of primary products and ideas.

But democratic impulses and spiritual energies had been released into colonial society. These impulses placed the merchants in opposition to producers (both those who owned new enterprises and the artisans who worked in them). These tensions would, from time to time, play themselves out in the Mechanics' Institutes. To understand the dynamics at work in the various Institutes, one has to do careful case-by-case analysis. The presence of these new adult learning sites is more wide-spread than one might think (if one has not yet heard of them at all). In Nova Scotia, Institutes rapidly spread from their base in Halifax (1831): Pictou (1834), Sydney (1837), Truro (1839), Windsor (1841), Antigon-ish (1839), Guysborough (1842), Liverpool (1842), Dartmouth (1842), Yarmouth (1835), Arichat (1842), and Stewiacke (1837). New Bruns-wick progressed somewhat more slowly—Hillsborough (1839), briefly in Fredericton (1842), Hampton Ferry (1843), Woodstock and Chatham (1846), Sackville (1847), Dorchester (1848), Bathurst, Maugerville, and Newcastle and Douglastown (1849), St. Stephen (1851), Upper Wood-stock (1852), Burton, Richibucto, and Dalhousie (1854), St. Andrews (1859), and St. John (1838). Prince Edward Island, like the other future provinces within the Confederation, created a riot of literary associations, mutual instruction societies, subscription libraries, and various kinds of debating societies. Charlottetown's Mechanics' Institute was formed in 1838, Georgetown (1842), followed by Stanhope (1843), Bedeque Liter-ary and Scientific Society (1844), Vernon River (1848), Eglinton (1854). Port Hill and Princetown created Institutes in 1850. A similar profusion, except on a larger scale, occurred in Upper and Lower Canada. The Institutes also spread across the country, with the first Mechanics' Insti-tute appearing in British Columbia in 1861 (even the gold rush town of Barkerville sported its very own Institute).

The appearance of these Institutes as an integral component in an emergent educational configuration to democratize knowledge produc-tion, but particularly dissemination, is a major cultural event of the nine-teenth century. In the earliest phases of the Institutes, particularly in the Maritimes, elites tended to dominate in attendance. But this changed as the producing class gained more strength in the middle to late nineteenth century, when skilled artisans predominated. Although the educational programming of the Institutes varied from place to place, we can identify the four primary forms of Institute pedagogy: lectures, libraries, classes, and museums (Frost, 1982). Lectures were particularly eventful, as the nineteenth-century taste for the spectacular and the sensational often took precedence over scientific investigation. But prominent scientists, thinkers, and reformers of the day—such as Joseph Howe in Nova Scotia and William Lyon Mackenzie of Upper Canada—lectured at these Insti-tutes. Hewitt's (1987) study of Mechanics' Institutes in the Maritimes indicates that about 60% of all lectures were on scientific topics, with history and travel a distant second at the Halifax Institute, and a similar pattern in Charlottetown (although by 1856-59, compared to the period between 1839-43, the number of lectures on history, travel, and biography had doubled). Interestingly, the percentage of lectures on science plummeted from 66% in 1839-43 to only 11% between 1871 and 1875 in the St. John Institute.

At the St. John Mechanics' Institute in New Brunswick, Abraham Gesner (1797-1864), a prominent geologist and scientific developer who participated in the Geological Surveys, taught lecture courses. He was rather conservative and imagined that the spread of knowledge would discourage rebellion: the revolts against Family Compacts were not far from his memory. The Institutes brought the new thinking and technological inventions into a public learning space. To be sure, there was an amateurish quality to these displays and lectures (some boring and ill-informed lecturers were booed off the stage), but the "book of nature" was being opened to more people. All of the Institutes created libraries that were accessible to the community (the earlier subscription libraries required fees, thus barring some people from access to books). Some—like the Halifax Mechanics' Institute—had a handsome collection of 2,450 volumes. But Halifax also had other libraries in the early nineteenth century. The Legislative Library, for example, had two hundred volumes in 1819. Churches like St. Andrew's Presbyterian had their own congregational libraries. It is quite understandable that George Renny Young thought Nova Scotians ripe for improvement and ready for a public library of their own.

The Institutes also held classes for artisans. The Toronto Institute provides a good illustration of the central focus of these classes. Ramsey (1999) comments:

> For Mackenzie and others involved in the Institute in the 1830s, the new facility was intended to address the needs of these skilled workers, providing them with much needed classes in reading and writing as well as technical skills, and including the more refined activities of classical studies and art. If workers were to be the backbone of the new community, and that community was not to be the narrow class society of the Family Compact and its followers, the agricultural and industrial workers required an educational and civil structure upon which to build democratic sovereignty and responsible government (p. 85).

This quotation highlights the importance of these Institutes to the evolution of the Canadian just learning society (Welton, 2005, contrasts the "just learning society" with conventional views of lifelong learning).

We must remember that the Institutes were made available to working men and women who often had not attended a public, or common, school. They would have learned basic literacy and numeracy at home (or from private or itinerate tutors), but they would not have had any kind of systematic instruction. Labour historian Bryan Palmer (1983) observes that Hamilton workers made good use of the reading rooms at the Hamilton Mechanics' Institute. There was much emphasis on art classes, but why? Ramsey (1999) says that "knowledge of art was understood to mean a full range of basic copy work for the elementary plan of the mechanic, through the more complex designs of mechanical and technical drawing for design and drafting" (p. 86). These lectures and classes had as their aim the improvement of mechanical and agricultural manufacturing. However, the Institutes, wherever they were, had a difficult time maintaining their classes. Indeed, the Institutes themselves struggled with problems such as financial insolvency, unstable membership (as workers came and went from various locales), and the general difficulties ordinary people had in finding time and money to slip out to an evening class.

Four large Maritime centres—Saint John, Halifax, Charlottetown, and Miramichi—attempted to amass large collections of curiosities. Charlottetown's small, and neglected, cabinet held a skull of a walrus or sea cow. Saint John inherited Abraham Gesner's collection, comprising minerals and natural history exhibits. The museums were expensive to maintain and required significant funds to sustain. Still, the museum was an important educational tool to illustrate geology and natural history. These "cabinets of curiosity," which would evolve into our modern, glistening, hip contemporary museums and art galleries, evoke the earlier period of European history when humanists wandered through European cities searching for collectibles. One can identify continuity from the stumbling beginnings of the Canadian learning society to our more conscious sense that we inhabit a society where knowledge literally explodes at us from endless directions and sites.

In sum, Mechanics' Institutes are a central component of an early industrial learning society (which includes the agriculture societies, common schools, museums, galleries, fairs, scientific institutes, libraries, universities, newspapers and magazines, and voluntary associations such as churches). This we have called the civil society learning infrastructure. Mechanics' Institutes appeared at an historical moment of transition to a new way of seeing and ordering the world. We captured a glint of the way science begins to restructure the way we work in the discussion of agricultural societies. This new ordering was in the service of improvement: of nature and human beings and their social organization. Thus, a number of the key Mechanics' Institutes—Halifax, Saint John, and Toronto—were intimately linked with reform movements against Family Compact forms of

The Montreal Mechanics' Institute was established in 1828 and was the first Mechanics' Institute in Canada. The building is still in use as a library today and was recognized as a National Historic Site of Canada in 2005. (Credit: courtesy of Michael Welton)

rule. W. Lyon Mackenzie and Dr. John Rolph, important reform leaders, were prominent members of the Toronto Institute. In Nova Scotia, the reformer Joseph Howe was a leading player in the Halifax Mechanics' Institute. He gave the first address at its opening, spelling out indelibly the theme of the essential need for an educated citizenry for responsible governance (Keane, 1975).

The Mechanics' Institutes, then, must not be interpreted simply as an educational project that failed to reach its intended audience of "mechanics." They are not simply instruments of elite social control. They are ambivalently democratic spaces. The Mechanics' Institute project was consciously constructed against the restriction of pedagogical space to the ruling colonial elites. These elites—particularly those of the merchant class—exercised tight control over colonial learning processes. They were unwilling to extend the conversation about public issues beyond their own group. These Institutes, as well, can be interpreted as signs that the entrepreneurial elites of the day and interested artisans and farmers were themselves exploring in amateurish fashion the new science and technologies of the day.

We can also conclude that the Mechanics' Institutes signify that the Liberal Order of Rule was being instituted in Canada. The ideology of equality of the Individual required that all men and women be permitted access to all forms of knowledge. Knowledge (of self, others, nature in all of its plenitude) could not be kept from adult learners, nor could the children and youth be subject to restricted forms of education. But many difficult lessons about the full meaning of this awaited Canadians as they marched towards and through the twentieth century. Elites do not give up easily their control over production and distribution of materials, goods, or ideas. And those below often resisted what elites offered as life-enhancing curriculum.

The Education of Public Opinion

The education of public opinion is another central theme in this epochal period of Canadian history. McNairn (2000) has provided a new and exciting reading of the period under consideration. He has shifted the focus away from the traditional, conventional focus on administrative systems. Instead, he has focused on the struggle for political power as a struggle for the control of public opinion and culture. The education of public opinion was one of the features of Victorian Canada. This luminous idea enables us to scan the cultural landscape to understand that the emergent voluntary associations (like literary societies [Dunlop 1973]) were nurturing a citizen identity and community consciousness. Canadian historians have turned attention to this theme. Heather Murray's *Come, Bright Improvement! The Literary Societies of Nineteenth-century Ontario* (2002; see also, 1999) is one illustration; Darren Ferry's *Uniting in Measures of Common Good* (2008) is another. What may be even more important about these literary societies is that they appear to be the locus of learning for some women in colonial Canada. They are gender specific. They are also race specific, as many African Canadian women in nineteenth-century Ontario created many literary societies. It remains to be seen if they can be understood within Nancy Cott's (1977) framework of the "cult of domesticity" manifest within the first wave of nineteenth-century feminism.

One early twentieth-century Canadian historian, D. C. Harvey, wrote about an "intellectual awakening" occurring in Nova Scotia in the late eighteenth and early nineteenth centuries. Harvey finds evidence for this claim in a flourishing publishing culture. In 1789, the date marking the French Revolution, Nova Scotia's first magazine appeared—the *Nova Scotia Magazine and Comprehensive Review of Literature, Politics and News*—whose purpose was to encourage "writing" and "gentlemen to offer their speculation on natural history, topography, and agricultural techniques." It only lasted two years, but was followed by the appearance of the *Acadian Recorder* in 1813. The emergence of the *Free Press* in 1816 projected something of the modern unrest into Nova Scotian life. Many others followed. In 1822, a public subscription library opened in Yarmouth and Pictou, one in Halifax in 1824 and the Halifax Athenaeum in 1834. This sort of close-to-the-ground observation of Canadian cultural life in one of its garden corners can also be carried out in other parts of our country. Wherever Canadians settled—whether in a very tough mining community or on the vastness of the prairies—the settlers never settled for bread over Brahms.

Contemporary adult education theory has oriented us to consider that learning occurs not just in spaces designated as such (a formal school or technical institute). We have made reference to museums, galleries, and exhibitions; we could also hasten to add gardens and zoos (the latter flourished in the nineteenth century). Today these learning sites consciously design educational programming, which takes on various innovative forms. In earlier centuries, the conscious educational intentions were not formalized. But still, gardens, zoos, museums, and exhibitions were "schools that did not seem to teach." Heaman (1999) writes of the way exhibitions eschewed verbal representation for a 3-D encyclopedia that appealed to the eye. Exhibitions appear to precede the common school as a popular pedagogical form. They are saturated with the ideology of improvement, but are not text based.

The ethos of the Victorian age was of investigation, collecting, displaying—all designed to improve on the human and natural stuff now apprehended through the scientific optic (it is also true that the Victorian age could spin away from the head to accentuating the sentiments and "warm heart"). In a sense, the "natural" was now constructed as a pedagogical learning site in itself. While the early explorers (such as Cartier and Champlain) were intensely curious about the new land they were encountering, recording their findings in journals and gathering samples of many things (including people), the collecting impulse broke out in fuller force in nineteenth-century Canada. Many men (mostly) mobilized considerable energy and resources to investigate and map nature, doing "inventory science." The Geological Survey was the main instrument of this science.

Benign Improvement or Persistent Antagonism? First Nations under Colonialism

The pedagogical encounter and antagonism between First Nations and white settlers from Europe began from the first steps of Jacques Cartier and his sailors. Locked from that moment on in a complex mutual learning dynamic (or wrestling match), each learned much from the other. Throughout the mercantile, fur trading era until the arrival of the early industrial society, Natives and whites co-existed, each dependent on the other. But this co-dependency ended as the mode of production transformed itself, marginalizing the Native people in ways previously unknown. During this period until the mid-nineteenth century, Brownlie (2009) argues incisively, Native leaders assumed that they did not have to abandon their traditions or communities. They would have room to direct their own affairs. However, the Canadian state's policy from the mid-nineteenth century onward well into the twentieth, "sought to turn culturally distinct, communally oriented opponents into individualistic, private-property owning liberal subjects" (p. 299). This statement captures the pedagogical nature of this vision precisely. In 1846 the state moved to subdivide the reserves; this met with immediate resistance from Natives. Their identity (and future existence as Aboriginals) was tied to maintaining, not dissolving, their land. Native communities, from this time on, appeared to be under assault.

In the 1820s and 1830s liberal humanitarian impulses (evident in the anti-slave movement [Hochschild, 2005] as well as Aboriginal Protection Societies) worried that Indians might become extinct if they weren't protected. Reserves seemed suitable for this purpose. And to maintain the reserve, legal protection was required. This established the principle of legal protection; a distinct feature of the Gradual Civilization Act of 1857. Now, though, with the rise of the Liberal Order regime, conflicting ideologies were at play. This made it very difficult, if nigh impossible, for the "cultural horizons" of Native and white to converge in mutual outlook and understanding. On the one hand, Natives were to be treated as separate from all other Canadians; on the other, the Liberal regime required the dismantling of the "Indian way of life." Natives were still, it must be said, the cultural other, presenting the state (and other pedagogues like Indian agents or some missionaries) with the challenge to find ways of coercing them into becoming liberal subjects. Thus, the Royal Proclamation of 1763 laid the legal ground for distinct status and treatment of First Nations. The Department of Indian Affairs (DIA) would administer what was "codified in the consolidated Indian Act of 1876, which institutionalized distinct status, rights, and disabilities for First Nations peoples" (Brownlie, 2009, p. 301).

While this surely made many Native peoples feel that they were being treated like children, their separate status was anomalous within the Liberal Order framework. From 1840-80, this specific vision enacted several projects to wrench the Natives from their legal status within the Canadian state. The first, the enfranchisement policy, offered Native individuals the full rights of citizens if they would renounce their status. They would also be given fifty acres of reserve land (apparently without consulting anyone). This was perceived by Native people as an insidious attempt to terminate their "distinction as Indian, dissolve reserves and abolish treaty entitlements by eliminating the groups who could claim them" (Brownlie, 2009, p. 302). The Indian Enfranchisement Act of 1869 would not be removed until 1985. Natives were bargaining with the devil, it seemed, and refused to play this dark game.

Today in our postmodern, uneasily multicultural society, we find it very easy to denounce missionaries at work in Canada since the beginning of the sixteenth century. It is not easy in our secular age to move inside the world outlook of fervent believers like Father Brébeuf, Father Albert Lacombe, Thomas Crosby, or William Duncan (or Native converts like Peter Jones for that matter) in order to see through their eyes. We would rather moralize and judge them. Even if some Canadian Christians of our time may feel queasy, it is fair to say, I think, that the Christianization of the Native peoples ("les sauvages") was perceived by colonizers as a key instrument in gaining indigenous peoples' adherence to colonial policy. Some missionaries may have agreed with the overlaying of Christianity and civilization, but missionaries are not always reliable. In Jamaica, some of the early nineteenth century missionaries held to anti-slavery sentiments, rooted in their understanding of the meaning of being free in Christ. It is true that in the early plantation culture of Jamaica that the Anglicans were in the plantation owners' pay, and deserved a Marxianstyled debunking. But Christian missionaries in Canada, while surely children of their age, held to ideas of equality before God that set them apart from those clinging to biological racist views or crude social Darwinism in the late nineteenth century.

The Canadian state, however, thought that Christianization would wean the Natives away from their pagan ways, leaving them with nowhere to go but into the hands of the Liberal Order. This view was of particular importance from 1840–80. The state wanted to improve the Natives: to transform them into deracinated Canadians. From the churches' perspective, Indians had to be saved from themselves and the evils of the newcomer society. In his famous book, *Up and Down the North Pacific Coast by Canoe and Mission Ship* (1914), Methodist Thomas Crosby laments profoundly the deleterious evidence of the evil newcomer: alcohol shipped into Native communities and prostitution in the alleys of Victoria. Brownlie (2009) comments that the missionaries and the liberal humanitarians allied themselves to defend Aboriginal peoples. They "decisively shaped Upper Canada's Indian policy in the 1820s and 1830s, and frequently intervened in Aboriginal affairs for many decades afterwards" (p. 302). Missionaries often advocated for Native peoples, taking action to protect their communities. They even criticized the popular idea that Natives were somehow doomed to vanish. They provided voice for those Natives living in a "culture of silence" when the government had turned a deaf ear to Indian voices. Brownlie (2009) argues that: "The churches and missionaries maintained a belief in Aboriginal potential for cultural and political equality long after such beliefs were effectively abandoned by the general Canadian population and by most DIA officials" (p. 303). As adult educators of Native peoples and educators of the government itself, the churches mattered to the state: Christianization was an integral part of the assimilation process.

The residential school was a chosen instrument of assimilation of children and youth. The churches thought they would be harsh, but suitable forms to transmit the necessary knowledge and skills to function in a white-dominated society. No schooling in the mid-to-late nineteenth century was much fun. Bruce Curtis' pioneering study (1988) dug into previously un-tapped archives of Upper Canada and discovered countless cases of violence against teachers and the burning to the ground of the schoolhouse. But the discipline, the regimentation, the work in surrounding gardens or laundries, and poor health care was radically unable to even do much of a job of assimilating Native youth to stand tall and speak their truths. The separation of the children from home was meant to make the assimilation process easier. Alas, children often returned from their schooling only to be absorbed into Native rituals and ceremonies. And Native parents came to some schools, complaining of an abusive teacher and withdrawing their own children (Gresko, 1980). But the residential school made complete and logical sense within the Liberal Order framework. Even though only a small percentage of children actually went to a residential school, they did not succeed in effacing Native cultures. They did, however, lead to considerable pain and emotional confusion (leading the Canadian government to offer an apology). Still, the school itself cannot take all the blame. The Canadian state must assume this burden of responsibility for the devastating consequences of their attempt to impose a way of being and doing on a particular community that holds to a different conception of the world, the land, of rights, of raising its children, of maintaining its own identity.

The colonial governing, elites, employers, and missionaries adhered to a monarchical, Tory tradition of paternalism. This benevolent paternalism meant that elites had to protect and provide minimal care for its subordinates. The treaties, reserves, and separate status of Native peoples reflected this paternalism; ironically, it enabled them to preserve crucial anchors of their cultural identity. The Liberal Order gradually set this colonial benevolence aside as the early industrial society expanded into a full-fledged corporate form. Indian Affairs was a kind of hybrid, with the enfranchisement project pure Liberalism, and the Acts protecting the Indians reflecting the early paternalism. At the heart of colonial paternalism, manifest in Africa, India, the Middle East, and Asia as well (Mishra, 2012), was the searing idea that the subjects were collectively unfit to govern themselves. Thus, resistant or oppositional pedagogies struggled against the cultural hegemony of the elites. Workers soon learned that their wages and working conditions would never change if they merely waited on the good graces of the bosses. Native peoples knew what the Canadian state was up to and resisted where and when they were able. In the movement for responsible government and the development of a more complex learning infrastructure in the nineteenth century, colonial subjects struggled to be recognized as citizens. For women, this meant they would not receive suffrage until around the end of WWI. And for Blacks the situation was bleaker.

Deeply transformative learning occurs when the parties to conversation, individuals or cultures, open themselves to learning something significant, something that might change the way they understand themselves, the social and cultural worlds, what it means to engage one another respectfully with full dignity. The science of anthropology in the Victorian era worked within a social evolutionary framework, with primitive peoples placed at a lower level on the scale than civilization at the apex (Harris, 2001). The respect for the other had to await the 1920s, when Franz Boas (1940) began gathering Northwest Coastal Indian ethnographic data on myths, practices, rituals, and art. Anthropology was, indeed, as Clyde Kluckhohn (1949) wrote, a "mirror for man." Victorians gazed at the mirror and saw themselves smiling back. But First Nations peoples did not reject liberalism completely. Natives believed in, and practiced, free speech, personal liberty and freedom of belief. Confronted by the Jesuits in seventeenth century New France, many Native philosophers and leaders could not quite understand why there seemed to be "one best way." Plains Indians, too, were no strangers to individual self-expression: their young men went on quests for their guardian spirits, a lonely, often difficult and painful, quest. Most Native cultures were egalitarian (the Iroquois being famous for their democratic practices), with the exception of the hierarchical chiefdoms of the Northwest Coast. Even there, the potlatch, in its purest form, worked to redistribute goods to those areas of the coast that had a rough winter or harvesting season. But one cannot press the comparison too far: Native peoples were reluctant to impose on others, including children; they respected the other's dignity so much that they did not interfere; they were more communitarian than pure Liberal possessive individualists.

Thus, the introduction of Liberalism (the political form most appropriate to an industrial, capitalist social, and economic order) threatened to "undercut this carefully balanced existence, for it suggests to the individual that the community has no inherent value, that others only have value in relation to one's own self-examined beliefs and that one has no inherent responsibility to any being other oneself" (Brownlie, 2009, p. 308). Natives also knew that even when they adopted Christian values and European ways, they were not received by white society as fully equal partners. One could abandon one's cultural values and still face a marginal, lonely existence. Then, too, always in the shadows of state attempts to unsettle Natives from their lands lay the capitalist entrepreneurs who wanted their resources. In response, Natives adopted two strategies. They used the master's tools to dismantle his house by using liberal precepts as instruments to fight colonialism. They even allied with the Family Compact in Upper Canada who still believed in the treaty rights. They embraced Christianity, too, because they thought the missionaries might be potential allies in the resistance to colonization. Conversion to a God who made all human beings equal provided semantic potential in their struggle for recognition as full citizens with collective rights. Becoming a Christian in this age of assimilation meant that they had access to Western education (which many Natives wanted, but often got something else) and a broad Christian public interested in their fate and future. Thus, Christianity provided more resources for their affirmation of identity than Liberalism did. It also opened up a global public space for debate and discussion about the fate of indigenous peoples.

The Canadian Liberal state may have wanted to play the role of confident, fatherly pedagogue who knew what the Native peoples needed to become. They were raw material, like a wilderness, that needed working over and improvement into something civilized. However, the very structure of treaties, reserves, Indian Act, federal responsibility for Aboriginal peoples set them apart. The government was forced, as Brownlie observes

Aboriginal students attending the Metlakatla Indian Residential School (Credit: William James Topley / Library and Archives Canada / C-015037)

poignantly, into keeping their obligations and maintaining their responsibility for Native peoples. The social learning processes within besieged Native communities—a kind of subterranean stream flowing through their histories—served as lifeworld resources to resist enfranchisement policies. The lifeworld curriculum prepared by the state tutors of the Native peoples was served up and resisted, even though the undermining (or damaging) of traditional native economic structures in the various sub-regions of Canada created vulnerabilities to the pathologies of failed modernization. Their own lifeworld curriculum rejected the two fundamental premises of the Liberal Order paradigm: individual rights as properties of the individual and the notion of universal rights that are blind to difference. Native peoples had to be constantly alert to the Canadian state's attempts to colonize their lifeworlds (Habermas, 1984, 1987): to turn Indians into rational men of the age of enlightenment and improvement.

In the wild and dark forests of northern British Columbia—captured vividly by Emily Carr's paintings—in a village called Metlakatla, William Duncan, an intrepid Church Missionary Society (Anglican) missionary, convinced a band of Tsimshian Native people to create a Christian utopian community in the wilderness of the early 1860s. Duncan can be seen as a symbol of the evangelizing and sentimental impulses of Victorian Christianity (Taylor, 2007, has labelled this period the "Age of Mobilization"). Christianizing was integral to the improvement ideology. Conversion to Jesus Christ was believed to provide the motivational energy for people to live disciplined, moral lives. The industrial age required conservation of moral energy as people adapted to the machine-age rhythms that were remote from the work rhythms of hunting and gathering or fishing or even farming. The consumption of alcohol, for instance, had to be restricted or considerably limited so that men could work their long days. And Christianizing the native peoples of Canada was an integral part of the Liberal Order Project to undermine Native adherence to non-liberal values and norms. The Metlatkatla utopian experiment weaves all of these themes together. Duncan and his Native followers wanted to establish a "type of commune that practices Christianity and also transferred education, industrial training, and Europeanized amusements" (Miller, 1989, p. 149). What a fascinating variant of the Liberal Order paradigm! Duncan's utopian experiment hints at different ways of being Indian and being Christian. There is no single homogenized way of "being Indian." The forms of Native Christian expression were often hybrids, incorporating elements from traditional spirituality. Nor would this be the last attempt to creating a "total learning community": the Finnish immigrant Matti Kurikka attempted to establish a utopian island co-operative community, Sointula, on Malcolm Island, BC, in 1901.

Learning Traditions Among African Nova Scotians Under Bitter Conditions

The African Loyalists, Maroons, and the refugees from 1812 who came to Nova Scotia bore the scars and psychological wounds of the bitter world of slavery. The whip and the Bible had been used to miseducate the Blacks on the plantations of the West Indies and the US south. They had been subjected to the pedagogies of dominance. But through embracing a liberating reading of the scriptures, they believed that their own exodus to a promised land would arrive one day (Genovese, 1976). Blacks fused remnants of traditional musical and cultural forms with a vernacular gospel that spoke of deep suffering and an even deeper hope. The Blacks arriving in Nova Scotia, scarcely a Promised Land at that time, from 1785-1813, had not learned their lessons of survival in classrooms. They encountered two harsh pedagogues: the environment and the hostile Anglo-Celtic settlers. They did bring some "cultural baggage" with them to Nova Scotia, but they certainly did not find that the rudimentary institutions of Nova Scotia were open to them. They were radically segregated, and had little opportunity for work and formal schooling for their children. Thus, African Nova Scotians faced their challenges in non-formal settings. Delvina Bernard (n.d) states that the "racially segregated Nova Scotian community became their classroom and each racist and or philanthropic encounter with the colonial rulers of the day, became their curriculum."

Africans, like First Nations and Chinese peoples, were forced into segregated forms of learning. The resistance of Natives to the Liberal Order colonial project (within a treaty framework) took the form of a discordant pedagogy, whereas it makes sense to consider the learning sites created by Black Nova Scotians an outcast form. Their lifeworld curriculum centred in survival and adaptation to hostile conditions; unlike First Nations, they had no form of legal protection whatsoever. Winks (1997; orig. 1971), author of *Blacks in Canada: A History*, identifies "sources of strength" as provided by church, press, and schools. As outcasts, the Blacks in Nova Scotia had to create their own separate learning infrastructure (or form of civil society). By the mid-nineteenth century the African United Baptist Association (AUBA) (founded in 1854) would become the keystone learning site within their infrastructure. Social clubs emerged (in Ontario in the late 1800s, Black women formed their own literary societies); and the powerful Negro Lodge of Free and Accepted Masons was established in 1856. Bernard (n.d.) vigorously states: "These institutions which still exist today, can be credited for having successfully provided a safe, culturally sensitive, democratic, and highly communicative learning site where Africans not only learned the skills, knowledge and social graces needed to function in Nova Scotian society, but also acquired the appropriate indoctrination, and African cultural assimilation needed to sustain a counter perspective, worldview, and pedagogy—all of which was essential to cultural survival." Throughout Black history in Canada the church would serve as the base from which many other projects would be launched. It was a kind of educational and political mobilizing centre (just as St. Francis Xavier would be in the Tompkins-Coady era of the 1920s to 1950s).

The Black rudimentary learning infrastructure grew and expanded into the 1970s. The Odd Fellows Lodge of 1890, the important Nova Scotia Home for Coloured Children in 1921; the African United Baptist Women's Institute of the 1930s; the Nova Scotia Association for the Advancement of Coloured People in 1945; the Brotherhood of Sleeping Car Porters in 1946; the movement to form the George Washington Carver Credit Union in 1950: these are a few of the associations created by Black Nova Scotians. In 1945 Nova Scotia formed a division of adult education under the brilliant leadership of Guy Henson. He initiated several adult education projects among the Black population; the Rev.

William P. Oliver, the formidable preacher at the keystone AUBA church in Halifax, the Cornwallis St. Church, a man in the Booker T. Washington tradition of self-help and education, worked with Henson. Bernard, herself an activist, musician, and proponent of Africentrism in contemporary Nova Scotia, wonders if African Nova Scotians actually developed some distaste for formal adult education because they associated institutional with a European way of life and non-formal and informal structures with the African/Black way of being and doing. Bernard also wonders about the limitations (as well as obvious strengths) of this preference and if this has disenabled them from functioning craftily and ably in white-dominant institutions.

Richard Preston, the Black Baptist minister and abolitionist, born in Virginia in 1791 or 1792, founded the AUBA. His voice must be recovered from our silenced past. In Black histories, Preston is seldom given credit as an adult educator, remaining invisible unlike the white adult educators Fathers Jimmy Tompkins and Moses Coady, Guy Henson as well as others. He has been labelled a preacher and an abolitionist—is that end of the story? Thinking of Preston through the learning lens may spark new forms of inquiry. Preston had purchased his freedom from Virginia slavery and learned to read and write before reaching Halifax, a rather dreary, damp, and gloomy Anglo-military base in this period. He immediately fell in with African brethren of Preston and Halifax who were in the spiritual care of John Burton, a former Methodist missionary from Durham, England, who had become a Baptist while in the US. He quickly revealed leadership talent and powerful oratorical skills and soon took charge of Christian missions among the scattered communities of African Nova Scotians. This was timely: the African community had lost some of its members, as they had sought a better (and sunnier) life in Sierra Leone.

The task facing Preston was arduous and difficult. Bernard (n.d) argues that Preston had to "transform their aspirations from the limits of being mere builders, on the periphery of white society, to that of proud architects of their own African social world." After racialized tussles with Burton's mixed race First Baptist Church, the African communicants were convinced that they had to form their own, separate Black church. With Burton aging, Preston seized the day and went to Britain in 1831 to be trained as a preacher and build support for an African chapel in Nova Scotia. He fell into the company of illustrious Abolitionists like William Wilberforce and Thomas Fowler Brixon during its historical high point: the achievement of the Emancipation for Black slaves in 1833. With his

preaching skills honed and his vernacular speech permeated with Abolitionist rhetoric, Preston arrived in Halifax after his year in London in
1832. He returned to England shortly after and was ordained, returning with funds to build the Cornwallis St. Church in 1833. Preston was
also involved in creating the Halifax African Abolitionist Society and
the African Friendly Society, establishing a pattern in Black culture of
using the church as a base from which to pry open public space for the
education of the public on matters of slavery and human rights. Though
short-lived, Bernard says that these ventures were "informal schools of
political education."

Preston's own high point came on September 1, 1854, when he
founded the African United Baptist Association (AUBA), a union of
twelve churches. The AUBA became a folk school in itself. There, people could be transformed from people consigned to menial tasks into
deacons, deaconesses, leaders, and superintendents of Sunday Schools.
They were transfigured into somebodies. They could be masters of their
own houses, brothers and sisters, children of God. Bernard argues that
the AUBA and its network of associations (such as schools for children)
was a learning site where they learned skills, dispositions, and attitudes
to express their full engagement in their communities. They learned to
account for money, raise funds for capital projects, organize and conduct
business meetings, make public presentations, carry out political lobbying activities (always in the face of much hostility such as white mobs
breaking up meetings in the 1840s), and practice democratic organizing
principles. Black Nova Scotians were under surveillance and they had
to demonstrate that they were moral people who could run their affairs
and control selected dimensions of their life situation. Heavenly salvation
was fused with earthly emancipation. From the 1930s to the 1970s, self-
help and communication development flourished in Black communities
in Nova Scotia, Quebec, and Ontario. The lifeworld curriculum of the
Black Nova Scotians was offered as a counter-pedagogy to the racist curriculum of Nova Scotia's rather selective induction of improvement for
some and not others.

Bernard sums up her own understanding of her history: "African
Nova Scotian adult education history is the same as the adult education
history of other great Nova Scotians in that it is a history of grappling
with issues of freedom and emancipation; it is a history that tackles issues
of commitment and responsibility. Most important, it is a history that
situates education in the context of the general good of the people." She
also believes that telling the Black story reveals how racialized the Nova

Scotian social, political, and economic climate has been. Drawing lessons from Preston's life, Bernard claims that his "curriculum of spiritual and political emancipation accords to a larger message of preservation, survival, and reproduction of the lifeworld." Thus, to "uncover this history of Father Richard Preston and the AUBA, is to uncover the early history of adult education in the African Nova Scotia community."

References

Allen, R. (2008). *The view from Murney Tower: Salem Bland, Victorian controversies, and the search for a new Christianity.* Toronto: University of Toronto Press.

Armour, L. (1980). Some agreeable minds. In *Canadian Forum,* June–July.

Bannister, J. (2009). Canada as counter-revolution: The Loyalist Order Framework in Canadian history, 1750–1840. In J. Constant & M. Ducharme (Eds.). *Liberalism and hegemony: Debating the Canadian liberal revolution* (pp. 98–146). Toronto: University of Toronto Press.

Bernard, D. (n.d.). "Learning traditions among African Nova Scotians" and "Rendering the invisible visible: The life and times of Richard Preston." Study papers for graduate seminar, Mount St. Vincent University.

Boas, F. (1940). *Race, language, and culture.* New York: The Macmillan Company.

Brownlie, R. J. (2009). A persistent antagonism: First Nations and the Liberal Order. In J.F. Constant & M. Ducharme (Eds.). *Liberalism and hegemony: Debating the Canadian liberal revolution* (pp. 298–321). Toronto: University of Toronto Press.

Cott, N. (1977). *Bonds of womanhood: "Woman's sphere" in New England, 1780–1835.* New Haven: Yale University Press.

Crosby, T. (1914) *Up and down the North Pacific Coast by canoe and mission ship.* Toronto: Missionary Society of the Methodist Church.

Curtis, B. (1988). *Building the educational state: Canada West, 1836–1871.* Philadelphia (PA): Falmer Press.

Dunlop, A. C. (1973). The Pictou literary and scientific society. *Nova Scotia Historical Quarterly,* 3(2), 99–116.

Ferry, D. (2008). *Uniting in Measures of Common Good.* Kingston/Montreal: McGill-Queen's University Press.

Frost, S. (1982). Science education in the nineteenth century: The Natural History Society of Montreal, 1827–1925. *McGill Journal of Education,* 17(1), 31–41.

Genovese, E. (1976). *Roll, Jordan, roll: The world the slaves made.* New York: Vintage Books.

Gresko, J. (1980). White "rites" and Indian "rites": Indian education and native responses in the West, 1870–1910. In D. C. Jones, N. Sheehan, & R. M. Stamp (Eds.). *Shaping the schools of the Canadian West.* Calgary (AB): Detselig Enterprises.

Gwyn, J. (1998). *Excessive expectations: Maritime commerce and the economic development of Nova Scotia, 1740–1870.* Montreal/Kingston: McGill-Queen's University Press.

Habermas, J. (1972). *Knowledge and human interests.* London: Heinemann Books.

Habermas, J. (1984). *The theory of communicative action. Volume 1: Reason and the rationalization of society.* Boston: Beacon Press.

Habermas, J. (1987). *The theory of communicative action. Volume 2: Lifeworld and a system: A critique of functionalist reason.* Boston: Beacon Press.

Harris, M. (2001). *Rise of anthropological theory: A history of theories of culture.* Walnut Creek (CA): AltaMira Press.

Heaman, E. (1999). *The inglorious arts of peace: exhibitions in Canadian society during the nineteenth century.* Toronto: University of Toronto Press.

Hewitt, M. (1986). The Mechanics' Institutes movement in the Maritimes, 1831–1889. Unpublished Master's thesis. University of New Brunswick, Fredericton and Saint John.

Hochschild, A. (2005). *Bury the chains: Prophets and rebels in the fight to free an empire's slaves.* Boston: Houghton Mifflin.

Keane, P. (1975). A study in early problems and policies in adult education: The Halifax Mechanics' Institute. *Social History,* 6(16), 255–74.

Kelly, J. (1998). *Under the gaze: Learning to be black in white society.* Halifax (NS): Fernwood Publishers.

Kelly, J. (2006). Black identity and community. In T. Fenwick, T. Nesbit, & B. Spencer (Eds.). *Contexts of adult education: Canadian perspectives.* Toronto: Thompson Educational Publishing.

Kluckhohn, C. (1949). *Mirror for man: A survey of human behavior and social attitudes.* Greenwich (CN): Fawcett Publishers.

Marshall, D. (1992). *Secularizing the faith: Canadian protestant clergy and the crisis of belief, 1850–1940.* Toronto: University of Toronto Press.

Marshall, W. (1796) The rural economy of the west of England.: Including Devonshire, and parts of Somersetshire, Dorsetshire, and Cornwall. London : Printed for G. Nicol, G.G., J. Robinson and J. Debrett.

McDonald, N. & Chaiton, A. (Eds.). (1978). *Egerton Ryerson and his times: Essays on history of education.* Toronto: Macmillan of Canada.

McKay, I. (2009). The liberal order framework: A prospect for a reconnaissance of Canadian history. In J.F. Constant & M. Ducharme (Eds.). *Liberalism and hegemony: Debating the Canadian Liberal Revolution* (pp. 35–63). Toronto: University of Toronto Press.

McKillip, A.B. (1979). *A Disciplined Intelligence: Critical Inquiry and Canadian Thought in the Victorian Era.* Montreal/Kingston: McGill-Queen's University Press.

McNairn, J. (2000). *Capacity to judge public opinion and deliberative democracy in Upper Canada, 1791–1854.* Toronto: University of Toronto Press.

Miller, J. R. (1989). *Skyscrapers hide the heavens: A history of Indian-White relations in Canada.* Toronto: University of Toronto Press.

Mishra, P. (2012). *From the ruins of empire: The revolt against the west and the remaking of Asia.* Toronto: Doubleday Canada.

Murray, H. (1999). Great works and good works: The Toronto women's literary club, 1877–83. *Historical Studies in Education,* 11(1), 75–95.

Murray, H. (2002). *Come, bright improvement: The literary societies of nineteenth-century Ontario.* Toronto: University of Toronto Press.

Paley, W. (1802). *Natural theology: Or, evidences of the existence and attributes of the deity, collected from the appearance of nature.* New York: Sheldon and Company.

Palmer, B. (1983). *Working-class experience: The rise and reconstitution of Canadian Labour, 1800–1980.* Toronto: Butterworth and Company.

Pentland, H. C. (1981). *Labour and capital in Canada 1650–1860.* Toronto: James Lorimer & Company.

Ramsey, E. (1999). Art and industrial society: The role of the Toronto Mechanics' Institute in the promotion of art, 1831–1883. In *Labour/LeTravail,* 43, 71–103.

Robins, N. (1987). "Useful knowledge for the workingman": The Montreal mechanics' institute, 1828–1870. In M. Welton (Ed.). *Knowledge for the people: The struggle for learning in English-speaking Canada, 1828–1973.* Toronto: OISE Press.

Said, E. (1993). *Culture and imperialism.* New York: Knopf.

Sheets-Pyerson, S. (1996). *John W. Dawson: Faith, hope, and science*. Montreal/Kingston: McGill-Queens University Press.

Sherlock, P. & Bennett, H. (1997). *The story of the Jamaican people*. Kingston: Ian Randle Publishers.

Taylor, C. (2007). *A secular age*. Cambridge (MA): Belknap Press of Harvard University Press.

Welton, M. (n.d.). "Extending the circle of conversation": Agricultural adult education in Nova Scotia in the eighteenth and nineteenth centuries. Unpublished paper.

Welton, M. (2005). *Designing the just learning society: A critical inquiry*. Leicester (UK): NIACE Publishing.

Winks, R. (1997). *Blacks in Canada: a history*. Montreal/Kingston: McGill-Queen's University Press.

Zweller, S. (1987). *Inventing Canada: Early Victorian science and the idea of a transnational nation*. Montreal/Kingston: McGill-Queen's University Press.

Zweller, S. (1996). *Land of promise, promised land: The culture of Victorian science in Canada*. Ottawa: Canadian Historical Association.

4

Adult Learning in the Age of the "Great Transformation" (1880-1929)

The period from 1880 until the outbreak of the debilitating depression of 1929 was enormously breath-taking, conflict-ridden (even brutal), eventful and turbulent. It was as if there had been a great tectonic shift beneath the floor of Western civilization. The Edwardian complacency and self-satisfaction of British imperialism and European culture was shattered in the gas-filled trenches of World War I (the war that was supposed to end all wars, but was merely a prelude to another a generation later). Poet Wilfred Owen's "sweet wine of youth" poured out in noble sacrifice for one's nation prior to 1914 had turned into Siegfried Sassoon's war poetry of nihilistic, hollow-eyed men staring into nothingness by the war's end. The capitalist ruling elites of Europe (and Canada) were under siege throughout this period: in Germany, for example, the German liberal synthesis of Protestantism and high ideals (particularly reflected in German theology) collapsed in the hell of WWI.

 This led youthful theologians like the Swiss Karl Barth to pronounce anathema on his teachers and the tattered culture of liberal Protestantism. The great socialist parties of Europe, particularly German Social Democracy led by Karl Kautsky and Eduard Bernstein, had imagined that the new socialist world could come gradually, through the ballot box and extensive adult education work filtered through numerous voluntary associations. But they had been discredited—the German SDP supported the German war effort, thus sundering the old Marxian cry for workers of the world to unite. The route taken by the Russian Bolsheviks—a vanguard seizing state power—broke out in the horrors of civil strife of 1917; and in the war's aftermath, left wing socialists (like Rosa Luxemburg) had tried to create "workers' councils" or soviets in cities like Berlin. She ended her life, dumped unceremoniously into a river.

The Russian Revolution sent shock waves throughout Canadian elite circles, and was greeted heartily by many Canadian workers, who had their great moment in the Winnipeg general strike of 1919. So did World War I: thousands of Canadians died in this war (some historians have suggested that Canada was a born as a "nation" at the battle of Vimy

Ridge in 1917), and those who returned were often determined to build a better and more secure world. That was the case with the Scots Watson Thomson and John Grierson, who would both play seminal and creative roles in the Canadian adult education movements of the 1930s and 1940s (Welton, 1983, 1987; Pollard, 1987). During this period the slogan "Knowledge for the people" became the watchword of a wide variety of truly remarkable adult education ventures in collective learning and action. If the "age of improvement" saw the beginnings of the democratization of knowledge in the emergent voluntary associations, visual pedagogies, and written publications, during the "age of great transformation" the floodgates were opened wide. Adult education became more conscious of itself, more formalized in sensibility. But the first federated association of Canadian adult educators would only be created in the mid-1930s, and the academic study of adult learning and education the late 1950s and early 1960s.

The mobilization of women—one of our greatest adult education movement in our history—occurs in this period as women awaken to their subjugation and restriction to the domestic household. Women literally explode with energy and motivation to be full citizens, actively engaged in the great debates about what Canadian society had to change to be a hospitable place for all women. The working class gradually found its collective voice by the late nineteenth century as the Knights of Labour, formed in Philadelphia in 1869, entered Ontario and Quebec in 1875, and organized 450 assemblies across Canada. They were strongest in Quebec, Ontario, and BC, but established locals in the Nova Scotia, New Brunswick, and Manitoba. They also offered a wide range of adult education activities (Kealey and Palmer, 1987). Workers everywhere in Canada faced tough bosses and dangerous working conditions: this was most evident in the coal fields of Cape Breton and little places like Cumberland on Vancouver Island. They organized trade unions, formed federations, and educated themselves during this time. Socialists had their own networks of people's forums; the socialist coal miner and union leader in the Cape Breton coalfields, J. B. McLachlan, even dreamed of creating a Labour College in the early 1920s. The Workers' Educational Association (the WEA), an import from Britain and the brainchild of Albert Mansbridge, was born first in Toronto in 1917/8, and later in other cities in Canada. This important voluntary association existed precariously in relationship to the staid, emergent extension divisions of the universities of Toronto, McGill, and Queen's. The most innovative venture in workers' education was initiated by Alfred Fitzpatrick, the quirky Presbyterian minister, who took knowledge to the camp men far removed from urban, polite society and university classes comprised mainly of elite, white males.

Universities, old and new, either developed their incipient extension programs, or, like the Universities of Alberta and Saskatchewan, made the extension of knowledge to its citizenry an integral part of its mission. In 1928/9, St. Francis Xavier University in Antigonish, Nova Scotia, would take some of its inspiration from these innovative universities for the people. The president of the University of Alberta, Dr. H. Tory, spearheaded another remarkable adult education project during World War I. Amidst some controversy with the YMCA over the control of army education, Tory headed up Khaki University which served fifty thousand men with courses and assisted with integration into civilian life. Classes were even held in the trenches—the University of Vimy Ridge—a stunning image of study before heading into enemy machine gun fire (Cook, 2002; Crearer, 1995). Although the prairie universities often had links with the farm movements, the Saskatchewan Grain Growers and United Farmers of Alberta in the early twentieth century organized themselves as learning sites, through establishing locals, organizing conferences, and publishing farm journals and papers. Agrarian radicals of this period believed that knowledge was power, and often were critical of conventional forms of democracy.

During this period Canadian Protestantism and a minority presence within Roman Catholicism (in Quebec and Nova Scotia) began to understand their faith in less transcendental terms, identifying "being Christian" as working to bring the "kingdom of God" down to earth. Religion was flattened out along the horizontal plane. Many of Canada's celebrated adult education initiatives—from Frontier College to the Antigonish Movement to many of women's projects—were impelled by a social gospel dynamic and ethic. Women's role in the social gospel movement has been neglected. We try to restore this lack in our examination of the adult education work of Beatrice Brigden and Nellie McClung as well as deepening our understanding of women's role and difficulties achieving equality in the Antigonish Movement. *Knowledge for the People*—the title of Catholic social gospel exponent Father Jimmy Tompkins' impassioned booklet written in 1921—captures the spirit of reform (knowledge was necessary to reform the world, to make it a better place) during the late nineteenth and early twentieth centuries. The world as Tompkins' expressed it was "fraught with wonderful possibilities." If extended to include women, the world was indeed fraught with wonderful possibilities. This period accentuates the importance of social movements as pre-eminent collective learning sites and the expansion of human possibility.

However, not every Canadian had the same wonderful possibilities. Fitzpatrick sought without great success to alert urban Canadians to the plight of the neglected camp men. First Nations continue their struggles against the Canadian state and imposed adult education. But important political organizations began to appear as early as 1941 with Andrew Paull's Native Brotherhood of BC (Paull had been educated by the Oblates). As well, Black Nova Scotians created various new organizations during this period, while continuing to face racist hostility and poor work and educational prospects. Black immigrating to Alberta in the 1910s also faced serious racism. Then, too, Chinese immigrants faced their own misery, working on railroads and as cheap labour in the Vancouver Island coal fields. European immigrants had to face, like these others, the suspicions of a still very Anglo-conformist society. The cry of "White Canada forever," shouted out at the turn of twentieth century in BC, still echoed through the following decades (Ward, 1978; Wang, 2006). For their part, Chinese immigrants first came to Canada in 1858, lured by gold in the Fraser Canyon, and, in the 1880s, to work as contract labour on the CPR. They faced legal, social, and racist prejudice against their very presence. They were driven to segregation: in their own communities they created benevolent societies and clan-nurtured forms of association that enabled them to maintain a Chinese identity (the Protestant missionaries, as Wang [2006] brilliantly shows, offered them a loving God but no possible way of becoming integrated into Canadian society). They were faced with the choice of rejecting their Chinese religious and cultural form of life in exchange for rejection by whiter society. These were harsh lessons to learn. Most turned away from the offer.

The seeds of the new industrial order, planted here and there in a still largely rural nineteenth century, began to flower in the late nineteenth and early twentieth centuries. In the first twenty-five years between the election of Sir Wilfred Laurier in 1896 and the resignation of Sir Robert Borden in 1921, Canada was a country being transformed (Brown and Cook, 1974). Our population increased by three million as immigrants flowed into the country, mostly into the west. Cities like Calgary and Vancouver leapt into existence almost overnight. Two new provinces were created, Alberta and Saskatchewan, and British Columbia was opened up, revealing vast new sources of mineral wealth and energy. In the early twentieth century, wheat—prairie gold—poured into the bakeries of Europe. Two new transcontinental railways were chartered. Highways and roads sliced up the landscape more systematically than in the days of horse and buggy. Canada was becoming a new place. But not any old place: after Confederation Canada was to become an "Anglo-Saxon culture that shared 'a heritage of political democracy, evangelical Protestant Christianity,' and of the Canadian nation as a vehicle for a moral imperialism that would spread Christian civilization around the world" (Wang, 2006, p. 7). We should be alerted, then, to noticing the way this overarching vision of what Canada was, and could become, filtrated into the work of adult educators in numerous reform movements.

Canadians faced at least three marked learning challenges in the late nineteenth century and the opening decades of the twentieth.

 First, *the peopling of the prairie west*. Two million and more Canadians added a new ethnic dimension to Canadian life in the prairie west. Contrary to popular mythology, a significant number of these immigrants found employment in the burgeoning agricultural and industrial sectors as wage labourers. Conditions of work in the camps, mines, and farm settlements were harsh, and daily life was often a scramble for existence. The massive influx of newcomers confronted Canadians—particularly those of Anglo-Saxon lineage—with this challenge: what kind of nation would we become? One of our leading social thinkers of the early twentieth century, J. S. Woodsworth, who wrote *Strangers Within our Gates* (1909), exhibited clear preference for "northern races." Chinese, he believed, were not easily assimilated. Even this progressive-minded man could not quite get beyond his ethnic and Christian heritage (see Mills, 1991). The anti-Chinese riots in Vancouver in the early twentieth century attest to this unease with Chinese immigrants.

Canadians were in the early stages of learning to live with diversity and building an inclusive pluralistic society. Adult educators working in settlement houses in Winnipeg or teaching night classes in some remote single-room school house believed that the "immigrant" ought to assimilate, to conform to what they thought were the correct norms (this is called Anglo-conformism: loyal to the Crown, British forms of law and governance, and liberal values). Others—notably women involved in Homemakers Clubs in Saskatchewan—also sought to integrate women from places like the Ukraine into their associations. But life for immigrants was not easy in the early years. Anglo-conformists did not like the sound of "foreign tongues"; they didn't like the fact that German Mennonites wanted their own schools; they were not sure about the new religious expressions appearing on the prairie landscape. Sometimes, too, men and women from non-Anglo backgrounds opted for radical politics (like the Ukrainian Labour Farm Temple Association or Finnish socialists who settled in the Lakehead area of Ontario). This fuelled hostility, with Anglo leaders of the day perceiving immigrant workers as "dangerous foreigners." The latter was the case in the aftermath of the Winnipeg General Strike when some immigrants were blamed for fomenting the strike and were deported.

Second, *altering the balance between city and rural dweller.* During this period Canada was becoming an urbanized country where people's livelihoods increasingly depended on industry, natural resources, and service occupations. Between 1881 and 1911, the combined population of Halifax, Montreal, Toronto, and Winnipeg tripled. Calgary went from 4,000 people in 1903 to 44,000 in 1911. There is a downside to the urbanization process, however. As cities populated, rural areas depopulate. Take note of the crisis in the Country of Antigonish in rural Nova Scotia in the late nineteenth and early twentieth century. Between 1901 and 1911 outward migration ("goin' down the road") had been continuous, with an estimated loss of 24,000 inhabitants. Indeed, the vacant farm symbolized the plight of rural society. In Nova Scotia, men and women left the rural areas, pulled inexorably into burgeoning coal mining towns like Springhill, Inverness, or Glace Bay (which grew from 6,945 to 16,562 between 1901 and 1910, and earned the nickname of "Little Moscow" because of its cohort of Communist Party members), or out to the "booming west." One of the fundamental learning challenges facing the Antigonish Movement reformers—spearheaded by Father Jimmy Tompkins—was rural depopulation. For Tompkins and many of his fellow religious folk, the people of Antigonish County needed to be wakened from their deep slumber. The Danish folk school movement caught the imagination of rural adult educators who saw in it potential to revitalize rural life and to stanch the outflow to the cities. The Danish folk school would also inspire adult educators in the 1930s and 1940s (revived today in the form of residential adult education).

On the Pacific edge, the city of Vancouver was a boom town extraordinaire in the late nineteenth and early twentieth century. Hunt (1987) meticulously documents the way largely Anglo-Saxon elites founded voluntary associations such as the Art, Historical and Scientific Association (AHSA) in 1894, the Arts and Crafts Association in 1900, and many more in order to bring a cultural and moral tone to life in this unstable materialist world of rough-and-tumble Vancouver. Imagining themselves as cultural missionaries, the elites (Hunt engages in an intricate and careful attempt to determine who attended what association) sought to infuse "culture" and "civilization" into the rough and crass industrial capitalist society that was emerging out of the dank west coast forests. These middle-class British men and women found it difficult to break out of their class (good intentions though they had to reach the masses and working people). They usually ended up educating themselves (what Hunt calls "mutual enlightenment") through lectures and conversaziones; art galleries and museums were available for ordinary people. Hunt calls this "bi-focal pedagogy." Founded in the early twentieth century, the BC Literary Club, to give one example, comprised of evangelical, non-conformist members (unlike the AHSA which was dominated by Anglicans and Presbyterians) was more egalitarian. Culture is class-based, and the drawing-room world of the AHSA and Arts and Crafts or the Women's Musical Club was far removed from the Cumberland or Nanaimo coal fields. In 1916, the Vancouver Institute would be created to bring order out of the fragmented number of voluntary associations (scientific, naturalist, musical, fine arts, archaeology, or mountaineering). It is still running today. Hunt's attentive work serves as a good reminder that voluntary associations do have class and gendered dimensions.

The impact of industrial and urban life on the lives of men, women, and children was profound. Many people who flocked into our growing cities did not find the Promised Land. Many lived in deplorable housing in urban slums, with the entire attendant "vices" associated with poverty and exploitation. In Montreal, between 1897 and 1911, one third of the babies died before reaching age twelve. During this period, reformers widely believed that urban growth was a serious menace to the nation. Some humanitarian reformers, such as J. J. Kelso of Toronto, concentrated on child welfare. Save the children and we can save the future! All reformers were motivated by an acute sense of moral crisis. They passionately believed in the possibility of improving self and society. Fuelled by confidence in the natural (and new social) sciences, their own values were distinctly progressive and Christian. Their social gospel outlook committed them to fostering civic community and social justice. We see continuity between the "age of improvement" of the nineteenth century and the progressive sentiments of the twentieth.

Knowledge was power, and adult education was the means to acquire really useful knowledge about the environmentally-rooted causes of human misery. However, as Ramsey Cook has so brilliantly explicated in his work, *The Regenerators* (1985), those adhering to the social gospel, like cleric-politicians J. S. Woodsworth, A. E. Smith, and William Irvine, or feminist activists like Beatrice Brigden or Flora Dennison, were shadowed by grave doubts in the old evangelical message of an authoritative Bible and the saving grace of Christ. This period, then, is a turbulent time of doubt and reform. And recent religious history has also intriguingly indicated that the working class often did not share its secular-minded leaders' antipathy toward revivalist forms of Christian self-expression (McKay, 2008).

Third, *stirrings at the grassroots*. Many Canadians—in factories, in mines, on farms, in offices, and in households—struggled with the demands of a new, unfamiliar, and often exploitative kind of society. They were, one could say, becoming enlightened about the causes of their suffering. They were becoming empowered to act to change their life situations. Although one might, perhaps, argue that the struggle for responsible government in Canada in the mid-nineteenth century was something like a social movement, it is not until the late nineteenth and into the twentieth that we see the significance of social movements as learning sites. They came into their own at that time. Unless we can perceive them as salient places where people were enlightened and strengthened to act to create a more just world, we will miss a central learning dynamic of the period under survey. On the prairies, we see the birth of agrarian protest movements. The rhetoric and literature of farm organizations such as the United Farmers of Alberta (UFA) and the Saskatchewan Grain Growers Association (SGGA) were replete with statements stressing the importance of adult education in the farm movement. These agrarian radical movements (Laycock, 1990) often harboured deliberative forms of democratic vision, placing them in opposition to liberal parliamentarism (and the dominant idea of the Liberal Order more generally). At its founding convention in 1909, the UFA declared that its purpose was to educate for collective action. Laycock has argued persuasively that farm men and women learned democracy by actively participating in meetings where they could learn to speak and act confidently. The farm local was a key educative form. But the movement culture was also sustained as an oppositional learning site through lectures, study clubs, farm newspapers, and the annual convention. One of Alberta's great farm leaders, Henry Wise Wood, believed passionately that farmers could combine their intelligences into a mighty force for good.

The industrial working classes in the age of transformation faced challenges no less daunting than did their compatriots in the farm movements. They had to contend with the likes of James Dunsmuir, the BC coal baron who objected to all unions because if the workers managed his mine, he wouldn't be able to. He didn't want any of that, but trade unions emerged doggedly in the 1880s. While the trade union was a voluntary association of working people with a primary purpose of bargaining for decent wages, the union itself carried learning potential as workers clarified their self-understandings and tried to understand what their work meant in the larger scheme of things. Along with unions came socialist political parties (including the Socialist Party of Canada), strikes, agitation, and unrest, culminating in the Winnipeg General Strike in 1919. These parties sponsored various educational activities as they contested the power of capitalist owners to have their way without any restraints or humanist sentiments.

The troubles and struggles in the Cape Breton coal mines and steel industry were very bitter. Company stores, feudal management, and bitter and violent strikes conducted while the army was seemingly camped permanently outside the gates marked the early twentieth century. Or we could look at Alfred Fitzpatrick, the founder of Frontier College, and the lumber, railway, and mining camps dotted across Northern Ontario. There we would find the "bunkhouse men" (see, for an empirical study, Edmund Bradwin's *Bunkhouse Man* [1928], living in poorly ventilated, dirty, and verminous living conditions. Fitzpatrick, in his famous book, *The University in Overalls* (1923) exclaimed: "We send our sons and daughters to schools and colleges, which are often endowed by the toil of men in conditions so degrading as to lead to the sacrifices of their manhood. What is needed by these men in the camps, buried socially, intellectually, and morally, is not charity, but more social justice" (pp. 36–37).

The early twentieth century saw an explosion of learning amongst women on farms and in urban centres. Women created a host of voluntary associations—from Women's Institutes to the Women's International League for Peace and Freedom. They began to challenge their consignment to the domestic sphere. But they did this innovatively. They used the word "housekeeper" as a metaphor for fundamental community-building and sustaining activities. They were not willing to be seen as second-class citizens. Feminist scholars identify the prevalent ideology as "maternal feminism." Women used their identification with the domestic sphere to offer a moral and ethical critique of societal organization. Women moved into the real world of politics and public spheres as well, using their location in the moral domain of the household to raise serious questions about the needs of their children and other vulnerable members of their communities and municipalities. Indeed, the theme of citizenship is central to this project. This is the time, after all, when women agitated and educated for suffrage. The struggles around suffrage can profitably be viewed as an important social learning process for men and women in the early twentieth century. Women were learning a new identity as female persons. Men had to learn that, too.

The Education of the Working Man

The world of workers' education in the early twentieth century is a rough-and-tumble and conflict-ridden world. In fact, Canada was in the throes (as were its European and American counterparts) of the evolution of capitalism from its early small-scale manufacturing stage toward what is often called "monopoly capitalism." This new form of capital is the "matrix-event" (McKay, 2008) generating society's new problems. As capitalism entered its monopolistic or corporate phase (the age of conglomerates, cartels, administrative efficiency, advertising agencies, Taylorism, professionalization, and labour unrest) the labour process was radically reshaped by widespread mechanization, incorporating research in the solving of production problems (the scientization of labour), the subdivision of labour (the deskilling thesis), the emergence of more centralized, efficient, authoritarian managerial systems (the bureaucratic control theme), and professionalization (the elite expert appears in many areas of social life).

The underlying objectives of workers' education are often complex since different bodies and individuals may involve themselves in workers' education with a mixture of motives. One British writer, P. G. Hopkins (1987), simplifies these motives this way: i) individual development for its own sake; ii) improved efficiency for workers' organizations; iii) improved socio-economic contributions from workers' organizations; iv) change and transformation in society (and work organization); and v) stability and coherence in society. We can make this basic distinction: the workplace itself (the "school of labour") and the education of workers (labour's schools) form the outlook and sensibility of the workers. We often do not consider the design of work itself as a curricular structure (Welton, 1991b; 2005). Workers' education highlights the contentious nature of adult learning and education. Stepping back into the past world of industrial worksites, strikes, and rancorous debate between liberals, conservatives, and radicals of different stripes forces us to think afresh about the issues of propaganda, indoctrination, and education. Some radical workers understood their educational project as propaganda. They sensed that the dominant institutions—universities, for instance—often fed them scraps of knowledge. The Workers Educational Association

(WEA), on the other hand, subscribed to the liberal value of enabling workers to think for themselves. Others—members of late nineteenth- and early twentieth-century socialist parties—called for nothing less than the creation of a new economic and social order. The intensity of these debates reveals that the organization and management of knowledge and skill at workplaces is central to societal reproduction and resistance. Let us highlight four initiatives: Frontier College, the WEA, the learning network of the Winnipeg working class, and Jimmy Tompkins' pre-Antigonish movement initiatives with workers. Our intention is to examine processes of industrial conflict and change through the learning lens.

The Winnipeg General Strike of 1919 is quite well known to many Canadians. There were massive sympathy strikes in many places across the country, including Amherst, Nova Scotia. Our basic assumption is that before persons can change their behaviour and their society, they must first be enlightened as to that possibility. Education must always be considered in attempts to understand the larger processes of social conflict and change. But education does not necessarily mean "formal schooling." Historian Richard Johnson (1981) examined what he called "self-initiated" forms of education of British workers. He demonstrated how individual workers in the late eighteenth and early nineteenth centuries drew upon educational resources such as the family, neighbourhood pubs, places of work, use of a knowledgeable friend, or discussions with a "scholar" residing in a village to help them acquire "really useful knowledge." They also invented educational forms such as communal reading and discussion groups, set up facilities for newspapers in pubs and coffee houses, and listened to travelling lecturers. They educated themselves through a kind of learning network.

The most eclectic of the workers' education projects in Winnipeg was the People's Forum. Originating with social gospel/social work activities in the city's legendary north end in 1910, the originators of the Forum included people who, during the war years, would become convinced of the need to create a fundamentally different society—a co-operative commonwealth. Labour's pedagogues included the Christian socialist pacifist J. S. Woodsworth, Frances Beynon, a radical feminist fired from the *Grain Grower's Guide* for anti-war and anti-capitalist activities, and A.V .Thomas, her brother-in-law, also fired from the conservative *Manitoba Free Press*. Operating independently of the Winnipeg school system until 1914, the People's Forum held regular Sunday evening meetings in local theatres until it floundered in 1917, largely because of the commitment of many of its leaders to radical political activities. Throughout the turbulent years from 1912 to 1917, *The Voice,* a workers' paper which criticized capitalist abuses from an essentially Christian ethical position, carried weekly reports of events at the People's Forum in Winnipeg, and in a host of others in surrounding communities. The workers' press announced lectures and meetings and often carried verbatim lecture texts. The People's Forum, evidence suggests, encouraged participatory engagement, discussion always following lectures. The workers' press did not provide equal coverage of the lectures of other educational forums— the YMCA and the University of Manitoba.

Judging from the reports of *The Voice,* the Forum debated a wide range of critical themes. Speakers called for increased political involvement because "our system of government … places great power in the hands of a few men," and numerous speakers addressed the issue of militarism, the need for social reconstruction, and the need to teach children in their own language. The latter theme signals the presence of an active ethnic presence in Winnipeg's north end. The anti-militarist theme offended some school board members, and forced the Forum committee into some compromises. But a number of forums, featuring men like the controversial Methodist social gospeller Salem Bland of Wesley Theological College (Winnipeg was the leading centre of the social gospel in Canada) continued to indict the war.

By the autumn of 1917, the leadership of the Forum had dispersed, but workers' education activities continued unabated. Rejecting the People's Forum's affiliation with the public school system and "bourgeois reformism," in September 1917 the Winnipeg Trades and Labour Council (WTLC) announced a series of Sunday afternoon lectures, featuring socialist and progressive speakers. The lecture series lasted only one season. But in 1918 the non-denominational Labour Church had begun, and included a program of Sunday afternoon lectures, featuring the "radical wing" of the People's Forum (J. S. Woodsworth, Fred Dixon, Salem Bland, and William Ivens, the Labour Church's instigator). The People's Forum and the Labour Church, bridged by the WTLC lecture series, form a continuum of educational activities. By the end of 1918, it seems safe to conclude, Winnipeg workers had been enlightened to the point where they believed that alternatives to capitalism were necessary and possible.

Perhaps the most significant development in Winnipeg in September 1919 was the Labour Church and the One Big Union's (OBU), the union that sought to unify all workers in a single union to achieve economic and political power, call for the formation of a Labour College for Winnipeg after the bitter defeat of the General Strike of May and June. A parallel initiative, several years later, occurred in Nova Scotia—particularly among the radical coal miners, who were very interested in workers' education. The workers wanted a permanent provincial Labour College that would draw on the expertise of teachers and college professors. Nova Scotian workers would not get what they wanted, and would have to wait until the early 1930s until St. Francis Xavier University provided educational services. But St. Francis had its own agenda, and one major item was to quell the insurrection of dangerous knowledge and political action in industrial Cape Breton. The OBU did, however, organize classes and lectures, and those in economics were most popular. The Winnipeg workers wanted a Labour College very badly, and wrote the Scottish radical "Red John" Maclean of the Glasgow Labour College and also to the Rand School of Social Sciences in the US. The more militant wing of the international labour movement clearly wanted a permanent school to nurture their brand of oppositional consciousness. But a Canadian Labour College would not materialize until the 1960s, and then only under the watchful eye of reformist trade union bureaucrats running the Canadian Labour Congress.

Radical political parties—an integral if fractious part of the configuration of labour's schools—were also involved in the movement in Winnipeg. The Socialist Party of Canada (The SPC), tracing its origins to Winnipeg in 1890, with deep roots amongst hard rock miners of BC's mountains, rigorously and dogmatically schooled its resolute vanguard in Marxist axioms. In fact, the SPC's chiliastic vision of the inevitable end of capitalism steeled them to educate their followers for this future. Their classes in understanding the need to abolish the wage system, for instance, did not encourage the kind of dialogue favoured by the WEA. Another small socialist party, the Social Democratic Party (SDP) also arranged evening classes during the 1912/1913 season. More reformist than the SPC, its brand of socialism was more palatable to the broad-based Winnipeg left. Other small labour parties—the Dominion Labour party and the Independent Labour Party—engaged in sporadic educational activities, but their members were involved in the educational programs of the People's Forum, OBU, and the Labour churches. According to Allen Mills (1984), J. S. Woodsworth believed that: "The making of socialists … was an intellectual activity, requiring for its success a constant appeal to the spoken and written word. Socialism would arrive … through voluntary action that derived from the power of clear, methodological, and rational argument itself" (p. 105). There was wide recognition amongst

A photo showing the interior of a frontier college classroom near Sudbury around 1912. (Credit: Library and Archives Canada / PA-061766)

workers and their leaders of the necessity of education for action. In fact, this luminous idea was shared, I would argue, across a wide spectrum of adult education in the period of the "great awakening" and "great transformation."

Frontier College is, along with the Antigonish Movement, probably one of Canada's best known adult education movements. In fact, it still exists today—doing its literacy work amongst society's vulnerable illiterates. Frontier College was founded by Alfred Fitzpatrick, a Nova Scotian from Pictou Academy, in 1899. First called the Reading Camp Association, after 1919 it became known as Frontier College. In the late nineteenth century, Fitzpatrick had been preaching in lumber camps (he was a Presbyterian missionary [see Fraser, 1988, for a study of the impact of the social gospel in the Presbyterian Church from 1875-1915]) in northern Ontario. It was there he became aware of the needs of the men in the camps and began to realize that conventional missionary approaches were not adequate. The gospel had to address the social and educational needs of the men. He can be placed in the "social gospel" paradigm emerging in Anglo-Protestantism (see Allen, 1971, 2008; Christie & Gauvreau, 1996). Fitzpatrick believed that adult education was the "daydream of visionaries." During all of his professional life he railed against establishment Canada—the elites who ran our universities, our churches, our trade unions, our governing bureaucracies—for ignoring the plight of the neglected men in the camps, the bunkhouse men. For him, education was a God-given right, and not the exclusive privilege of a few favoured persons.

In 1899 the Reading Camp Movement began with the setting up of a reading room at two logging camps at Nairn Centre, in the Algoma Region, with the help of local library boards, plus a travelling library from McGill in Montreal. By 1902, Fitzpatrick had recruited instructors from the universities to work as labourer-teachers; and by 1909, the Reading Camp Association had been formally created. (It would become Frontier College in 1919.) This really was an epochal event in adult educational history. The teacher was no longer apart from, or above, the students. They shared the work and world of the men in lumber, railway, and mining camps. For Fitzpatrick, the instructors were living the gospel and were learning to integrate mental and manual work. Fitzpatrick, writing in his unpublished book, *Schools and Other Penetentiaries* [sic], written around 1930, really was a kind of educational radical. He believed in holistic learning and thought that the universities distorted the mind "out of all proportion to … hand and heart" (n.p). He elevated ordinary work and experience above book-learning and called for the integration of head, heart, and hand. Today we would call him a "humanist" educator. And he was prescient: "We must teach them," he declared in *The University in Overalls* (1923), "not only how to cut trees without destroying the forest, how to stump and till the land scientifically, and how to catch fish in the proper seasons without threatening their extermination—in other words, show them how to wrest a living from Nature without becoming her slave or destroyer" (p. 42). Technical-instrumental forms of learning were not satisfactory for Fitzpatrick. Concern for the environment is not new.

Before Ivan Illich wrote his notorious text, *De-Schooling Society* (1970), Fitzpatrick had advocated de-schooling society. He worked ceaselessly to convince universities to release their faculty members for half-time experiential learning and half-time book learning. He worked tirelessly to convince the elite institutions of the day to turn their gaze to the poor and vulnerable. He well knew that some conservative-minded folks believed that he was treading on dangerous ground because education breeds discontent. If educated, the masses will become lazy and lawless. No educated man will work in the woods, or handle the pick and shovel in mines and on railway construction. For Fitzpatrick, the remedy for this discontent lay with educating them, while at the same time improving their environment. The men who produced the wealth do not get any educational benefits. The toilers of the forest, mine, and railway construc-

re being robbed. Their treatment was nothing short of criminal.
ere the utterly neglected citizens of the camps.

Fitzpatrick criticized the universities for their ivory tower separation
from the real world and the state for its laissez-faire postures. He thought
that churches and government did not really care much about the fate of
these immigrant men working in camps scattered across the land. Fitzpatrick, the early twentieth-century social gospel proponent, thought that
the solution to the structurally rooted problems of the bunkhouse men
lay primarily with the redemption of individuals through empathetic
provision of basic adult education and citizenship training by labourer-
teachers. There are traces of paternalism (some have criticized his focus
on men only) and Anglo-Saxon elite surveillance in his vision. He taught
the men in the camps what today we would call ABE and ESL: but he
also did not want the OBU radicals who tramped through these camps,
too, to steal these men for revolutionary politics. This fear of "dangerous
knowledge" from below is a prominent theme in educational work of
Father Jimmy Tompkins in the early twentieth century. Yet Fitzpatrick
stood outside the establishment, with the forgotten, the voiceless, and
the neglected. He was an adult educational visionary who stood outside
the establishment and cried out incessantly that all people had the right
to the cultural resources of our society and were entitled to full citizenship. His distinctive contribution to adult education in Canada, one that
many scoffed at, was his insistence that there could be no healthy growth
of the brain without the concurrent work of the hands. His rejection of
"education" as a sphere apart from life was very radical and visionary. He
died a broken-hearted man.

Another adult education visionary who railed against the establishment was the pesky, agitational presence, Father Jimmy Tompkins of
Nova Scotia. Beginning in the early twentieth century, spearheaded by
Tompkins, a cadre of reform-minded priests (dubbed as "Bolsheviks of
a better sort") as well as women and lay community leaders began to
shape a new "social Catholicism" in response to the plight of the poor
and the plight of the Roman Catholic Church in Nova Scotia. For the
Antigonish reformers, recovering the Church's lost influence was intimately linked to the educative and political struggles to emancipate the
oppressed peoples labouring in the mines, at sea, on the farms, and in
households. This vision of emancipation of the oppressed fishermen was
also shared by William Coaker, the founder of the Fishermen's Protection Union in 1908 in Newfoundland. Like Tompkins, the self-educated
diamond in the rough Coaker had to face feudal conditions in the fishery

and a conservative Catholic hierarchy. But Newfoundland had been, and was ruled, by the St. John's merchants. They controlled politics and the church as well. The fishermen were subjected to an ugly oppressive mode of payment called the "truck system." They lived on starvations' edge. Coaker was not as conscious an adult educator as Tompkins, but he organized the fishers of the north-east coast into unions. He gave them hope and voice. Coaker created night schools and his unions served as a rough form of deliberative democracy. They even elected some members of parliament. But the Roman Catholic Church opposed them severely, as did the merchants. The Fishermen's Protective Union was finally crushed in 1928 (Macdonald, 1987). Newfoundland's harsh landscape matched its politics in the nineteenth and early twentieth centuries (see Overton [1995] for an acerbic critique of Newfoundland adult education).

Throughout the nineteenth century, the Roman Catholic Church had been reluctant to respond to the urgent new questions posed by industrialism and modernity. The Roman Catholic Church's social ethics had been shaped in the context of a rural, patriarchal, and hierarchical society. As Catholic workers grappled with the new realities of widespread poverty in the midst of excessive wealth, union organizing, cyclical economic depression, socialist parties speaking with secular accents and women's insistent demands for social equality, Catholic identity was under severe strain. Church dogma, homilies, and charity for the individual poor seemed utterly inadequate responses to the new kinds of problems (or learning challenges) twentieth century men and women were facing. The Catholic Church desperately needed to provide a new cultural synthesis for changed times. Behind the walls of "fortress Catholicism," Catholics hoped to ride out the storms of secularism and socialism seeking to invade their walls. The diocesan newspaper, *The Casket*, condemned the evils of socialism, suffragettes, Protestants, and assorted infidel movements. Suffragettes were depicted as "wild creatures," who, if given the vote, "would raise problems not yet thought of …" (July 17, 1912). Yet towards the end of 1913 a new spirit percolated through the ultramontane Catholicism. The Rev. Andrew Egan, writing on the subject of "The Catholic Church the friend of the working man" (October 23, 1913), called upon Catholics to stand for the "right of the employed against the injustice from all sides, and for any movement that makes for social betterment …" Egan's words are inexplicable outside Pope Leo XIII's epochal encyclical, *Rerum Novarum*, delivered in 1891. Pope Leo lowered the drawbridge of fortress Catholicism to the plight of the suffering workers. Laissez-faire Catholicism was no longer acceptable, and

Catholics were encouraged to understand the modern world in order to bring a Catholic influence to bear upon the major problems of the day, particularly the social problem. Yet the papal prescription against socialism and for private property constrained the possible solutions to the social crisis. Thus, the Church was under considerable pressure to move toward the world to restore lost influence over secular affairs by competing directly with other ideologies (socialism or Protestantism).

The Antigonish reform-cadres who clustered around Tompkins—a spearhead minority—were impelled into action. The reformers in the first decades of the twentieth century had much to be concerned about. The "vacant farm" symbolized the plight of rural society, exacerbated by the migration into the coal towns of Glace Bay and Dominion as well as the steel mills in Sydney and the subsidized Eastern Car Company in New Glasgow. Tompkins began his work at St. Francis College, in the small town of Antigonish, in 1902. The college was a modest, parochial institution at that time and Tompkins would go on to become its vice-president in 1908. In 1912 Tompkins returned from a British university meeting held at Oxford ablaze with desire to carry the university to the people. It was dawning on Tompkins that adult education could precipitate a cultural awakening in men and women's minds, hearts, and souls. Tompkins maintained that workers would be exploited and dominated unless they got knowledge for themselves.

Education was the way to power. But how were they to proceed? The leadership of the diocese—Bishop Morrison and Rector Hugh Macpherson—were neither sympathetic to Tompkins' radical intuitions nor his importunate nature. Beginning in late 1913, impatient of noble theorizing, Tompkins plunged into feverish social action on two fronts. He opened a column on the "Forward Movement" in *The Casket*, and began to orchestrate action to booster civic awareness and responsibility. The period of the Antigonish Forward Movement in 1913 to its gradual dissipation by the end of 1915, is particularly important for our understanding of adult education and the New Catholicism. Tompkins intends to focus his concern on the plight of the rural areas, open dialogue with Protestants, to speak out against the political bosses oppressing the people. The Forward Movement sought to repopulate the country, beautify the towns, dredge the harbour, and find an adult educator to work with farmers (he found "Little Doc" Hugh Macpherson, a St. Francis professor, to enlighten farmers about the new science of agriculture). The future seemed "fraught with wonderful possibilities."

The Forward Movement precipitated important social learning processes to counter "commercial pessimism" and "citizen lassitude." Tompkins opened up significant public space for dialogue about Nova Scotia's plight. Aware that post-WWI people were hungry for knowledge and wanted to have a say in how the society was run, Tompkins opened up space in *The Casket* for avant-garde Catholics thinkers like Henry Somerville of England and Father John Ryan, famed in the US for proposing a "living wage" for workers. A strong commitment to adult education characterized the new discourse flowing through public space. Pedagogical activism, or transformation through self-activity, is placed at the heart of the populism now part of Tompkins' language of reform. Significantly for the future of what would become the "Antigonish Movement" of the 1930s to 1950s, Tompkins opened up dialogue with the industrial workers. In the "Education and Social Conferences" of 1918 and 1919, he succeeded in opening up dialogue on questions of industrial democracy. On his own, he spoke with the "red" leaders of the workers in Cape Breton. He tried to foster a WEA-styled adult education for the industrial workers, rather than the Plebs League favoured by communist workers in the United Kingdom (Simon, 1992).

One of the most iconic of Canadian adult education projects, the People's School, held at St. Francis, was launched in 1921, to demonstrate the power of adult education to change people's way of seeing and acting within the world. Attended by fifty-one men, it turned out to be a great success for the reformers' agenda. Moses Coady, who taught mathematics at the school, found the students "anxious for knowledge and desirous of improvement. … The time is ripe, it would seem, for a vigorous program of adult education in this country." And the progressive *Halifax Herald* (May 28, 1921) commented: "For many years universities everywhere have been, and most of the time still are, laboring under the misconception that they, by divine right, shall serve the wealthy and privileged classes, and in no degree promoted popular education." Tompkins also spearheaded an enormously controversial and acrimonious effort to create a University of Nova Scotia. The poor, under-resourced religious colleges could not really fund high-level university and graduate work. But the Bishop and Rector would have none of this: they were not going to submit to secular forces waiting to destroy Catholic faith in universities like Harvard or Dalhousie. Tompkins was banished to Canso, a poverty-stricken but technologically advanced remote fishing town, where there was mostly "fish, fog and fornication" (in Father Jimmy's lively phrase).

From 1923 until St. Francis Xavier actually agreed to create an extension department in 1928, Tompkins agitated amongst the fishermen, a terribly exploited sector of the working class. By 1927 his pedagogical activity and seed-sowing took root, and many fishermen helped along by reform-priests in the fishing villages, forced the government of Nova Scotia into inquiring into the state of the fishery. The MacLean Commission sided with the plight of the fishermen, recommending "adult education for cooperation" as solution. The reform-cadre also agitated for an extension department in the 1920s meetings of the "Education and Social Conference." By 1928 the efforts to press the Church hierarchy to create an extension department and to launch a coherent attack on social and economic problems had succeeded. Moses Coady was appointed as first extension director. The years of behind the scenes mentoring had paid off for the pesky Tompkins. His second cousin was now ready to become "mighty Moses" who would lead his people to the Promised Land of Co-operativism (Welton, 2005; and Welton, n.d.)

In 1903 the British-born Albert Mansbridge initiated the Association for the Higher Education of Working Men in Great Britain. Within five years, this fledgling organization grew into the Workers Education Association. Mansbridge was a passionate advocate of liberal studies for working people. Within five years of the establishment of the WEA, operating out of Mansbridge's home, fifty branches, with over nine hundred affiliated organizations had been formed. In January 1908, R. H. Tawney of Oxford's Balliol College began his three-year tutorial class in economic history with forty students, all pledged to attend regularly and write fortnightly essays. The main educational form of the WEA, which drew upon university professors to teach working people, was the tutorial. It was there that men and women, many of them with only a few years of formal schooling, were led into the realm of liberal studies. The WEA was committed to fostering critical thinking amongst its members. It valued objectivity, reason, and argumentation. The WEA was sometimes perceived by militant workers as too liberal and not radical enough.

Mansbridge first travelled to Canada around the time of the outbreak of the First World War (his second visit was to Newfoundland in 1929). He was trying to encourage Canadian universities to sponsor WEA classes. The Winnipeg workers were actually suspicious of any kind of classes that the university might sponsor for them. They thought that the universities only fed the workers scraps of knowledge. This tension or friction point between university and working people has roots in our history. For instance, Father Jimmy Tompkins thought that a WEA-like form of workers' education could inoculate the Cape Breton workers from communist influences (he was no doubt aware of this antagonism in British society). Guy Henson started a chapter of the WEA in Halifax in 1938. He told the story of trying to get a classroom in a high school in Halifax for a WEA meeting, only to be informed that the school board refused because they thought that the workers might bring in venereal disease and thereby contaminate the youth.

The WEA originated in a time of labour militancy and radicalism on an unprecedented scale. Workers' education is contested space. The Canadian university extension movement emerged in the first two decades of the twentieth century. It, too, recognized the potential of adult education in resolving the social conflict. Although Queen's University organized some tutorial classes in 1889, the University of Saskatchewan created its Agricultural Extension Department in 1910 and was really the first in the field (closely followed by the University of Alberta in 1912). The University of Toronto organized its Extension Department in 1920. It provides a useful focal point, since it sponsored the first WEA tutorial classes for workers and is considered Canada's most prestigious centre of higher education. In a three-page document simply entitled "University Extension," written in 1922, the University of Toronto presented its understanding of the nature and purpose of adult education. From its opening lines, this text is pervaded by a profound sense of danger and crisis. "At this moment," the anonymous author(s) declared, there is a "crisis in the whole world of education." Public schools and the technical training provided by universities have left out the "most important part" of the education. Neither has developed the "power of thinking" or "useful criticism," but more significantly, neither had built a "thoughtful, comprehending human spirit." The task had never been more urgent.

They thought that adult education could foster harmony between capital (or business), labour, and the state. They saw an "immense danger to a country in the existence of two languages, the language of the cultivated and the language of the street, neither of which is really comprehensible to the other." The choice of the street/cultivated metaphor is significant. The languages of social transformation—products of workers' own learning and experience—are consigned to the street, the realm of the undisciplined, the untrained, the untutored, and the rebellious. Indeed, one catches in the text's identification of adult education with "formalized" instruction by "trained" tutors (real adult education is authorized by the university). Thoughtful and cultivated people did not organize strikes and challenge the government's policies. It was imperative, therefore, that the university extend its higher education to those classes previously neglected. Because the "whole basis of national unity rests upon the theory of the nation being an aggregation of persons who, on the whole, think alike, and it is very difficult for two sets of people to think alike who speak more or less different languages and think in different categories," a "large expansion of adult education is called for." Working men (and women) had to be incorporated into higher culture—defined implicitly as Anglo-conformist (Welton, 1991a).

The WEA was successfully established in Toronto at the end of the First World War because the key professorial players—W. L. Grant, principal of Upper Canada College, Professor R. M. McIver, and W. S. Milner; and Arthur Glazebrook, an exchange broker—believed that the foundations of democracy were under siege in a crassly materialistic age. Clearly alarmed by the Russian Revolution, the Winnipeg General Strike, and the OBU, and startled by the enormously increased strike activities, rapid growth of trade unions, these middle-class academics "sought to use the Association as a means to curb the spread of radicalism." All the educators who supported the WEA insisted that the teaching be done by university professors. "It is the University, after all," declared Glazebrook, "that contains the treasury of knowledge and the training in method that are required." This would be a matter of some controversy. Writing to Grant on October 13, 1921, classics professor W. S. Milner thought that the "success of the WEA as an educational ideal was seriously imperiled." The controversy, one of many to dog the WEA's path until its demise in the late 1940s, was over union activist James Ballantyne's desire to teach a course in Marxian economics. Though not denying the right of the university to deal with Marx, Milner thought it unwise and absurd to exercise this right. How could the university support a teacher from the workers' own ranks? Despairing and disconsolate, Milner took his stand for the "culture of mind and spirit." The "unhappy truth," as he saw it, was that the WEA had "fallen into the hands of Labour that is more anxious for power than for culture, and the spiritual force of the movement is on the ebb" (Welton, 1991a).

The WEA was contested terrain throughout its history. Conflicting visions of adult education—its purpose and process—would be articulated by multiple voices. In the early years of the Association, a number of working men (like the Irishman Alf MacGowan of the International Typographical Union) believed that workers with more knowledge could help to improve the existing political and social systems. They hoped it would be improved through a workers' educational movement that increased workers' understanding of political and social issues. These worker activists shared the academics' faith that truth could be examined in an unbiased way—the grand vision of the British WEA tutorial movement.

Workers agreed that they needed access to broader knowledge than technical education. Some workers emphasized the need for social justice and attacked the limitations of education in a class society and insisted on the social and collective purposes of the WEA. The redoubtable Winnipeg labour movement shared this latter conviction. In 1915 they had met with University of Manitoba Professor A. Dale to discuss the formation of a chapter of the WEA. From the start they were suspicious. The University of Manitoba, the committee claimed, was for the rich and provided only "scraps of knowledge" for workers. After the meeting the Winnipeg Trades and Labour Congress (TLC) decided not to support the WEA because they had to deal with professors who were in the grip of capitalist ideology. The WEA was unable to establish itself in Winnipeg until 1938 (in 1937, Watson Thomson would work with the Calgary WEA, and in the late 1930s with the Edmonton branch as part of his extension work with the University of Alberta; Vancouver only created its WEA in 1942). This mutual suspicion between the labour movement and the university is one of the important subtexts in the history of Canadian and global workers' education. The university professors (with a few exceptions) saw the WEA as a way of exercising social control; they wanted to maintain existing power. The labour movement activists wanted to shift the balance of power and further labour's cause. In the rancorous history of the Vancouver WEA (1942-48), opposing political parties, the CCF and the Communist Party battled for control of the organization and ended up destroying it.

Drummond Wren, one of our great Canadian workers' educators, summed up WEA philosophy this way: "The Workers' Educational Association, therefore, must not attach itself to any ideology, nor become the proponent of any particular philosophy, political, economic or otherwise. Therein lays the educational policy of the WEA, 'to teach how to think, not what to think.' Don't misunderstand me—such a policy does not presume an acceptance of the status quo. It is revolutionary, because to teach how to think and the application of critical judgment to existing social and economic wrongs, would eventually eliminate for our society all injustices…" (Welton, 1986).

Educating for a Brighter New Day: Women's Organizations as Learning Sites

"In times like these"—this was the title of Nellie McClung's best seller feminist text of 1915. What were these times, from the tail end of the 1890s to the early decades of the twentieth century, like for women? The simple answer is pretty dreadful. Women's situation was so dreadful that they were not even recognized as legal persons in the BNA Act of 1867. They weren't, until the ecstatic cry of Emily Murphy "We've won! We've won!" broke the stillness in 1929. During these years Canada was convulsed and confused by seemingly overwhelming problems. Old scripts specifying precisely what men and were to do in the world were no longer applicable. By the 1880s commentators in press and magazine (the literary public sphere) were noticing that women were straining against their restriction to the domestic sphere. The old idea that "women's place was in the home" didn't really make sense when women were beginning to enter university to gain entrance to select professions such as law, medicine, and teaching. Women were also working in factories and sweatshops, often at one half or one third of men's wages. Life was not at all lovely for working class women. They were usually too exhausted from waged work and domestic duties to join many groups. Canada was in the midst of a massive transition to a new phase of industrial capitalism, that of the rule by the large, monopolistic corporation. These massive economic changes unsettled women's ability to manage the lifeworld. Indeed, it seemed that this modernizing world had placed them at the mercy of the state without any power of influence.

Farm women faced their own peculiar problems. Many women had arrived on the prairies lured by the promise of free homesteads. Some had little clue about lay ahead of them. They faced physical isolation (in southern Saskatchewan, during the settlement period until WWI; in the north, into the 1930s). Women were isolated and lonely. Often times they were left alone to care for the farm and the children while their husbands were off transporting grain or getting needed materials. Loneliness bred depression and assorted mental illnesses. Eline Morrow, a farm woman who had immigrated to Shell Lake, Saskatchewan, in 1917, tells the story of being so utterly bereft that she would find herself going down to the slough and saying, "Should I drown myself now or later?" (Steer, 1992, p. 162). These traits—isolation and loneliness—were exacerbated by farm women's lack of access to medical care and midwives. The advantage that farm women had over urban women (both middle and working class) was that their pioneering work of farming was obviously a partnership. Most men could see that their farms couldn't survive without their wives. So it is not surprising that men in the farm movement were basically supportive of female suffrage and expanded roles for women in the public sphere. Even so, some farm men remained thick-headed around women's proper sphere and purpose in life.

Rural and farm women in the early twentieth century were exceedingly vulnerable. Urban environments were wracked with numerous social problems, including poor housing, poor sanitation, and absence of green spaces, crime, and intemperance. As industrial work conditions ground men down, they turned easily to drink to drown their sorrows. But this simply added to women's troubles: men drank away meagre wages and often beat their wives. Women had no legal recourse; and if their husbands died, they had few options for any kind of support. Indeed, the ethos of reform, animated by a Protestant social gospel perfumed the utopian air they breathed. The Methodist Church was in its heyday; and its message turned its followers towards the flattened horizon of an imminent coming of the kingdom of God. Floating on the energy generated by a booming Canada—anything seemed possible—reformers imagined that a brighter, new day was inevitable. Knowledge was power; and education and agitation could make a better Canada. And feminist reformers (of various tendency, some more left, some more to the right) were surely at the head of this great march upward and onward. Times were tough; there was much suffering, but reform was possible. Protestant missionaries saw their work in messianic terms: God had chosen Canada as His dominion of a new world (MacBeth, 1912; Osterhout, 1929). And the feminist reformers had little doubt, either, that as women they were in some way morally superior to men; and that the household, their domain, was the primary base

That an awakening of consciousness amongst women had been percolating throughout Canadian society was reflected in the formation of the National Council of Women in 1913. Their exclusion from male organizations impelled women to create numerous associations to meet their needs and change aspects of a world perceived as flawed by male privilege and power. The Women's Christian Temperance Union (WCTU) originated in Owen Sound in 1874 by Letitia Youmans (Cook, 1995). It spread rapidly across Canada, and in 1885, the WCTU was formed as a national organization. This movement served as a vital training ground for female activists. In 1876, Dr. Emily Stowe, Canada's first female medical doctor, created the Toronto Women's Literary Club. It served as a ruse for suffrage ideas. In 1897, Adelaide Hoodless formed the first Woman's

Institute in Stoney Creek, Ontario. These three organizations are rather well-known to many Canadians. We hear echoes of their voices into our present. Forgotten voices—such as the revolutionary socialist Margaret Haile—were amongst a small group of women active in early social-ist organizations such as the Canadian Socialist League. Haile was the first candidate to run for a legislature in Canada in 1902. Thus, when the Canadian Suffrage Association was formed in 1910, it had numer-ous activists and advocates who had learned the ropes of organizing for enlightenment and organizing for action.

The suffrage movement was the keystone theme for feminists in the first two decades of the twentieth century. Even when engaged in other pressing matters, women like McClung, Haile, Brigden, Mur-phy, McNaughton, Stowe, and many others campaigned for suffrage for women. By 1900, to be sure, propertied women had gained municipal voting rights. However, women faced formidable anti-feminist attacks from prominent intellectuals like Stephen Leacock, politicians such as Sir Rodmond Roblin, the tainted premier of Manitoba from 1900 to 1915 (tainted, in that his Conservative government had vested interests in the alcohol industry and feared women would vote for prohibition), and McClung's nemesis as well as Sir Almoth Wright, a pioneer in vaccina-tion therapy and rabid critic of women's desire to provoke a "domestic revolution" (Warne, 1993).

The battle for suffrage waged in the public sphere—print and in civil society spaces opened up for deliberation and debate—were supported by the WCTU, who well knew that prohibition required legislation. The National Council of Women supported suffrage, as did a wide range of farm organizations on the prairies (including their publications, such as the influential *Grain Growers Guide*). Indeed, the women's reform move-ment had facilitated the creation of able feminist journalists, like Lil-lian Beynon Thomas, who began writing for the *Winnipeg Free Press* in 1906 in support of suffrage and women's rights. Women succeeded, one might argue, in turning Canadian society into a giant, bumptious study circle. They were educating themselves in this social movement learning site. They were struggling for recognition as full human persons. In this process, they were acquiring voice and identity as the "new women" of a better, more equitable Canada. They were also educating the pub-lic and, in doing so, challenging long-standing notions, often supported by appeal to the divine, of a natural sphere for women. Among other pedagogical innovations, the Political Equality League (formed in 1912), with Thomas as its first president, cued by a skit mocking Roblin's anti-feminist antics, created the Mock Parliament Skit at the Walker Theatre. This early form of popular theatre reversed the roles with men coming to the parliament to gain the right to vote. They were curtly informed that such beautiful and cultured men should not receive the right to vote.

From among the hundreds of women's organizations and learning sites created by women from the late nineteenth to the mid-twentieth century, we select three that illustrate the range and variety of women's interests and manner of educating themselves and the public. The Women's Institutes crafted its curricula for women around the pressing needs of women in the domestic sphere. So did Home and School Associations (Delhi, 1992) and the Saskatchewan Homemakers' Clubs (Welton, 2003). They educated for home and community, and have been labelled as "civic housekeepers" (Veinott, 1992) and "housekeepers of the community" (Dennison, 1987). The Woman's Institutes have a secure place within conventional narratives of Canadian adult learning and education history; the Homemakers and the Women's International League for Peace and Freedom and various women's co-operative initiatives, less so. Even less attention has been given to women's educational and organizing work within socialist formations (Kealey, 1979; Sangster, 1989; McKay, 2008). Each organization worked in a particular zone, moving from home to province, and to the entire world.

As modernizing forces, technological, scientific, and cultural, sent shudders through rural Canada, perhaps it is not surprising, given the ethos of reform permeating the air that women would search for answers to their pressing problems of loneliness and the need for recognition of their unpaid labour. Agriculture was, itself, professionalizing as new scientific and technical inventions changed the way farming was being executed. Science ruled the day! Women skillfully entered into this discourse, and worked it for their own ends. Their work could be understood as "domestic science": it required domestic ways of knowing, skill, attitudes, and sensibility. Men had, in fact, responded to the learning challenges posed by the changes in production and shift to mixed farming by creating the Ontario Agricultural College in 1879. But only men could enroll; and even the Farmers' Institutes (important adult male learning sites in their own right) had few women involved. And the big farm organizations, the Patrons of Industry, and the Farmer's associations, excluded women. Rural de-population added to everyone's travail. By the 1890s, as already noted, women were entering higher education, and women were working outside the home in factories, as domestic servants and in the new retail industries and offices. The neatly packaged "two spheres" had cracked; women had to sort these matters out. Why couldn't education not only enable women to gain entry to professions, but also enable them to bolster their traditional roles? Women needed practical training in household skills to manage increasingly complex lifeworlds (including the scientific rearing of children). How could they change the world if they didn't know how to run a meeting?

The Hamilton socialite Adelaide Hoodless had been advocating for domestic science training for girls in the secondary schools since the early 1890s. The new forms of knowledge regarding nutrition, sanitation, and hygiene had filtrated into the lifeworld. Young women needed to learn these new forms of knowledge. There was a significant gap between their common sense and their new approaches. If household work gained a new dignity, then girls would not be lured into more dangerous forms of work. But women running households needed education too. Hoodless founded the Woman's Institute in 1897 to do just that. The Institute's purpose was "to promote household science which leads to improvements in home architecture, with special attention to home sanitation, to better understanding of the economic and hygienic value of foods and fuels, and to a more scientific care of children, with a view to raising the general standard of health of our people" (Crowley, 1992, p. 4). This captures admirably the educational vision of the Woman's Institutes. It was comforting to women and not threatening to men. It was also, in its own way, brilliant. Hoodless herself would play little role in the actually running of the Institutes (she died in 1910), which very quickly spread throughout Ontario, to other parts of Canada, and, eventually to Great Britain.

Why did the Institutes grow so rapidly? The simple answer is that rural women wanted them. They filled a void and permitted women to come together for mutual edification and social activity in a non-sectarian environment. The farm women shared a common form of life, and their organization enhanced social solidarity and created social capital in their communities. In this safe and secure milieu, reticent farm women could acquire a confident voice. Listening to the lectures provided by the Farmer's Institutes (women adult educators such as Dr. Margaret Patterson, Ethel Chapman, and Dr. Caroline Brown were hired to give lectures on the circuit), women's intellectual horizons widened. In their own reading circles, women grappled with making sense of the new science of bacteria and how to increase their own dairy production and, perhaps, the novels (such as *Sowing Seeds in Danny* [1908]) written by Nellie McClung. The annual convention provided another, larger, learning site for Institute women. There, women engaged the larger issues (such as suffrage and the need for legislation change). But not all locals could dream up vital programs. The Department of Agriculture had to step in by sending out educators to teach short courses.

Women plunged into community projects. For the first decade or so of their history, the Institutes pressed hard to have Domestic Science taught in the schools. Health projects were central to this community-based action. They wanted (and got) medical and dental inspectors—social surveys revealing shocking problems. World War I and the influenza epidemic of 1918 heightened women's concerns over health (and particularly, high infant mortality rates). They pressured the newly created Department of Health to establish well-baby clinics in churches and free children's clinics. The Institutes, though they eschewed partisan party politics, were forced—as they defended the domestic domain—to become, as Crowley (1992) observes, "interested in public questions [that] increasingly involved them in politics as the political realm itself was expanded in the early twentieth century. Under pressure principally from women's groups, farmers and labour, governments slowly assumed new responsibilities, not only in the areas of health and welfare" (p. 10). Here, then, cast in theoretical discourse, we see the brilliance of Woman's Institutes (as well as other organizations) way of doing politics. The collective learning processes in civil society associations crystallizes women's understanding of particular issues, and they move to the gates of governing bodies to enter and gain desired changes. This form of political engagement would, however, be contested by the United Farm Women of Ontario who accused the Institutes of a weak orientation to politics (Crowley, 1992).

If the Woman's Institutes were like tea parties, the Woman's International League for Peace and Freedom (WILPF) was a boisterous rally. It had been founded in The Hague in April 1915. Immediately thereafter, a branch was formed in Toronto by a small band of suffragettes; it was disbanded in 1917, but re-established in May 1919. By the mid-1920s, branches were added in Vancouver (1921) and Winnipeg (1925) with general support of individual farm women in Alberta and Saskatchewan. During the 1920s the WILPF offered an expansive and radical vision of a co-operative world of international and sexual equality—a vision remarkably articulated by the "mighty mite" of Saskatchewan, Violet McNaughton (Steer, 1992; Taylor, 2000). Women's concerns were interwoven and interconnected: if women fought for temperance to stem the tide of violence and articulating a caring vision of home and community, it made sense to fight for a peaceful and co-operative world. They took as their main educational goal the education of public opinion. Boutilier (1992) states that the "educational emphasis and the strategies which it adopted to attain its goals reflected both a strong faith in the powers of education to change society and reflected its own membership's past activities in feminist politics" (p. 89). Vision engenders projects and projects find methods: for the WILPF, this meant focusing on personal and group study, public education as well as the education of children and youth.

The WILPF had taken on a fierce enemy: militarism intertwined with a competitive capitalist system, underpinned, they believed, by a skewed understanding of masculinity. This confrontation separates them from more liberal feminist organizations. How would one change such historically deep-rooted structures of war and male character? Is it even possible? The WILPF thought their educational radicalism could erode the acculturated habits and attitudes of war instilled in children by story books glorifying war and the egregious cadet parades in the schools. Their educational reform strategy was two-fold: they worked to prepare curricular materials to counteract militarism in the schools to create a form of perspective transformation in the minds of youth and their teachers; and they engaged in a wide range of projects to unsettle the regnant ideology of militaristic capitalism. Perhaps the WILPF can be characterized as the most utopian of feminist reform movements in this era. They wanted to overturn the "spirit of hatred" polluting men's (and women's) souls, and demanded nothing less than "moral reconstruction of society." Theirs was a civilizing mission in a most difficult of times— post-World War I ultra-nationalism and fear of radicalism (the infamous "red scare" poked its ugly head in people's affairs). This utopian search for peace in the lifeworld and the system was perceived by most feminists of the time as a natural female preoccupation. Thus, many women's organizations turned attention to the educational system. But could children really be society's redeemers?

The public education of the WILPF used several devices or methods. They produced and distributed a wide range of peace literature. For instance, between 1919 and 1921 the Vancouver and Toronto branches produced eight different pamphlets that were distributed to other branches and women's organizations in western Canada and Toronto. The emergent core of feminist journalists wrote newspaper articles. They organized public speeches. But the most innovative social pedagogical form used by the WILPF was the all-day peace conference. In 1928 the

Vancouver branch led by the indomitable Laura Jamieson, opened up this public sphere to influence the Canadian federal government, as signatory to the Kellogg-Briand Act, to act upon its disavowal of war; other conferences were held in Saskatoon and Winnipeg. Women's groups, once hostile to each other joined to deliberate in a series of round-table discussions. Here, the WILPF has expanded communicative action towards the creation of a global public sphere. Women learned to challenge their own viewpoints as they listened to those of others. Vancouver and Winnipeg branches even held pageants bringing together a variety of ethnic associations in order to create "good will" between nations and cultures. But it was the insistent and dogged efforts to de-militarize the schools that distinguish the WILPF from other groups. Jamieson's persistence paid off: in 1927 the provincial government of BC eliminated cadet drills in the schools. Her political supporters, Agnes MacPhail, the first woman elected to national parliament, and J. S. Woodsworth, the Co-operative Commonwealth Federation (CCF) leader, would have been pleased.

To highlight the innovative pedagogies of female reformers and adult educators during this period, let us examine the educational work of Beatrice Brigden, Violet McNaughton, and Nellie McClung. Although both McClung and Brigden's world outlook and moral and ethical framework were filtered through Methodist Protestantism and bear the marks of the tensions between faith and secularism, we cannot understand their feminism apart from their personal faiths and internal struggles. What does stand out, however, is their tendency to see the world through a moralizing lens. On the other hand, McNaughton's early formation in North Kent, England, in the late nineteenth century appears to be more free thinking and secular in orientation (Taylor, 2000). Brigden, born in Belleville, Ontario, in 1888, acquired early on a love of recitation and public speaking. Encouraged to apply her Christian faith for the social good by leading social gospellers, she was hired by the Methodist church to speak to women about purity, marriage, and motherhood. From 1913 to 1919 Brigden criss-crossed the country, giving countless lectures and recitals for the Methodist Church's campaign for social purity. In itself, the recital is an arresting pedagogical form. Feminists like Brigden and McClung realized that to capture audiences, they had to combine entertainment with their message. This form of adult educational work, requiring vocal and rhetorical skills, was extraordinarily difficult and important—girls and women had very little access to "scientific" knowledge about sexuality and contraception, relations with men, marriage, and the birth and rearing of children. But her work was often dismissed as trivial or even as "socialist" by skeptics within the church. In 1918 and the aftermath of the war, Brigden was swept up in the messianic, socialist zeal of the People's Church (one of the Labour churches) of Brandon, under the leadership of the Rev. A. E. Smith. She played a central role as an adult educator there, leading discussion groups for women, and touring the "Forum circuit" where she gave recitals from the radical texts of the day with dashes of literature thrown in. On the road again, she toured, this time her recitals and speeches demanded structural change to the economic and political order (Sangster, 1992; Mitchell, 1990).

Violet McNaughton deserves recognition as one of our greatest and most formidable adult educators in the twentieth century. For sixty of her eighty-nine years, she was involved in educating others, with time left over to make quilts and strawberry jam. She learned her techniques of organizing and teaching skills working in Kent, in the late nineteenth century, as a school teacher (her mantra was "Organize! Organize!). By the time she arrived in Saskatchewan in 1909 she already had embraced the values of co-operativism, women's, and reform movements. She plunged into the tide of reform surging across Canada from sea to sea. This adult educator shared much in common with her sisters in the WILPF and reform movements. Radical changes could be achieved non-violently and co-operatively. This required learning how to co-operate. No advocate of radical separation, McNaughton believed that each gender had to play its part, sometimes together, sometimes in their own associations.

Like Father Jimmy Tompkins, she believed that people had the capacity to self-organize. For her, the first step was awareness and understanding of the issue; the second required making a decision for action based on their understanding of the issue; and, thirdly, to act in such a way as to improve their own and the lives of others in the larger community. This was an expansive and generous vision, a form of deliberative democracy in practice. Steer (1992) states: "This unshakeable belief in the ability of education to shape the society in which she lived, together with her belief in the equality of women and the need for a society based on co-operative principles, provides both the force and rationale for her numerous activities" (p. 139). McNaughton was like a mighty windmill, and generated almost endless projects.

Three organizations created between 1913 and 1920 owe their existence largely to her. Like other feminists of her day, Violet responded to the problem of isolation and loneliness by imagining the possibility of an auxiliary to the Saskatchewan Grain Growers Association (SGGA). She wasn't opposed to the Homemakers' Clubs, or the work churches did

Women's editor of the Western Produce Violet McNaughton (sitting in the foreground) alongside her fellow Community Progress judge, and University of Saskatchewan President, Walter Murray, with eight women in ethnic dress standing to the rear. (Credit: W.C. Murray fonds, MG 1. Records of the Community Progress Competitions #17)

in providing socializing and educational opportunities. Her eyes were focused on creating co-operative economic structures for all, an auxiliary (WGGA) would enable the SGGA to mobilize the energy of men and women. With the assistance of the radical journalist Francis Beynon (Lillian's sister), the WGGA was created at the annual meeting of the SGGA (the first farm organization to do so) in 1913. Her speech proclaimed that women's weapons were organization. Her second significant initiative emerged from her belief that those many groups working for suffrage needed to be consolidated. The franchise for women would improve their social conditions—in fact, absolutely for tackling problems like prostitution, consolidated schools, or medical aid. However, economic change had to precede social and cultural changes. If women's work was sheer drudgery and they remained ignorant of bookkeeping and finance, they remained helpless. So she formed the Provincial Equality Franchise Board in 1915. Saskatchewan became the second province in Canada to grant women the vote.

The third organization McNaughton helped launch was the International Council of Farm Women in January 1919. Like other feminist educators and moulders of public opinion, she wanted farm women to have the pedagogical form to express themselves nationally. The needs of women and children could not be muffled or repressed. McNaughton didn't always find the farm movement hospitable to her desire to the have the WGGA and the SGGA to create a special study branch where

they could study subjects like international relations. But the "intellectual development of the masses" was overshadowed by the economic
interests of the SGGA, though Henry Wise Woods, legendary leader of
the UFA, was amenable to using the locals for study. It was a hard slog:
by the mid-1920s, interest in the SGGA and WGGA had waned. Violet's
educational vision accentuated the need for radical transformation in
the self-understanding of women's labour. They had to value themselves,
otherwise nobody else would. They were wives and housekeepers; they
were also producers in the economic sphere. McNaughton never fully
subscribed to the popular idea that women were more nurturing and
self-sacrificing than men. For her, this had only bred inferiority com-
plexes amongst women.

McNaughton exemplifies another important pedagogical form. Like
other feminists, she took up their pens to educate ordinary women. In
April 1916 she became the editor of the *Saturday Press and Prairie Farm*, a
small weekly paper she used to challenge and chide the established paper,
the stodgy *Grain Growers' Guide*. Her paper soon evolved into a forum
for discussing issues vital to achieving a better world. She sought to re-
educate women to take up their responsibilities to build this new world.
She carried reports of women's organizations (and the CCF, which she
ardently supported), thus creating a network for communicative action.
Later, she would write for *The Western Producer*, an influential farm journal. She found her journalism an effective pedagogical vehicle. At the
heart of this women's vision was the luminous idea that women and men
had to "live a life" as well as "make a living." But to "live a life" material
needs first had to be met, which happened through co-operative efforts.
Ideally, this would leave sufficient free time for women to develop their
"higher selves." A potent vision of human flourishing is the cornerstone
of her work as an educator and activist (Steer, 1992; Taylor, 2000).

Nellie McClung is the best known of these three remarkable female
adult educators and accomplished organizers. Her voice reverberates still
in Canadian memories and contemporary feminist scholarship (Strong-
Boag, 1972; Warne, 1993; Hancock, 1986). Like Brigden, McClung (b.
1873) was raised in a devoted Methodist family and was a proponent
of the social gospel. She can be thought of as an educator whose work
was akin to that of a performative artist. For her, the performance had
two interwoven components: one was the orally performed lecture and
recitals; the other, her writings. She had received some of her training
for performative pedagogy in the normal school and learning leadership
skills in Methodist youth groups. And she learned how to get and hold

audiences in the school of hard knocks. She had discovered the power of speech for good and bad; and knew that humour laced with caustic wit could handle the disbelievers and hecklers in rough and tumble community halls. McClung's performances were in the service of the women's reform movement. She had persuasive power; temperance, peace, suffrage, church, and political groups wanted her. A poster produced by the WCTU for a recital, December 3, 1912, offered McClung as reader of her own stories interspersed with songs and harp solos. Another meeting, at the O.I. Say Town Hall, declared that it would be the "scene of the greatest rally to hear Nellie McClung," acknowledged as Canada's "greatest entertainer and oratoress [sic] and will be heard in her best form on the much discussed Drink Question." These sorts of activities were reproduced hundreds of times over many decades. Indeed, one can hear the speech rhythms and honed wit and polished story on every page of *In Times Like These*. If her lectures were "sermons in disguise" (Hancock, 1986), then "literature was her pulpit" (Warne, 1993).

McClung was a didactic writer. She wrote novels, short stories, newspaper articles, and autobiography with one intention in mind: to shape the moral sensibilities of women (and men) to work for a better Canada, to create, as she said in *In Times Like These*, a "land of the fair deal." Collected, these works consist of sixteen volumes. Her works can be situated in an incipient female literary sphere. Canadian women, since the early nineteenth century, had been writing memoirs and accounts of pioneering life (Susanna Moodie and Catharine Parr Traill); and novelists like Agnes Machar appear in the late nineteenth century. Often neglected, these works must be re-thought in new terms. All of McClung's writings were committed to dissipating the fog surrounding the ideas, structures, associations, and laws that were unjust to women. She wrote for "religious and moral edification" (Warne, 1993, p. 55) to awaken moral consciousness, which in turn would lead to direct action at the institutional level. She was aware that her Pearlie Watson Trilogy (*Sowing Seeds in Danny* [1908], *The Second Chance* [1910] and *Purple Spring* [1921]) was melodramatic in literary form. These novels reflect the moral high ground of early twentieth century Methodism: the dangers of alcohol to the unsuspecting woman, the necessity of kinds to cement human community. She committed to awakening women's consciousness, not in the production of a sophisticated pretty literary text.

McClung caught the attention of the African Canadian community, a thousand of whom had arrived in Alberta from Oklahoma between 1907 and 1911, and settled in small rural communities like Pine Creek north of Edmonton. Like the African Canadians in Nova Scotia, the church—the Emanuel African Methodist Church—led by Rev. George Slater, was the crucible for identity formation and adult learning and action. Slater wrote a column, "Our Negro Citizen," for the *Edmonton Journal*, and references to Nellie McClung and Emily Murphy appear often. He also mentions the formation of the Phillis Wheatley WCTU—composed of Black women—who appear in the Annual Report of the Alberta WCTU in 1916. These African Canadian women, like their counterparts in the "coloured" Women's Institute in Nova Scotia, participated in the larger debates of the day and educated themselves as the equals of their white counterparts (Cui and Kelly, 2012).

In Times Like These, written almost one hundred years ago at the outbreak of WWI, is still a powerful testament to a feminist humanist world-outlook. The label of "maternal feminist" does not seem appropriate to this frontal attack against an androcentric society (Strong-Boag, 1972; Bacchi, 1983). Permeated by a prophetic form of Christianity (which also adopts themes later articulated in feminist theologies), McClung excoriated the idea that militarism was inherent in our species and the Christian churches' reading women out of the gospels and full participation in church decision-making and right to preach and be ordained. She declared: "The church has deliberately set its face against the emancipation of women, and in that respect it has been a perfect joy to the liquor traffic, who recognize their deadliest foe to be the woman with a ballot in her hand" (1915, p. 74). In fact, McClung fought for years to gain ordination rights for women in the Methodist church, gained only in 1937. Unlike Brigden she stayed within the Methodist, then the United (formed in 1925), churches until her death in 1951. McClung (1915) knew only too well that through most of history "women have always got things that they did not want" (p. 56)—whether that was war, the alcohol business, less pay for equal work or the vote. Her vision of radical democracy broke through partisan politics: she wanted women to "share in citizenship" (p. 56)—this meant, for her, that "women's specificity provided a powerful challenge to the androcentric imagination, particularly in its denial of the public sphere become accountable to women's experience, as defined by women" (Warne, 1993, p. 187). Her performative pedagogy was in the service of deliberative democracy and the full emancipation of women from their inertial state. Feminist historian Dolores Hayden (author of *The Great Domestic Revolution: A History of Feminist Design for the American Home, Neighbourhoods, and Cities* [1987]) captures well the struggles of Canadian (and American) women to use adult education pedagogies to emancipate themselves from the "split between domestic life and public life created by industrial capitalism, as it affected women. Every feminist campaign for women's autonomy must be seen in this light" (p. 4).

Pioneers and Pedagogues: Carrying the University to the People

Historians of Canadian adult education generally agree that the idea of extension was borrowed from the English universities of Cambridge and Oxford. Cambridge launched formal extension classes in 1873, and Oxford is intimately, if ambiguously, bound with the emergence of workers' education in the late nineteenth and early twentieth centuries. The famous document, *Oxford and the Working-class* was published in 1908. Five years earlier, the English WEA had been created under the dreamy leadership of Albert Mansbridge. English developments form one stream of influence into the Canadian worlds of higher education. The other influence, constantly referenced by the pioneering university builders in Alberta and Saskatchewan, was the American University of Wisconsin (Kett, 1994). Indeed, the older, more established eastern universities such as Toronto, Queen's, and McGill were influenced by English developments. They defined extension primarily as the offering of courses in non-traditional ways (what is termed the extra-mural function of the university).

The University of Toronto did not form its extension division until July 1, 1920, under the directorship of W. J. Dunlop. It exemplifies the course-giving approach. The University of Toronto's extension service (which began in a small way in 1858 by offering library services to the public) during the period from 1890 to 1920 offered an irregular fare of adult education—local lectures (off campus), public lectures (on campus), credential courses for teachers, summer classes for teachers, and, as we have seen earlier, tutorial classes for the WEA (which did not involve any kind of formal certification). The University of Toronto professors were rather resistant to extension; one told Dunlop, "I like you, Dunlop, but I detest what you are doing." Although Dunlop was a social conservative (he didn't much like the WEA at all), and was an "empire builder," he shared the ethos of the early twentieth century that was able to imagine "extension" as a form of "public service" (Knoepll, 1967). The Mechanics' Institutes, Corbett (1952) says, "provided universities and colleges with the first organized opportunity to relate the thinking and the research going on within the universities to the problems of the community they served" (p. 5). Some university professors, particularly those with an interest in natural history or the new technologies, would lecture at the Institutes. As university historian Robin Harris (1976) observes, by the mid-nineteenth century "free public lectures were provided by Dalhousie, McGill, Queen's, Acadia, and Laval" (p. 147). The Institutes opened up some social learning space for the amateurs out to explore the new sciences and inventions. This knowledge, however, was hardly diffused widely through the population, and the university lectures were mainly "affairs of the moment" (Dunlop, 1981, p. 5). With the gradual disappearance of Mechanics' Institutes in the late nineteenth century, universities moved, some reluctantly, into vacated public space and began to offer lectures on a variety of subjects, mainly consisting of scientific, literary, and historical nature.

Queen's University is often considered a conservative and traditional university. Yet it is Queen's that assumed the leadership of the extension movement in the 1880s and 1890s (the universities of Saskatchewan and Alberta did not yet exist). George Munro Grant, a Nova Scotian by birth and Presbyterian minister by vocation, left his prestigious parish of St. Matthew's Church in Halifax in 1877 to assume the principalship of the floundering Queen's University. By all assessments, Principal Grant was a man of vision (he was a staunch but stodgy advocate of the British imperial linkage) and openness for his time (he opposed the Toronto Trades and Labour Council's anti-Chinese sentiments in the 1890s), and he struggled, like so many recalescent reformers of the day, with the Capital-Labour conundrum. One of the leading proponents of the Protestant social gospel, Principal Grant believed that the university and the church were "vital forces in national development, not refuges shielding scholars from the world" (Berger, 1970, p. 183). Why did Grant want to build an extension program at Queen's? He believed that the university had a responsibility to extend its edifying influence to as wide a constituency as possible (the public service ethic). Here, we are reminded of the rhetoric used by the University of Toronto when it first created its extension division: the university had the role to disseminate "legitimate knowledge" and suppress "dangerous forms" that might erupt from the uncultured and rebellious working class and citizenry. Like Dr. Henry M. Tory, the first president of the University of Alberta, he knew that Queen's fragile predicament (they faced pressure to become an affiliate of the University of Toronto) required some innovative steps to permit extramural students to gain university credits. During the 1880s, Queen's held summer schools for teachers. This permitted men, and particularly young women, to attend regular classes. Grant wanted—as Tory did—to create a loyal following in the competitive world of universities and boosterish cities.

Though hardly revolutionary, this sort of departure from the normal pattern was for its time significant enough (not significant enough, as we have seen, for Alfred Fitzpatrick), and the university had to grapple with the nuts and bolts administrative issues of how students would gain access to books and who would serve as examiners in Queen's outposts scattered throughout Ontario and Canada. By 1894, sixty-seven extramural students were registered. There was great demand for these services and Queen's had to recruit special correspondence tutors beginning in 1894. Queen's would go on to be widely recognized for its correspondence courses. The university also reached out to other constituencies in search of credentials, offering courses for prospectors and miners in association with the Kingston School of Mining. These latter courses, extending as far as Sault St. Marie and the Rainy River District, were intended to promote the study of elementary mineralogy and geology, and to diffuse knowledge that would be useful to those exploring and developing mineral lands. By 1898, these courses would be discontinued for lack of significant interest.

Ned Corbett (1952) observed that the "administration and staff of many of our Canadian universities regarded extension work as an entirely unnecessary activity and not properly the function of an institution whose first responsibility lies in teaching and research" (p. 7). This turned out to be the case even with Queen's. Between 1900 and 1910 there was growing concern over standards for extension work (these courses watered down the content) and university administrators, including Principal Grant, became worried that university professors could not play the dual roles of professor and extension teacher. This sentiment was nicely captured in a *Boston Herald* article reprinted in the influential *The Canadian Education Monthly and School Magazine* in the summer of 1892. "No man occupying a professor's chair at Harvard or Yale or Princeton or Johns Hopkins," the writer pontificated, "can give his nights to university extension in the cities, without destroying or impairing the usefulness of his days at the university" (Dunlop, 1981, p. 62). Another conflict, with deep analogues to our time, occurred when economics professor O. D. Skelton conducted a rather aggressive campaign to entice the thousands of bank clerks to take extramural courses. By September 1913, in cooperation with the Canadian Bankers Association, 680 had registered in an associate's course, with 375 in a fellow's. This development received a tart reply from Dean Cappon, who scolded Skelton: "In the midst of all our practical modern developments … training a larger-minded citizenry, remains properly the chief function which distinguishes it from a technical or business college" (Dunlop, 1981, p. 102).

This course-giving approach, building on the foundation of traditional university work, was rejected by the emergent universities of Alberta and Saskatchewan in the early twentieth century. It was also rejected by St. Francis Xavier University in the late 1920s. A different vision was offered by these three universities: that of beginning in the life situation, in the interests and problems of people in their real lives. Although one can see a mild democratizing tendency in Queen's University's openness to making arrangements for practicing teachers to work for a degree without attending classes in the 1880s, the eastern universities' approach to extension did not break with the traditional model of the university. We have already seen something of the trouble Alfred Fitzpatrick ran into when he tried to get university professors to spend part of their time in the field (or to simply take responsibility for extending knowledge to those who were forgotten, existing far from privileged, legitimate, knowledge-centres). We will highlight the origins and development of the extension departments at the Universities of Alberta and Saskatchewan. First, we offer some background thoughts.

In sharp contrast to Queen's or Toronto, the leaders of the Universities of Alberta and Saskatchewan, which emerged simultaneously with the birth of these provinces in 1905, decided that their new institutions would carry useful knowledge to the people and respond to the needs of people hungry for cultural enlightenment, scientific and technical insight, and for human solidarity. Why did university extension appear in Canada when it did? What social conditions called forth this particular form of adult education? The idea of extension is anchored in historic processes whereby work and, increasingly throughout the twentieth century, psychological and social processes became amenable to scientific understanding and control. From the 1830s to 1900, scientific investigation and discourse shifted from an inclusive amateurism to exclusive professional elites. By 1900, most Mechanics' Institutes had dissolved, or transmuted into libraries. Professionalized scientific investigation, in both the natural and social sciences, was taking its place within specialized nooks in the academy. Expert knowledge was now set over against common-sense knowledge, learned in the school of hard knocks and trial and error pragmatic problem-solving, even more decisively than in the beginnings of "scientized agriculture" in the early nineteenth century. The universities, then, had to first gain a monopoly on scientific knowledge before they could think of extending this newly-discovered knowledge, be it why rust infects wheat, how workers can produce more efficiently, or what is causing unemployment or how children should be raised. We can, I think, link the professionalization process to the gradual secularization of the university. Protestant intellectuals like Tory and Murray may have wanted to create a synthesis of the liberal university and the emergent scientific one. But over time, the liberal ideal of personal development succumbed.

The University of Alberta deserves a special place in the litany of Canadian adult education firsts. It was the first non-agricultural extension department created in the country in 1912. Two years earlier, the University of Saskatchewan had created its Agricultural Extension Department. The Alberta story is replete with larger-than-life characters who were brilliant and bold pedagogues who carried cultural forms of knowledge to the people of Alberta: Dr. Henry M. Tory, university president; A. E. Ottewell, the first director of extension and the inimitable raconteur; E. A. (Ned) Corbett, the second director. Henry Marshall Tory, born in Nova Scotia in 1864, arrived in Alberta to assume the university's presidency in 1908. Highly educated in the sciences, physics, and mathematics (BA and gold medal in 1890 from McGill) and theology (BD from Wesleyan College in Montreal). He preached for a few years, graduate work quickly followed, culminating in a DSc in mathematics in 1903. Tory's Methodist faith infused his world outlook: he was a man of high principle and egalitarian sentiments. But the classic separation of "faith" and "knowledge"—rent apart in the Enlightenment—permeated his work as university builder. The world of the "practical" (instrumental forms of knowing) triumphed as scientific method, in laboratory or empirical technique, came into prominence (Creet, 1981). This was also true for Walter Murray.

Tory exuded enthusiasm and had great energy. He was an institution builder who commanded the loyalty of those he worked with. And build he did: from the beginning of the birth of the University of Alberta, Tory was enmeshed in the controversial struggle over where the new university was to be built: Calgary or Edmonton. He was also trying to build a university in a pioneering province where practical needs and concerns dominated time and imagination. Tory, like Walter Murray, president of the University of Saskatchewan, believed deeply in the idea that the university has to serve all the people. It had to be a public university, and the extension department integral to its functioning and meaning. Like

Grant of Queen's, he, too, had to make the university known in the many scattered rural towns and villages.

The University of Alberta opened in 1908 with five professors. Tory quickly had them teaching in Edmonton and travelling down endless bumpy roads to provide lectures. Roads were terrible, sometimes non-existent, and branch lines of the railway didn't always extend to the farming villages. But the settlers were pouring into the province, including about a thousand African Americans from Oklahoma, filling fertile farm lands and ranch country. In his convocation address delivered in 1908, Tory proclaimed that extension "would carry its ideals of refinement and culture into their lives and its latent spiritual and moral power into their minds and hearts" (Yule, 1963, p. 12). Not a man to burrow into a study for secluded meditative hours, Tory and his little band of professor-extension pedagogues took their secular gospel into, as English professor E. K. Broadus put it, "every little rabbit-path of a settlement in the province" (Yule, 1963, p. 13). They were often surprised to find well-educated men and women hungry for communication and intensely interested in the scientific, literary, and social issues of the day. Stories abound of lecturers staying up all night in some small farmhouse talking into the wee hours of the morning. In 1912, the Extension Department was officially established. Tory selected Albert E. Ottewell, a member of the first graduating class, as his director. He was a huge man, 6'3" tall and weighing around 300 pounds. Born and raised in tough farming conditions in Clover Bar, Alberta, he didn't complete schooling and receive his degree in Classics until he was almost thirty. He thought he was headed for the Methodist ministry. But like Corbett, he fell into the company of adult educators. It may not be pressing matters too far to think of adult education in this period as a form of secular missionary work for the purpose of creating a civilized, just, and Anglo-Saxon Canada.

If Father Jimmy Tompkins is the "Johnny Appleseed" of Canadian adult education, then A. E. Ottewell is our "Paul Bunyan." Tory told Ottewell and Corbett that he wanted Albertan citizens to feel that the university belonged to them. Carry the university to the people giant Ottewell did, extraordinarily so. With boundless energy, he would down a few cans of salmon in the morning and would get to some small village by any means possible. He had a rickety old Model T Ford, he figured out how to use its engine to pull him out of the many mud holes of the spring rains. His pedagogical style was boisterous and humorous: Corbett (1953) says that he would begin will rounds of singing "The Old Grey Mare" and other such ditties to loosen up his audience (students) and then launch into his lecture—or lantern slide show—on "Evolution." Corbett, who first met Ottewell through the Khaki University in England in 1918 (Ottewell went there to assist Dr. Tory, who directed this remarkable innovation in adult pedagogy), recalls him holding 1,200 soldiers filling a machine-gun depot spellbound. Corbett left his mission field work after World War I and joined the Extension Department in 1920, becoming its director in 1928. He recalls the great skill with which Ottewell assembled his organization. By 1920 there were three hundred travelling libraries (managed admirably by Miss Jessie Montgomery) and an open-shelf library circulating to citizens by mail. Ottewell nurtured critical thinking and inquiry by assembling packages of debating materials (for topics such as "Oriental immigration"). He had a massive collection of the old lantern slides; short courses and lecture courses were provided. Corbett (1953) states that their job "was to bring to the remote places of the province whatever cultural and entertainment values the University could offer as a means of encouraging community solidarity, strengthening morale, awakening the civic conscience in regard to better home and school conditions; to bring color and some kindliness into the hard and lonely lives of frontier people" (p. 72). That captures the vision of the University of Alberta's Extension Department beautifully.

Corbett was a marvellous raconteur, a man of elegance, wry humour, and sardonic wit. He is also, perhaps, our first real historian of Canadian adult education. His stories are recounted in *We Have With Us Tonight* (1957). He tells of being asked to travel to a small pioneering community in 1924. Setting out early, Corbett made his way through quagmire roads, finally arriving at his small hotel to find a note posted on his door instructing him to meet everyone out at the fairground where a stampede was in full swing. Corbett was told that nobody had ever seen a picture show, and they looked forward to watching one. But, to his surprise, he was informed that the hall normally used for meetings had been used to store wheat and had been hauled away. But the hall would be brought to the site soon and the fun could begin. Now, in this strange turn of events, the meeting hall was brought to the professor!

Ottewell was fearless and his lectures on "evolution" (and many other subjects) stirred up some trouble. Some fundamentalist Bible-belt Albertans were nudged towards critical thought and reflective learning. He also knew that one had to make a lasting impression; he tried to dig the roots deep by organizing "Farm Young People's Week." One hundred youth from round the province would spend a few weeks at the University of Alberta in the summer. They were being trained in community leadership and active citizenship. Ottewell perceived the importance of radio early on as a pedagogical instrument for adult education. In 1925 he convinced the provincial government to engage in an experiment in radio education. Corbett (1953) comments: "In musical interpretation, in drama, in round-table discussion techniques, in the teaching of French, and in the use of radio to serve the everyday needs of farm people, CKUA was the pioneer in Canada" (p. 76). Ottewell assumed the job of Registrar in 1928 and was in constant demand as lecturer across the province.

Between 1886, when Sir Wilfred Laurier assumed prime ministership and Clifford Sifton began to craft his western settlement policies, millions of immigrants poured into the prairies, aided by the building of the transcontinental railway and lured by the dream of riches of a new beginning. This placed further strain on Natives, who faced the despair of the end of the buffalo era. The Riel Rebellions (1870 and 1885), in fact, had only intensified white fears of the Native "other." The Canadian state attempted to provide agricultural education for prairie Natives, but never did enough, and did not want Indians to acquire the skills and know-how to compete with white settlers. In 1895 there were only 73,500 settlers in the entire North-West Territories; by 1911 Saskatchewan would have a population of approximately 490,000 (about 95,000 farms with almost five million acres of wheat), scattered over of almost 100,000 square miles. Over two-thirds lived in the southern, treeless plains, or in the parklands of the northern section. Most of the immigrants from Central Europe chose the wooded sections of the northern part of the province. Bloc settlements were common, be they Ukrainians or Mennonites, and some Anglo-conformists like Saskatchewan Premier J. T. M. Anderson would find this troubling and a bit sinister (Anderson, 1918). The basic settlement pattern was put in place during this boom period. Those who flooded into the new land faced several learning challenges as they struggled to adapt to their new worlds. Not only did they confront problems pertaining to crops and livestock, they also had to build new forms of solidarity in a land of great isolation and ethnic diversity. Anderson was queasy about any religious outlook that strayed too far from the British Protestant norm.

The Saskatchewan Liberals, who won the election in 1905, wanted their new university to be practical and to serve the whole province (Hayden, 1983). For whatever reason, the pressure in Saskatchewan for the university to meet pressing practical problems seems to have been more intense than in Alberta. Dr. Walter Murray, a New Brunswicker, was chosen to be the first president of the University of Saskatchewan. In choosing Walter Murray as their first president, Saskatchewan had found a fierce idealist, disciplined and tempered by the many assaults to his bedrock Christianity in the modernizing culture of the late Victorian era. Murray was born in 1866 in rural Kings County, New Brunswick, into a middle-class, stern Presbyterian family. From his late teens, Murray seemed imbued with the progressive spirit of the social gospel. Murray graduated from Dalhousie in 1886 with honours in classics and mathematics. After a year of teacher training, he went to Edinburgh, acquiring a first-class honours MA in philosophy in 1891. While there, he met other men like the University of Toronto's Robert Falconer who, steeped in Hegelian idealism, became a stalwart advocate of the moral and service functions of the early twentieth century Canadian university. Falconer, Murray, and H. M. Tory found common ground in their struggle to blend the absolute and the empirical in an age puffed with the glories of science and technology (all too evident in World War I [Hochschild, 2011]). To education was transferred the role the Church had once played. For Murray, the university's fundamental task was to provide a unifying cultural orientation for the people of Saskatchewan in the age of progress. The university had to help men and women acquire the means of livelihood and resources for everyday meaningful living. Culture had to be fused with utilitarian interests. The university could brook no opposition as the emergent imperial centre for knowledge dissemination and legitimation in the pioneering and professionalizing society.

In a series of revealing presidential reports written between 1908 and 1920, Walter Murray set out his vision of the role of the university in society. The University of Saskatchewan had to be undivided and nonsectarian; agricultural education had to be central to its mission; it had to fuse culture and utility, and it had to serve the people. Perhaps his experience as a Presbyterian progressive in Halifax and professor of philosophy at Dalhousie had made him scoff at the sectarian politics of the cloth and cloak. Murray railed against the sectarian spirit of the Maritimes, where all of the little universities were begging for support from American millionaires. In his no-holds barred presidential report (PR) of 1908/1909, Murray wrote: "If our university is to serve the province in the things that abide, it should provide both the school of the humanities where men learn the purpose of life and the art of living. It should conserve the best of the past, and meet the needs of the future" (p. 11). The Church and Christian gospel as ultimate source of meaning appear to be sidelined: in its place, the humanities positioned as purveyor of meaning.

Murray was particularly opposed to a separate college of agriculture. A traditional university like Oxford would not have incorporated a college such as this. But a university "created by the people, supported and controlled by the people could not afford to neglect the chief interest of the people." This sentiment was very much in tune with Murray's attempted reconciliation of idealism with the practical. Having the agriculture college under the university's roof would put it in close touch with people's needs, infusing agriculture with a scientific spirit and preventing the professions, literary, and scientific interests from becoming "self-centred and indifferent to the great practical interests of the people" (PR, 1912/13, 1913/14).

Murray believed that the Great War had revealed the awesome power of science—a potent instrument, he thought, for "extending human power, supplying human needs, and alleviating human pain." Indeed, the world appeared to be on the "verge of an era of reconstruction, more profound in its principles, more far-reaching in its effects than any since the introduction of Christianity." But this surge of optimism was deeply tempered by the horrors of the First World War—captured so poignantly by Timothy Findley's *The Wars*. Who can forget scenes of yellow gas slowly creeping into the muddy bombed out mud holes? Humankind was called upon to "think out anew those fundamental principles and laws which should regulate the conduct of nations no less than of individuals" (PR, 1916-17, pp. 4-5). The emerging sciences of human society (history, law, economics) would be appealed to as never before. Men and women would turn to literature, philosophy, art, and religion with ever greater passion to discover the secret to living moral and ethical lives. By the end of the twentieth century this enlightenment vision would seem touchingly innocent, not yet tarnished, the ideology of progress still wearing emperor's clothing.

Murray worried about the power of emergent technical-instrumental reason (reason oriented to efficiency). But he was pulled inexorably towards solving agricultural production problems foremost. The "schools of practical science" were the necessities, and the "schools of liberal arts or humanities" were the luxuries. Like the University of Wisconsin, the University of Saskatchewan had to be a service university. Scientific agriculture had to be an integral part of the new university. It was entirely fitting that the university "through correspondence classes, extension courses, supervision of farmers' clubs, traveling libraries, women's institutes or musical tests to place within the reach of the solitary student, the distant townsmen, the farmer in his hours of leisure or the mothers or daughters in the home the opportunities for adding to their store of knowledge and enjoyment, as it is that the university should foster research into the properties of radium or the cause and cure for swamp fever…" (PR, 1912-13, p. 3).

When the Agricultural extension Division was created in 1912, it entered into an educational field already occupied by numerous agricultural societies. In 1884 the federal government was conducting scientific research, and in 1886 they established experimental farms at Ottawa (Ontario), Brandon (Manitoba), and Indian Head in Saskatchewan. The Department of Agriculture of the North-West Territories had noticed that farmers were demanding information on problems such as weed eradication and gopher destruction. Thus, the "Agricultural Societies Ordinance" of 1884 arose out of the recognition for a state-approved farmers' organization to encourage improvement in agriculture, horticulture, arbor culture, manufacture, and the useful arts. Their mandate also embraced key lifeworld domains of the home and community. The architects of the agricultural societies were the main educational and pedagogical form for channeling knowledge to the farmers. They became important learning sites, hosting industrial and agricultural exhibitions (the centre piece of society activity), introducing new varieties of seeds and plants, eradicating noxious weeds, encouraging plowing competitions and promoting farmers' institutes. "The pioneering farmers of Saskatchewan," W. B. Baker observed, brought "with them a rich and varied agrarian heritage from many old and established countries of the world [and] had transplanted the seeds of a new agriculture which was already emerging as a social and economic force at the turn of the century" (Baker, n.d, p. 3).

Once the College of Agriculture was created (with William John Rutherford as first dean) a significant amount of the educational activity previously directed by the Department of Agriculture could now be assumed. On March 1, 1910, the fairs and institute branches were transferred to the College of Agriculture, and the Department of Agriculture Extension was born, the first of its kind in the Dominion of Canada. F. H. Auld, who had supervised the fairs and institutes branches of the Department, was transferred to the university. He became the first director of Extension. Auld articulated his vision for the extension movement in his first annual report (1910/11). Scientific agriculture had to be mediated in popular form to the common farmers (some of whom were suspicious of universities and "book farming"). Auld informed his extension workers that he thought that many workers lacked the knowledge of scientific agriculture, and their speeches did not manifest "fundamental principles" underpinning methodological choices. Auld and other directors who would follow him (Greenway and Rayner) earnestly believed that agricultural knowledge was moving ahead of practice, rendering the common sense of farmers inadequate to the farming tasks of the day. This view echoes that of the voice of John Young of Halifax in 1822. With scientific knowledge (of disease and inefficient use of the soil) running ahead of the ordinary famers' indigenous knowledge and understanding, the extension leaders pressed ahead with missionary zeal.

The Extension Depart of the University of Saskatchewan was dynamic and creative. In 1919, Dean Rutherford divided the extension work into two categories: "organized" and "unorganized." By organized he meant the work the extension department did through the agricultural societies, homemakers' clubs, boys' and girls' clubs and the Grain Growers Association. The extension department furnished judges for competitions and short courses at the College, organized institutes in co-operation with various organizations and excursions to the College experimental farm. Unorganized extension work—the better farming train, the dairy and poultry car, etc.—in contrast, was not directly under the oversight of the Department of Extension. The extension service was financed through monies from the provincial legislature through the Education Department: it was part of the regular university budget. The Agricultural societies received grants from the Department of Agriculture for carrying one or more of the various activities outlined in the Agricultural Society Act—membership, exhibitions, seed grain fairs, standing field competitions, plowing matches, and stallion shows.

The agricultural societies were the anchor point for extension service. They were the most important site for learning about the solutions or practical problems' origination in the everyday process of raising stock, planting various crops, and marketing one's goods. Each of the activities attempted to motivate farmers to be more effective and efficient farmers and to encourage them to be more reflective in attitude towards their production activities. The exhibition was the "major activity in the historical development and impact of the agricultural societies" (Baker, n.d., p. 7). The fairs were costly, and some societies teetered on edge of dissolution trying to maintain them. The societies promoted a dizzying array of activities—many of which were designed to encourage farmers into developing better products (animals or farms). Agricultural societies were voluntary associations run by ordinary people who were acquiring knowledge and skills pertaining to democratic self-organization. By

1915, farm leaders recognized that they had to teach the youth the principles and practices of good farming in order to ensure the future of rural life. J.G. Rayner, who became director of extension in 1920, labelled the work amongst farm youth "one of the most striking developments in Extension work" (Rayner, n.d.). Boys and girls held their own camps, receiving valuable citizenship training.

The Extension Division also pioneered in the use of the "good farming trains"—an innovative adult education venture (falling into Rutherford's "unorganized" category), operated by the Department of Agriculture in co-operation with the railways and the extension department. These "schools on wheels" started rolling in 1908. Each train had fourteen cars and coaches. Some carried well selected animals, while others contained things like mechanical appliances. Others were fitted for teaching and demonstrating tillage and crop production and for home management demonstrations. There was even a nursery car where the children could be cared for while mothers attended lectures. They were equipped with the best instructors the college could provide, covering the CPR lines east and west of Saskatoon from Alberta to Manitoba.

In the early twentieth century, small groups of rural women felt the need for some organization which "would draw them together socially and give them opportunities to discuss questions of mutual interest" (Retrospect and Prospect, 25th anniversary of Saskatchewan Homemakers' Clubs, 1936, p. 13). Isolated women's clubs—like the Prosperity Homekeepers Society in the Rocanville District (organized in 1907) and the Open Door Circle of Mair (organized in 1909)—existed. But in January 1911, after an agricultural society-initiated organizing tour by Lillian Beynon in the fall, representatives of isolated women's clubs convened in Regina. Out of these discussions emerged the Saskatchewan Homemakers' Clubs, dedicated to the "promotion of the interests of home and community" (ibid.). Miss Abigail DeLeury was appointed as director of women's work for the university (the Extension Department had oversight responsibilities) in 1913, a position this able women held until 1930 when she was succeeded by Bertha Oxner. The domestic-sounding name of this organization belies its presence in Saskatchewan affairs as a powerful, and at times, even radical voice in defence of life-world interests.

In her opening address at the founding conference, Lillian Beynon ("Lillian Laurie" was her pen name as author of the women's page for the *Manitoba Free Press*) noted that there had been some dispute regarding "separating the work of men and women," but if women were to succeed, they had to specialize. "The farmer will not have time to learn all the secrets of housekeeping, nor will his wife have time to learn all about farming, if she is going to master her own profession of homemaker." If men needed to study—fewer were now laughing at book farming than in the old days—so much more "should women study the minds of their children that the soil there may be prepared to learn rightly the lessons of life." The secrets of Homemaker ideology are contained in these few excerpts. Women accepted the bifurcation of the world. By no means did they accept their inferior status and their exploitation by the male-dominated world. Indeed, the theme of the drudgery of farm women's life, with constant reference to men's deafness to their needs, pervades the conference proceedings of Homemaker assemblies through the tens and twenties. Beynon's adoption of the discourse of professionalization signals several important social and ideational developments. For one thing, farming was clearly being constituted as an "expert culture" and the new forms of knowledge and technology had very high status (to be scientific and efficient was highly valued). Secondly, women recognized that these developments rendered them powerless and inferior in status. To gain equality with men, they have little choice but to argue that "woman" is not a natural born housekeeper and that their work is a domestic science. Thirdly, the lifeworld was being rationalized and opened up to reflective public learning processes. Traditional, common-sense notions about health, nutrition, child-rearing, hygiene, gardening, consuming, ventilation, raising chickens, or architecture were all subjected to criticism.

In the first two decades of the twentieth century, Saskatchewan farm women almost exploded with desire to learn about themselves, others, and their immediate and far flung worlds. Nothing, from international relations to church union, was outside their ken. The local clubs—they grew from fourteen in 1914 to two hundred by 1924—were the educative hub of the Homemakers' organization. Women also attended district conventions and the annual meeting held on the University of Saskatchewan campus attracted around two hundred each year. For overworked rural homemakers, the trip to the university was one of the year's special events. Obtaining "hired help" was a persistent problem for farm women, and the week away was highly treasured. There they conducted their business meetings, listened to lectures, participated in recreational activities, and tasted the delights of city life (including a leisurely soak in the tub free from distractions). No doubt farm women returned home energized for the arduous tasks of meeting the cavilling needs of children and men and the work of the farm.

Women were encouraged to study all manner of subjects and situations. But health concerns of children and mothers were the centrepiece of the Homemakers' lifeworld curriculum. The educational process was anchored in this simple assumption: the life of pioneering farm women was extremely exhausting and time-consuming, and this situation was not simply in the nature of things. Homemakers' leaders like Mrs. Dayton, president of the Manitoba Home Economics Clubs, spoke boldly about the way farm men had all they needed in the way of machinery. Women, in sharp contrast, did their washing by hand. "We should see it," Mrs. Dayton declared to the 1916 annual convention, "that the mother and the child have at least as good a chance in life as the little colt and its mother" (Report of the Proceedings of the Homemakers' Clubs of Saskatchewan, 1916). Women could neither be healthy nor have the time to learn how to care for their children more effectively if they were consumed by farm labour.

By World War I, Homemakers' clubs were increasingly demanding knowledge about child welfare. In 1919/20, for instance, they held fifty-two short courses of two to five days duration on home nursing, eugenics, household science, child welfare, and dressmaking and millinery; child welfare exhibits and clinics were now a general feature of Homemaker fairs. The Homemakers' leadership agitated incessantly for more and better maternity care for women. This demand meant establishing community nursing programs and hospitals. By 1921 Abigail DeLeury could celebrate the Homemakers' pioneering role in getting medical inspection of schools and nursing care. In fact, they were among our earliest advocates of preventative approaches to health care. The School Hygiene Branch in 1921/22 reported many cases of bad teeth, adenoids, enlarged tonsils, malnutrition, TB, defective sight, and hearing. Early twentieth century women in organizations such as Homemakers were developing a different idea of politics. In the still pertinent words of Thomas, "We women have not gone out to politics; they have come in, and troubled our children, and our homes, and we cannot get away from politics" (Proceedings of the annual Convention of Homemakers, 1916). These women were discovering that democracy was not solely about representative politics or control over economic processes.

References

Allen, R. (1971). *The social passion: Religion and social reform in Canada, 1914–1928.* Toronto: University of Toronto Press.

Allen, R. (2008). *The view from Murney Tower: Salem Bland, Victorian controversies, and the search for a new Christianity.* Toronto: University of Toronto Press.

Anderson, J.T.M. (1918). *The education of the new Canadian.* Toronto: James Dent and Sons.

Bacchi, C. (1987). *Liberation deferred? The ideas of the English-Canadian suffragettes, 1827–1918.* Toronto: University of Toronto Press.

Baker, W. (n.d). The historical development of extension in Saskatchewan. J. Rayner Papers. Addresses. 1920–51. Extension Division Papers. University of Saskatchewan Archives, Saskatoon, Saskatchewan.

Berger, C. (1970). *The sense of power: Studies in the ideas of Canadian imperialism.* Toronto: University of Toronto Press.

Bernard, D. (n.d.). The African Union Baptist Association (AUBA) as a women's learning site. Unpublished paper, Mount St. Vincent University.

Boutilier, B. (1992). Making peace as interesting as war: The educational strategies of the Women's International League for Peace and Freedom in Canada during the 1920s. In M. Welton (Ed.). *Educating for a brighter new day: Women's organizations as learning sites.* Halifax (NS): Dalhousie University School of Education.

Bradwin, E. (1928). *Bunkhouse man: A study of work and pay in the camps of Canada, 1903–1914.* Toronto: University of Toronto Press.

Brown. C. & Cook, R. (1974). *Canada, 1896–1921: A nation transformed.* Toronto: McClelland and Stewart.

Christie, N. & Gauvreau, M. (1996). *A full-orbed Christianity: The protestant churches and social welfare in Canada, 1900–1940.* Kingston/Montreal: McGill-Queen's University Press.

Cook, G. (1987). Educational justice for the campmen: Alfred Fitzpatrick and the foundation of Frontier College, 1899–1922. In M. Welton (Ed.). *Knowledge for the people: The struggle for adult learning in English-speaking Canada, 1828–1973.* Toronto: OISE Press.

Cook, R. (1985). *The regenerators: Social criticism in late Victorian English Canada.* Toronto: University of Toronto Press.

Cook, S. (1995). *Through sunshine and shadow: The Woman's Christian Temperance Union, Evangelicalism and reform in Ontario, 1874–1930.* Montreal/Kingston: McGill-Queen's University Press.

Cook, T. (2002). From destruction to construction: The Khaki University of Canada, 1917–1919. *Journal of Canadian Studies,* 37(1), 109–43.

Corbett, E. A. (1952). *University extension in Canada.* Toronto: CAAE

Corbett, E. A. (1953). A.E. Ottewell. In H. Rouillard (Ed.). *Pioneers in adult education.* Toronto: Nelson and Sons.

Crearer, D. (1995). *Padres in no man's land: Canadian chaplains and the Great War.* Montreal/Kingston: McGill-Queen's University Press.

Creet, M. (1981). *H.M. Tory and the secular university.* Distributed by ERIC Clearinghouse, Washington D.C. Retrieved from http://trove.nla.gov.au/work/153557947.

Crowley, T. (1992). Educating for home and community: The genesis of the Women's Institutes in Ontario. In M. Welton (Ed.). *Educating for a brighter new day: Women's organizations as learning sites.* Halifax (NS): Dalhousie University, School of Education.

Cui, D. & Kelly, J. (2012). "Our Negro Citizens": An example of everyday citizenship practices. In A. Finkel at al. *Working people in Alberta: A history.* Athabasca (AB): Athabasca University Press.

Delhi, K. (1992) "The role of home and school association in the education of women in Toronto, 1916–1940." In M. Welton (Ed.). *Educating for a brighter new day: Women's organizations as learning sites* (pp. 79–88). Halifax (NS): Dalhousie University School of Education.

Dennison, C. (1987). "Housekeepers of the community": The British Columbia Women's Institute, 1909–1946. In M. Welton (Ed.). *Knowledge for the people: The struggle for adult learning in English-speaking Canada, 1828–1973*. Toronto: OISE Press.

Dunlop, E. A. (1981). *The development of extension education at Queen's University, 1889–1945*. Unpublished Ph.D dissertation, University of Toronto.

Fitzpatrick, A. (1930). *Schools and other penitentiaries [sic]*. Unpublished manuscript. Frontier College Papers, National Archives of Canada.

Fitzpatrick, A. (1923). *The university in overalls: A plea for part-time study*. Toronto: Frontier College Press.

Fraser, B. (1988). *The social uplifters: Presbyterian progressives and the social gospel in Canada, 1875–1915*. Waterloo (ON): Wilfred Laurier University Press.

Habermas, J. (1984). *The theory of communicative action. Volume 1: Reason and the rationalization of society*. Boston: Beacon Press.

Habermas, J. (1987). *The theory of communicative action. Volume 2: Lifeworld and a system: A critique of functionalist reason*. Boston: Beacon Press.

Hancock, C. (1986). *No small legacy: Canada's Nellie McClung*. Winfield (BC): Wood Lake Books.

Harris, R. (1976). *A history of higher education in Canada, 1663–1960*. Toronto: University of Toronto Press.

Hayden, D. (1987). *The great domestic revolution: A history of feminist designs for American homes, neighborhoods, and cities*. Cambridge: MIT Press.

Hayden, M. (1983). *Seeking a balance: The University of Saskatchewan, 1907–1982*. Vancouver: UBC Press.

Hochschild, A. (2011). *To end all wars: a story of loyalty and rebellion, 1914-1918*. New York: Houghton Mifflin Harcourt Publishing Company.

Hopkins, P. (1987). Difficulties involved in (researching and) writing about workers' education. In *CASAE History Bulletin*.

Hunt, I. (1987). Mutual enlightenment in early Vancouver, 1886-1916. Unpublished doctoral dissertation, Department of Educational Studies, UBC.

Johnson, R. (1981). Really useful knowledge: radical education and working class culture 1790-1848. In J. Clarke et al. (Eds.). *Working class culture: studies in history and theory*. London: Hutchinson and Company Publishers.

Kealey, G. & Palmer, B. (1987). *Dreaming of what might be: the Knights of Labour in Ontario, 1880-1900*. Toronto: New Hogtown Press.

Kealey, L. (1979). *Not unreasonable claim: Women and reform in Canada, 1880s–1920s*. Toronto: Women's Press.

Kett, J. (1994). *The pursuit of knowledge under difficulties: From self-improvement to adult education in America 1750–1990*. Palo Alto (CA): Stanford University Press.

Knoepll, E. (1967). An overview of the development of the Division of University Extension at the University of Toronto since 1920. Paper for Drs. Harris and E. Sheffield. University of Toronto Extension Papers. Box Director of University Extension, file 2.

Laycock, D. (1990). *Populism and democratic thought in the Canadian prairies, 1910–1940*. Toronto: University of Toronto Press.

MacBeth, R. G. (1912). *Our task in Canada*. Toronto: The Westminster Co.

MacLeod, D. (1990). A maturing of purpose: Recent publications in the history of technology and the physical sciences in Canada. *Acadiensis*, 20(1), 225-249.

Mills, A. (1984). Cooperation and community in the thought of J. S. Woodsworth. *Labour/Le Travail, 14*, 103–20.

Mills, A. (1991). *Fool for Christ: The political thought of J. S. Woodsworth.* Toronto: University of Toronto Press.

Mitchell, T. (1990). Beatrice Brigden and radicalism in the Methodist church. *Manitoba History.* 19 (Spring).

McDonald, I. (1987). "To each his own": William Coaker and the Fishermen's Protective Union in Newfoundland politics, 1908–1925/St. John's: Social and Economic Studies No. 33. Institute of Social and Economic Research. Memorial University.

McKay, I. (2008). *Reasoning otherwise: leftists and the people's enlightenment in Canada, 1880–1920.* Toronto: Between the Lines.

McClung, N. (1915). *In times like these.* Toronto: University of Toronto reprint (1972).

Osterhout, S. S. (1929). *Orientalism in Canada: The story of the work of the United Church of Canada with Asiatics in Canada.* Toronto: United Church of Canada Press.

Overton, J. (1995). Moral education of the poor: Adult education and land settlement schemes in Newfoundland in the 1930s. *Newfoundland Studies,* 11(2), 250–81.

Pollard, J. (1987). Propaganda for democracy: John Grierson and adult education during the second world war. In M. Welton (Ed.). *Knowledge for the people: The struggle for adult learning in English-speaking Canada, 1828–1973.* Toronto: OISE Press.

Radforth, I. & Sangster, J. (1987). The struggle for autonomous workers' education: The Workers' Educational Association in Ontario, 1917–51. In M. Welton (Ed.). *Knowledge for the people: the struggle for adult learning in English-speaking Canada, 1828–1973* (pp. 73–96). Toronto: OISE Press.

Rayner (n.d.). The Extension Department University of Saskatchewan, 1905–1940. Extension Papers. University of Saskatchewan Archives.

Report of the proceedings of the annual convention of the Homemakers Clubs of Saskatchewan (1916). Extension Papers, University of Saskatchewan.

Sangster, J. (1989). *Dreams of equality: women on the Canadian left, 1920–1950.* Toronto: University of Toronto Press.

Sangster, J. (1992). "The making of a socialist-feminist: The early career of Beatrice Brigden" In M. Welton (Ed.). *Educating for a brighter new day: Women's organizations as learning sites* (pp. 113–138). Halifax (NS): Dalhousie University: School of Education.

Simon, B. (1992). *The search for enlightenment: The working class and adult education in the twentieth century.* Leicester (UK): NIACE Press.

Steer, S. (1992). Violet McNaughton and the struggle for the cooperative society. In M. Welton (Ed.). *Educating for a brighter new day: Women's organizations as learning sites* (pp. 139–59). Halifax (NS): Dalhousie University, School of Education.

Strong-Boag, V. "Introduction." In N. McClung. *In Times Like These.* Toronto: University of Toronto Press.

Taylor, G. (1992). Should I drown myself now or later? In M. Welton (Ed.). *Educating for a brighter new day: women's organizations as learning sites.* Halifax (NS): Dalhousie University, School of Education.

Taylor, G. (2000). "Let us co-operate": Violet McNaughton and the co-operative ideal. In B. Fairbairn, I. MacPherson & N. Russell (Eds.). *Canadian co-operatives in the year 2000: Memory, mutual aid and the millennium* (pp. 57–78). Saskatoon (SK): Centre for the Study of Co-operatives, University of Saskatchewan

Veinott, R. (1992). "Civic housekeepers: The Halifax Local Council of Women, 1910–1921." In M. Welton (Ed.). *Educating for a brighter new day: Women's organizations as learning sites.* (pp. 17–46). Halifax (NS): Dalhousie University School of Education.

Wang, J. (2006). *His dominion' and the "Yellow Peril": Protestant missionaries to Chinese immigrants in Canada, 1859–1967.* Waterloo (ON): Wilfred Laurier Press.

Ward, P. (1978). *White Canada forever: Popular attitudes and public policy toward Orientals in British Columbia.* Montreal/Kingston: McGill-Queen's University Press.

Warne, R. (1993). *Literature as pulpit: The Christian social activism of Nellie L. McClung.* Waterloo (ON): Wilfred Laurier Press.

Welton, M. (n.d.). "Fraught with wonderful possibilities": Father Jimmy Tompkins and the struggle for a Catholic progressivism, 1902–1922. *NALL Working paper #57.*

Welton, M. (1983). "To be and build the glorious world": The educational thought and practice of Watson Thomson, 1899–1946. Unpublished Ph.D dissertation, Department of Social and Educational Studies, University of British Columbia

Welton, M. (1986). The depths of despondency: The struggle for autonomous workers' education in the Vancouver WEA, 1944–1948. *CASAE History Bulletin.*

Welton, M. (1987) Mobilizing the people for socialism: The politics of adult education in Saskatchewan, 1944–1945. In M. Welton (Ed.). *Knowledge for the people: The struggle for adult learning in English-speaking Canada, 1828–1973* (pp. 151–69). Toronto: OISE Press.

Welton, M. (1991a). Dangerous knowledge: Workers' education in the decades of discord. *Studies in the Education of Adults,* 23(1), 24–40.

Welton, M. (1991b). *Toward development work: The workplace as a learning environment.* Deakin, Australia: Deakin University Press.

Welton, M. (2003). Pioneers and progressive pedagogues: Carrying the University to the people of Saskatchewan, 1905–1928. *The Canadian Journal for the Study of Adult Education,* 17(2).

Welton, M. (2005). "Fraught with wonderful possibilities": Father Jimmy Tompkins and the struggle for a Catholic progressivism, 1912–1922. *Studies in Continuing Education,* 27 (2) 117–34.

Wilson, L. (1979). Educational role of the United Farm Women of Alberta. In D. Jones et al. (Eds.). *Shaping the schools of the Canadian West.* Calgary (AB): Detselig Press.

Woodsworth, J. S. (1909). *Strangers within our gates.* Toronto: University of Toronto reprint.

Yule, D. L. G. (1963). *Educational pioneers in university extension in western Canada.* An essay for Unit 102, graduate course in Education, Ontario College of Education, February. Extension Papers 75-149. Archives of the University of Alberta, Edmonton.

5

Adult Learning and the Crisis of Democracy (1929–1960)

The global depression broke out in 1929, propelling Canadians (and other countries throughout the world) into a bleak and grim time. Millions were out of work and on relief; many were hungry and anxious for the future. The R. B. Bennett government, though it had abolished the notorious relief camps in 1935, was widely perceived as callous towards suffering, as hysterically anti-communist, and to be bereft of practicable social policy. For those on the left the struggle of the destitute farmers, the itinerant hobos, the miner's strike in Estevan, Saskatchewan, in 1934, the Dominion Day riot in Regina in 1935, and the critical strike at the Oshawa General Motors plant in 1937, were the central symbols of a capitalist society with neither a human face nor much of a brain. The great awakening and transformation of Canadians that had occurred over the last fifty years had enabled many men and women to acquire a deeper understanding of what it meant to be active citizens and the range of obstacles they faced to build a better world. They wanted to be knowledgeable human beings, standing tall and speaking with other Canadians in public spheres about the kind of world they wanted to make. They had won significant rights to deepen their knowledge of how to live well and what constituted a just society. They had learned very valuable lessons in translating knowledge into action. They did not want elites to impose upon them from high above.

In the years between 1850 and 1929 Canadian society became rather haltingly a "better society" (women were declared to be "persons" in 1929), but the working class had been defeated in 1919. First Nations peoples, African Canadians, Chinese and European immigrants had created associations to defend their identities and resist the erasure of their own life forms. But they were scarcely welcomed as full citizens and human beings. Canada still had many miles to travel to become an authentic multicultural society. For their part, many women would travel into factories during the War. This gave them a taste of this industrial work and boosted their confidence. It also prepared them for the post WWII struggles against government propaganda to get women to stay in the home and produce four children. And the economic crash of 1929

until 1929,, greater power for women

only deepened Canadians' sense that the capitalist form of economy and polity was still inequitable, designed to serve interests other than those of ordinary citizens. We needed a planned economy. The world of 1929 further revealed the absence of social welfare nets. They would have to await the post-World War II world of welfare capitalism.

Canadians' learning capacities were under siege. They had to make sense, individually and collectively, of Hitler's and Mussolini's rise to power, the ambiguous presence of the communist Soviet Union, and the fractious Spanish Civil War. Watson Thomson had arrived in Canada from Scotland in April 1937, he immediately fell into the company of adult educators. Through an old army acquaintance from WWI, Thomson was put in touch with Corbett. Through Corbett, Thomson met H. H. Hannam, an ardent spokesperson for co-operative activities who had sparked the development of United Farmers of Ontario study clubs and made a modest beginning in residential adult education in the early 1930s. He also met Drummond Wren, former United Auto Workers' activist and militant socialist who had become the secretary-organizer of the national WEA in November 1929. When the WEA was formed in Ontario in 1918, its main purpose was to organize non-credit night classes for workers. By the late 1930s, the WEA had evolved into a pro-labour organization whose purpose was to provide workers with more knowledge to help them improve the political and economic system. Both Wren and Hannam were part of a lunch group of fifteen to twenty persons who met weekly with Corbett for discussion. Listening to these men filtered through his experience of Europe's angst and crisis, Thomson was persuaded that the 1930s was a period of massive contradictions for Canadians as well. Millions were out of work and on relief. But this spiritual and economic dislocation had precipitated a new cultural awakening. Thomson would play an exciting role from 1937 to 1946. He is one of our most unusual and visionary of Canadian adult educators and public intellectuals of his time.

Corbett had finagled a job working for Thomson with the WEA in Calgary in 1937. While there, Thomson had integrated himself into progressive farm circles, meeting farm leaders like Norman Smith. In 1938 Thomson went to work for the Department of Extension at the University of Alberta, Corbett's old stomping grounds. The Munich Crisis—British Prime Minister Neville Chamberlain abandoned the Czechs by permitting Hitler to annex Sudetenland—horrified Thomson. Their correspondence reveals that they both perceived the geopolitical scene as "blacker than it had been at any time during the century" (Welton, 1983,

p. 140). But Thomson believed that the crisis opened up educational possibilities for social re-constructionists. The educational goal was nothing less than a "new and deeper justice, a more co-operative way of life … to be established within our own bounds internally" (Welton, 1983, p. 141). Smith thought that Canadian indifference to global affairs had been shattered.

Canadians faced enormous learning challenges in the Depression, war years, and the ensuing Cold War period. In 1938, Dr. Henry Munro, president of the recently-founded Canadian Association of Adult Education (CAAE), spoke for many social observers when he said that "Canada, like other democracies, had been caught in a tidal wave of social awakening" (p. 14). The evidence was everywhere. New political parties, including the Cooperative Commonwealth Federation (CCF), a political synthesis of farm and labour groups, had been created in Regina in 1933 to articulate the aspirations of the dispossessed and exploited. A number of eastern intellectuals had already broken with their timid colleagues and created the League for Social Reconstruction (LSR), a Fabian-inspired think tank for the emergent democratic socialist CCF. Nor were the churches exempt: they were pressed to examine how their Christianizing project could be furthered. Sir Robert Falconer, former president of the University of Toronto, was appointed by the Board of Evangelism of the United Church of Canada to determine how the social order could be Christianized. This was an old dream not yet fulfilled. His report, *Christianizing the Social Order*, was published in 1934. The Fellowship for a Christian Social Order (FCSO), appeared in 1934. The FCSO, fusing two small groups, the Movement for a Christian Social Order in Toronto and the Fellowship of Christian Socialists in Montreal, was founded in Toronto in April 1934. Christian socialist thought crystallized in *Toward the Christian Revolution*, edited by left-wing theologian and hymn-writer Rev. Robert B.Y. Scott, and published in 1936. Both the FCSO and the LSR carried on a busy round of adult education activities. An "agit-prop" workers' theatre emerged in the mid-thirties, first in Toronto, later spreading across the country, to dramatize the plight of Canada's working class (Souchotte, 1987).

Everywhere voluntary organizations—some old like the Canadian Institute for International Affairs (CIIA), the Women's Institutes, and the WEA, some new like the Canadian Youth Congress and the Canadian League for Peace and Democracy—were engaged in the study of all sorts of things: government and economics, co-operatives and credit unions, child psychology and public speaking, health and community service.

In 1938, E. A. Corbett, director of the CAAE since 1936, estimated that 100,000 people were involved in non-formal adult education. Canadians studied in groups, listened to lectures, and gathered around their radios as they never had before. Sensing that individualistic, laissez-faire values were collapsing, many Canadians struggled to find new ways of making sense of their worlds and new solutions to the host of problems flowing in the wake of capitalism's global crisis. In the peripheral parts of the country, Canadians were most innovative because they had the most to lose. Paradoxically, it was the golden age of adult education, a time of inspiration for contemporary adult educators—even for exemplary models of practice to enable us to confront our own dispirited time.

Canadian adult educators seemed exceptionally intellectually alive and alert to the learning challenges of their era. They created a national adult education organization, the CAAE, experimented with community development projects, created a world famous co-operative adult education project, continued with various worker education efforts, used the "great, new instruments" of radio, film, and the arts brilliantly as learning instruments, and initiated two state-sponsored comprehensive programs to mobilize the people for active citizenship, in Saskatchewan under Watson Thomson's imaginative, bold leadership in 1944 and in Nova Scotia under Guy Henson's resolute vision of an educative democracy in 1945/6. None of this heightened awareness of the role that adult education could play in the world would have been possible without the great awakening and transformation occurring in the previous hundred years.

Indeed, the periodization of history is arbitrary; history simply flows onward and humans slice it up and give it names. We need markers, but they can lead us to miss the continuities of past and present. During these crisis-ridden years from 1929 to 1960, it was as if Canadian adult educators and community leaders woke up and noticed what had been and was, in fact, happening in civil society and public spheres. Adult education became conscious, we might argue, of Canada as an incipient learning society. The CAAE's high moment was the declaration of its Manifesto in 1943. Some fifteen years later, in the mid-1950s, several Canadian adult educators, J. Roby Kidd and Alan Thomas, met with their American counterparts in the Commission of Professors to design an academic program for the study of adult education. Ironically, the creation of an academic field of study occurs in a deeply conflicted time for Canadian adult education. The social reform adult educators' vision and commitment met with hostility in a changed culture and political world. To steal a line from Bob Dylan, the "idiot winds" of the Cold War were

The Coady International Institute was opened at St. Francis Xavier University in 1959. The Institute is world-renowned as a centre of excellence in community leadership education.

sending a chill through Canadian life and culture. Some think that the CAAE was derailed from its more radical purposes in the 1950s (as many of the movement's leaders from the 1930s and 1940s, including Thomson, Wren and Grierson were ousted from key leadership roles, accused of being "reds"). An emerging leader like J. Roby Kidd steered a safe course through infested waters and took a tamed Canadian adult education to the global scene. Kidd hosted the second UNESCO conference in Montreal in 1960, a time of extreme Cold War uneasiness, melancholy, and global distress. In the late 1960s Kidd would become director of OISE's graduate program in adult education. In 1973 he would play a key role in creating the International Council of Adult Education (ICAE). He became Canada's leading figure in international education (to be followed in the 1980s by Budd Hall, who assumed the directorship of the ICAE).

This chapter highlights the widely recognized adult education accomplishments of Canadians in this period. The Antigonish Movement is particularly renowned and well known in many parts of the world. After Moses Coady's death in 1959, St. Francis Xavier University created its Coady International Institute. Many students from different parts of the world have come to the Institute for training in co-operative ideals and practices. The experimental Farm Radio and Citizens' Forums were also exported world-wide (as was the Women's Institute). The first two government departments of adult education, created in very different political climates, one conservative and the other democratic socialist, deserve our attention and consideration. We will also highlight women's role in the Antigonish Movement, and meet many brilliant adult educators who rose to the challenge to educate the citizenry for deliberative democracy. Here we underscore the historical significance of the presence of this current within Canadian democracy. It has been manifest from the very beginnings of the "education of public opinion" in Upper Canada in the nineteenth-century, in agrarian radical movements, in co-operatives, in the many voluntary associations where men and women listened to one another's insights and thoughts about various problems and matters of general concern, and in the creation of public spheres for citizen deliberation. A significant minority of Canadians did not believe that parliamentary democracy was the climatic achievement.

On the Eve of a Great Mass Movement

The adult educators who gathered at the epochal seminar convened by University of Toronto director W. J. Dunlop in Toronto in late May 1934 to consider the formation of national association of adult education were themselves trying to define their mission in a context of economic distress, spiritual dislocation, and emergent social movements. At the seminar eighty-six delegates from forty-six organizations learned that Canada was "literally pulsating with adult education activity" (Dunlop, 1936, p. 302). Edmund Bradwin who succeeded Fitzpatrick as director, told of the outreach of Frontier College, Angus Bernard (A. B.) Macdonald of St. Francis Xavier University's catalytic linking of adult education, self-help, and co-operative development, and Corbett of the University of Alberta Extension Department's innovative cultural and pedagogical work in rural areas. Three of the six men attending the seminar who had toured the Scandinavian countries in 1932/33 told delegates that the high standards of democracy in the three small Scandinavian countries was a "result of the progress of popular adult education so well established in the last century by the great Danish educator and philosopher Grundtvig" (Cameron, c. 1936-38, n.p.).

The mood of the meeting was electrifying. Popular adult education was playing a pivotal role in resolving the crisis of democracy. Peter Sandiford, chief investigator of the national survey, *Adult Education in Canada* (completed in April 1935), articulated the Canadian adult education community's growing self-consciousness:

> Now, to combat present social organization, a much more comprehensive program is needed—one that envisages the whole of the adult education community in place of the hand-picked few. And if our diagnosis is correct then we are the eve of a great

mass movement in Adult Education, the like of which the world has never seen. The reform of society will come, not through the indoctrination of the young, but from the intellectual conversion and convictions of the adult. If this is true, then Adult Education has an important future. It is the agency whose sole purpose is to provide the people with vision (p. 17).

Sandiford's prophetic words signalled something new in Canada's journey from colonialism to the information age: a deepening awareness of adult education as an instrument of consciousness-raising and collective action to make the better world. This period, then, is the time when men and women begin to analyze and reflect on the role that adult learning and education play in creating a deliberative democracy. It is time of intellectual awakening. It was the time of "amateurs out to change the world"—Alex Laidlaw's memorable phrase penned in 1970 when he looked back to the 1930s amateurs who never had one university-based course in adult education but changed the world.

Canadians were indeed on the eve of a great mass movement. But when the CAAE was formally organized in the summer of 1935 at Macdonald College in St. Anne de Bellevue, Quebec, the adult education movement lacked a coherent vision and a strategy for reforming society. The idea of a national association of adult education had been percolating in adult education circles since 1891. Called the Canadian Association for the Extension of University Teaching, it sought to "bring within the reach of people, opportunities of sharing in the benefits of higher education" (Armstrong, 1968, p. 11). This association died in infancy. Adult education historians generally agree that the main impetus came from Frederick Keppel, president of the Carnegie Corporation, and his assistant, Morse Cartwright, director of the American Association for Adult Education (AAAE), founded in 1926. Keppel wanted to bring order out of the chaos of American adult education. He had also expressed interest in the Canadian adult education movement, specifically in the development of a national association. Perhaps, since requests for money were coming in from various Canadian projects, he thought it best to deal with a coordinating body. Keppel and Cartwright began to talk with some of the Canadians who attended the AAAE's meeting in Buffalo, New York, in 1932 (Father Jimmy Tompkins was the only Canadian who attended meetings in the 1920s). It was there that the idea of creating a national clearing house was discussed. In the ensuing years, Keppel and the Carnegie Corporation discussed the question of just what kind of person might be appropriate to lead the new Canadian organization in a time of economic and political crisis. Cartwright, for instance, did not want Drummond Wren, director of the Workers' Education Association, to lead the CAAE because of his alleged partisan commitment to workers' education.

Cartwright had, in fact, been talking with conservative people like Vincent Massey, W. L. Grant, and Dunlop. Each of these men was politically conservative in outlook and opposed to anything that smacked of social action (or socialism). It is also clear that Dunlop wanted to control the direction of the CAAE. Elite paternalism was manifest once again. Dunlop favoured a neutral clearing house to exchange ideas and practices, but did not win the day. An alternative vision, fostered by E. A. Corbett, then the director of the University of Alberta Extension Department, who was appointed as the CAAE's first director in 1936, would take the CAAE in a direction not exactly favoured by Morse Cartwright of the AAAE. Corbett quickly moved beyond a passive clearing house role in favour of a coordinating and mobilizing mission for the CAAE. The tension between two ideals, conservative and liberating, education for individual self-development and education for social reform, present at the CAAE's birth, weaves through the Canadian adult education movement's philosophy and practice to this present day. This tension, as we have seen from the beginning of our history, between elite control of the learning of adults and the autonomous development from below, is a perennial issue. For Corbett and the educational radicals he would work closely with, the Depression had revealed how little control men and women really had in economic, political, and cultural affairs. During the war, Corbett believed that the western democracies were languishing and besieged. Canadians lacked a unifying vision worth fighting and dying for. People were in a structural bind because they were excluded from society's decision-making processes and economically dependent on forces beyond their control.

Adult education, Corbett insisted, could be a "vitalizing force in any movement toward the realization of social justice through democratic methods" (Corbett, 1939, p. 12). People everywhere had to be involved in "fearless and open-minded study and discussion" (Corbett, 1941). His working philosophy was based on the conviction that through study, discussion, and planning together people could change their social and economic environment and in so doing, he thought, change themselves. He believed that the adult education movement could be not be satisfied with either "enlightening individuals" or "disseminating technical knowledge" to isolated farmers. In a brutal world that had witnessed the "successful mobilization of the Russian, German and Italian masses for totalitarian ends," Corbett was convinced that Canadians must "acquire somehow the realism of the dictator and establish our educational system in accordance with the principles of democracy. In that task adult education can help" (Corbett, 1936). Between 1936 and 1945 the Canadian adult education movement would be animated by a vision of participatory and economic democracy based on the principle of self-education in groups and direction action in local communities. In fact, Corbett would have known already of how the adult learning sites of women's groups and farm organizations had issued in various policy changes. This vision reflected the educational radicals (many of whom were Christian socialists, or in Coady's case, a communitarian syndicalist) who believed in the liberating power of dialogue and the potential of persons to change, personally and in social relations. They believed that well-organized adult education could unite the citizens of the community, promote economic rehabilitation through co-operative action, and develop a participatory civic consciousness.

In 1936, when Corbett was shaping a strategy for the CAAE, the Antigonish Movement was in full bloom. By 1939, when the movement peaked, 19,000 people were enrolled in 2,265 study clubs. "Antigonish," Corbett told an Alberta audience in 1938, "represented adult education at its best when working along economic lines" (Corbett, 1938). Coady believed that adult education had to start with the simple material things. What could be more vital to impoverished eastern Nova Scotians— farmers, fishermen, unemployed coal, and steel workers—than credit unions, producer and consumer co-operatives, insurance and buying clubs? In the late 1930s Corbett's strategy involved travelling throughout Canada to encourage Antigonish-style grassroots community oriented adult education. A networker par excellence, Corbett wanted to establish a decentralized but linked network of educational mobilizing centres throughout the country. Wherever possible, Corbett favoured using extension departments as centres for revitalizing rural communities. This might be called phase one of Corbett's strategy; in the early 1940s, Corbett would initiate phase two, the development of the CAAE-initiated national projects (first the Farm Radio Forum, then the Citizens' Forum), which involved Canadians in "open-minded study and discussion" (Corbett, 1941) of the kind of social order they wanted in the postwar world.

The Manitoban situation illustrates well Corbett's *modus operandi*. In January 1937 Corbett met with his old friend Sidney Smith, president of the University of Manitoba and genial ally of the adult education movement, to discuss the feasibility of conducting an experiment that would spearhead cultural and economic revitalization in the rural areas. By the end of January, a Sidney Smith-initiated report called for a program that would "arise out of, or at least be related to, the life of the people" (University Extension Program and Budget, 1937). Traditional university extension programs were urban-biased and unilateral and the United Farmers of Manitoba and the Co-operative Conference failed to attract a cross-section of the rural communities. The report argued that rural communities should be provided with the tools for community self-help. By so doing, the rural way of life could be upheld, supported, and revitalized. Study groups, the report contended, could be the "spearhead of the extension program." Smith envisaged that the program would require a director who would travel throughout the rural areas to correlate existing activity, make available community resources, and instruct local leaders. Corbett was convinced that the Rev. Harry and Mary Avison were the two people who could direct such a program.

Harry Avison had impeccable Christian socialist credentials: he had been active in the Student Christian Movement (SCM), where he had met Corbett, and had ties with the FCSO, LSR, and progressives within the United Church. Smith and Corbett believed that the university should sponsor, and legitimize, an experiment in community development through adult education. But they could not find the finances. The University of Manitoba would not be able to open an Adult Education office until January 1941 when the visionary Watson Thomson arrived from the University of Alberta's Extension Department to assume the directorship. In January 1938, however, the Avisons had decided to go to The Pas, a northern Manitoba lumbering town of three thousand inhabitants, to initiate a folk school-style experiment. Corbett was elated: he hoped that The Pas experiment would serve as an inspirational model for Manitoba and would encourage Carnegie to finance a major thrust within the province. Receiving financial support from David Winton, a Minnesota industrialist who owned a mill in The Pas and symbolic support from the CAAE, the Avisons attempted to build a "spirit of community" in an "amorphous and disjointed town" (Avison, 1957)

Three main challenges confronted the Avisons. First, the community was riven by numerous racial, religious, and social barriers; second, most people lived below or near the poverty line and much of the labour force was transient; third, there were few social services—no planned recreation, no night schools, no library facilities, few services for children. The Ukrainian Labour Farmer Temple organization, a left-wing organization affiliated with the Communist Party, carried on any organized study clubs. The Avisons moved quickly to establish training courses for unemployed youth, study clubs for men and women on the nature of democracy, recreation, and handicraft (very popular in this era) groups, a library, and they networked with local community organizations. The Avisons believed that adult education could "help people to meet adverse economic conditions," break down "social barriers that work against a unified community," and encourage the "appreciation of music and arts and crafts." (Avison, n.d.). The Pas experiment was a classic attempt to involve whole communities in the resolution of local problems.

This turned out to be an ambitious but ill-starred undertaking. From the outset the project was suspect among certain sections of the community. Who was financing, and supporting, the project? This had not been transparently evident to the community. Some suspected David Winton of wanting to use adult education to dampen worker unrest (the left-leaning segment of this rough and tumble town), others thought that Avison was using adult education to foment revolution (the right-leaning priest and members of the Roman Catholic Church). In fact, the Avisons became victims of a "rabid campaign of red-baiting led by the French-Canadian clergy" (Thomson, 1943a). Moreover, the war undermined the modestly successful Youth Training Program as well as exacerbating tensions between different ethnic groups. On February 13, 1940, Harry Avison wrote to Corbett: "The limits of the community as a field of work became increasingly clear ... There remains only isolated individuals who are interested in books or their own development. We have been singularly unsuccessful in bridging the sad gaps between the racial groups" (Avison, 1944). When the opportunity arose for Avison to join the staff of Macdonald College in 1940 as an English professor and editor of the Macdonald College journal, he left the wrangling and chaos of a northern Manitoba town for a more secure future in Quebec. Avison would remain at Macdonald College for twenty years, working closely with Dean W. H. Britain, head of Macdonald College, promoting libraries and publications as well as playing a key backroom role in CAAE strategy.

With Avison ensconced at Macdonald College, the way was open for the wily Corbett to convince Smith to secure the services of another innovative educational radical. Freed from his work in the University of Alberta's Extension Department, Watson Thomson arrived in Winnipeg in the uncertain winter of 1941 to assume the directorship of the Adult Education Office at the University of Manitoba. Carnegie financing had been secured. The Pas experiment clearly revealed the need for a global strategy of development. Community development without personal transformation was superficial and, ultimately, communities could not be transformed without structural change in regional and national political economy. Thomson was an avant-garde intellectual who had been engaged in experiments in deep spiritual transformation in small groups while living in London, England, in the 1930s before he left to come to Canada. In fact, while living in Edmonton, Thomson had created a co-operative living situation for a number of radicals (including Stan and Doris Rands and George and Margaret LeBeau). He believed that those who wanted to change the external world had to learn to break with their own egoism to be open to others. He anticipated the T-group (and consciousness-raising) phenomena of the 1960s, such as encounter groups. One had to be what one desired to build. Thomson's commitment to building up from below a voluntary co-operative society placed him in critical sympathy with the Avisons' experimental project. But the challenge was to bring citizens together to reflect on appropriate development strategy for the region. In modern idiom, Thomson was a deliberative democratic, an adept practitioner of communicative action.

Unlike the Antigonish radicals, who succeeded in linking adult learning to co-operative economic action, Thomson was working in a less fertile milieu. Parts of Manitoba had been severely hit by drought; many rural towns and villages were demoralized; farmers mistrusted the university, and the Manitoba Federation of Agriculture mistrusted the towns people. Initially, after a leadership training program held in late December 1940, Thomson's strategy involved using the study group to establish a beachhead in the community—creating centres of light and reflection. He hoped that the study groups, though at first self-contained, would become the nuclei of responsibility for general community education. By the spring of 1941 Thomson concluded that study and discussion of "What the war means to me" brought considerable individual enlightenment, especially in understanding the foundations of a democratic world order. But the important social role of the study group in breaking down social barriers and working toward general community integration had hardly begun.

A beginning had been made in laying the foundation for a systematic program of citizenship education aimed at creating more fully co-operative communities. Thomson believed that the process of working together, first in small face-to-face study groups and then in community projects, could perhaps set in motion a movement, deeper and broader, towards a fundamental restructuring of the social order. These assumptions anticipate theoretical reflection on civil society (social movements and public spheres) as the locus of consciousness transformation and structural change. But it was painfully clear to Thomson as well as members of the Adult Education Committee of the University of Manitoba, that even if the study groups proliferated significantly, the main problem facing the Department was just how to reach a wider cross-section of the rural population than the usual small numbers who respond to adult education projects. To reach a wider cross-section of the rural population, Thomson's assistants, Stan Rands and George LeBeau (former members of the Edmonton co-op house, and now living with Thomson and others at 139 Roslyn Road in Winnipeg) evolved a strategy that moved in several directions. They continued to build up a network of reflection/action centres in local communities, encouraging groups to conduct research on their own situation (later, called participatory action research). By the spring of 1942 Rands observed that many voluntary groups were "formulating thinking on community issues and bringing about appropriate constructive action either by pressure on the existing authorities or by voluntary action" (Rands, 1942, n.p.). And they developed a citizens' conference structure which brought delegates from the various study groups together to discuss the economic prospects for western Canada and what men and women could do out of their own initiative to build communities fit for veterans to return to.

By far the most exciting development in the University of Manitoba's Adult Education was the experimentation with documentary film as an educational tool. After brief experimentation with documentary film in the fall of 1941, Watson Thomson was soon convinced that effective work could only be done in the rural areas by using documentary films, especially those dealing with the war. Thomson was in touch with John Grierson, now director of the National Film Board (NFB). They had known each other at the University of Glasgow after the devastating First World War. The Board was planning, in co-operation with the Canadian Council of Education for Citizenship, a wide scheme of public information in the rural areas. A dapper man with left sympathies, Grierson became the centre of a youthful avant-garde group of filmmakers in Ottawa during the war years. All of Grierson's experimental work with documentary film was motivated by one central conviction: it was imperative, in a brutal world that had witnessed the Nazi's brilliant use of film for evil purposes, to "inform, to motivate and to involve people everywhere in the country in a grand common project of discussion, action and co-operation—and films were the best available tools to do the job" (Cited in Gray, 1973, p. 39). Education, for Grierson (1966), was

John Grierson (left), Chairman of the Wartime Information Board, meeting with Ralph Foster, Head of Graphics, National Film Board of Canada, to examine a series of posters produced by the National Film Board of Canada. . (Credit: Ronny Jaques/National Film Board of Canada. Photothèque/Library and Archives Canada/PA-179108)

the "key to the mobilization of men's minds to right ends or wrong ends, to order or chaos. … If men's minds have not been mobilized aright; the educational process has not been good enough" (p. 262). Art, Grierson was fond of saying, was a hammer and not a mirror aimed at rousing the civic heart and will. This was propaganda for democracy: a delicate matter, indeed, for astute participatory democrats like Thomson and the educational radicals (Pollard, 1987).

While the ostensible purpose of the NFB was to keep the public informed about the war (with the inevitable bias), the people at the NFB had a long-term purpose in mind. John Grierson, in Stan Rands' considered view, had chosen adult education organizations to sponsor film circuits because they recognized that war-time efforts were short run. By establishing a national network of rural (and later industrial and trade union) circuits, Canada was laying the basis for their perpetual use in communities, both to promote national unity and to stimulate action on community problems. Grierson (1944) argued that it was

> integral to the democratic idea that constructive action shall bubble up all over the place. Initiative must be not only central but local. By the mere acceptance of democracy we have taken upon ourselves the privilege and the duty of individual creative citizenship and we must organize all communication which will serve to maintain it … And, in the process of creating our democratic system of communications, in bridging the gaps between citizen and community, citizen and specialist, specialist and specialist, we shall find we have in the ordinary course of honest endeavor made the picture of democracy we are seeking (p. 4).

Grierson was attempting to counteract a popular idea articulated by the American Walter Lippmann that society had evolved into an entity so complex that only the elites could manage affairs. The people, as Coady would express it, were consigned to the bleachers.

Thomson and Rands threw themselves into film distribution enthusiastically, using film as a stimulus to social change and conscious-raising. Thus, another Canadian invention, the projectionist-animateur, would arrive in prairie towns in the early hours of the morning. Educators like George LeBeau took their heavy equipment to the nearest hotel. Then they were up in the morning for a showing at the local school, followed by afternoon and evening events. Their ultimate dream—that the production of films would be integrally related to distribution and use, with both closely related to the needs of the communities—would be fulfilled only in part. They did, however, develop the "film-forum," which was integrated into NFB practice throughout the rural circuits. The evolution of the film-forum, Thomson contended, turned the "one-way traffic of the mass-conditioning process into the two-way traffic of a sturdy democracy," bring "active participation and personal contribution back into the picture" (Thomson, 1944, pp. 133-4). Rands (1946) believed that: "Hundreds of communities have been stimulated to face their problems with a greater measure of responsibility and co-operative action; thousands of groups have come to think of documentary film as among their most valuable tools for accomplishing given purposes" (p. 8). The potential of the film circuits in quantitative terms was indicated by the fact that, in Manitoba alone, the rural audiences for 1943 totalled more than one-third of a million. Alex Sim (1943), an expert on rural community and adult education practice (he did community development work in the eastern townships of Quebec in the 1930s), captured the vision behind the film circuits, Farm and Citizens' Forums. "Adult Education programs must be conceived in terms of the masses. Education must be for all the people all the time. The end goal of any program must be to give the people a voice, to develop skills in tackling their own problems, to foster an understanding of the world (society, economic, and scientific) in which they live, and to train them that they must increase their control over this environment" (n. p.).

An Authentic Instrument of the Democratic Process: Outward to the Nation with the Citizens' Forum

The Citizens' Forum was the most visionary and ambitious of all the projects created by the educational radicals linked with the CAAE.

When the CAAE Council met in Toronto on November 6, 1942, to plot the organization's future, Canadian society was in ferment. The Depression had weakened faith in free enterprise; war and collective control had restored some prosperity and a sense of common public purpose. To many the importance of the rough equality of wartime seemed to demonstrate the real possibility of social justice in the postwar world. Canadians were increasingly confident that "collective action could and should create a far more stable and equitable society," (Creighton, 1976, p. 78). Popular demand for a new social order reflected itself in the dramatic increase in support for the democratic socialist CCF party. In 1941 the British Columbia CCF had won a plurality of votes, forcing the Liberals and Conservatives into a coalition and becoming the official opposition. In 1944 Saskatchewan would elect the first democratic socialist government in North America. CCF popularity symptomized the "massive shift in public opinion toward the left—a shift which was, on a much smaller scale, even sweeping a few communists to electoral success in some of the larger cities" (Whitaker, 1977, p. 59).

By the fall of 1943, when the Citizens' Forum was launched, the Liberal government appeared to be headed into a political abyss; indeed, in the late years of the war it seemed that Canadian politics and society might change significantly. The ruling Liberal party, facing an internal organizational and ideological crisis, was not providing decisive leadership to the Canadian people. E. A. Corbett and the educational radicals believed that unless postwar plans had the support of informed and vigorous public opinion, the Canadian people could easily be manipulated. The CAAE hoped to guide the process of public enlightenment towards a more just social order: a bold desire indeed. Phase two of Corbett's strategy, then, extended the vision of a participatory democracy outward to the national society. This project was both conceivable and practicable because a decentralized but linked network of educational mobilizing centres and voluntary associations had been built in the previous decades.

The Council chose Watson Thomson to direct the Special Committee on Education for Reconstruction. The choice was significant. Only a few months earlier Corbett had collaborated with Thomson on the Northern Plains Project. This imaginative project, with funding from the Rockefeller Foundation, had engaged farmers and agriculturalists in critical dialogue about the need to create a decentralized bio-region and eschewed educational neutrality (Welton, 1983). With this experience in creating the bases for communicative action, Thomson's role now shifted to helping provide the CAAE with philosophical leadership at a critical historical moment. The fundamental mandate of the Special Committee was to prepare policy for the CAAE. The resulting *Report of the Special Committee* set the tone and direction for the London Conference in May 1943 and the Education for Reconstruction Conference in September 1943. The CAAE was poised to embark on its most contentious phase of learning and action. The essential premise of the Citizens' Forum—that popular initiative could lead to the formulation of policy on the great issues of the day—was a bold attempt to influence the political discourse of Canadian capitalist society. The educational radicals of the CAAE, without actually advocating support for a particular political party (the CBC forbade this), wanted Canadians to make political choices based on ethical norms and not on expediency or self-interest.

The Committee believed that unless Canadian public opinion and the public will was mobilized through every available agency and medium, Canada would drift into the postwar world without any clear social purpose. The Committee thought that this critical situation demanded courage to pool what vision ("without which the people perish") they might have, and to face realistically the facts of their existing situation. After affirming the personalist principle that social institutions ought to serve the ends of general human welfare and not frustrate human personality, the Committee examined some of the formidable practical problems facing re-constructionist education. *The Report of the Special Program Committee,* a major document in Canadian adult education intellectual history, declared that never was the term "democracy" in greater need of re-definition and re-vitalization than in contemporary Canada. The Committee contended that people believed that behind the "façade of democratic procedures" there were narrow controlling interests. The great ideals of political equity were almost meaningless in the face of the oligarchic control of Canadian life. The meaning of democracy had to be examined, and the role of the "co-operative movement, community planning and 'collective action from below' as a counter-balancing force to maximize the danger of bureaucratic control carefully scrutinized" (Report of the Special Committee, 1943, pp. 15, 17).

After considering the possible roles of French Canadians, labour, the farmers, business, armed services, and women in postwar reconstruction, the Committee set out its recommendations for a CAAE reconstruction educational program. Any project that remained aloof from the "urgent necessities of the moment" was foredoomed to failure. The new program must take its stand favouring change. It had to be willing to align itself with those social forces committed to social change. The CAAE saw its special role as creating the public space to examine their future in the light of fundamental ethical principles. At the same time, the Committee recognized that it was "necessary to link the long-term goals with actual situations and trends in the present" (Report of the Special Committee, 1943, pp. 27-28). War phenomena such as Civilian Defense Units, farmers' production committees, and labour-management committees were "potential cells of the permanent democratic planning" of the future (Report of the Special Committee, 1943, pp. 27-28). To arouse national interest and integrate new groups with the CAAE, the Committee agreed that a conference should be held in early September 1943. The main purpose of this conference would be to give the co-ordinated campaign national publicity and to secure the close co-operation of interested organizations. Before this could occur, however, the Special Committee had to place its reflections before the Canadian adult education community at the London Conference in May 1943.

The challenge facing the Committee came through clearly in Sidney Smith's opening presidential address. "As an organization," Smith declared, "we are at the crossroads. If we do not, in this annual meeting, formulate new plans and initiate new projects ... we will be guilty men and women." Smith's message was unmistakable; the CAAE should make its own stand clear on the basic issues of western civilization. If it did not, the CAAE would become "one of the war's casualties because the swift-moving life of our times would find its existence unnecessary" (Smith, 1943, p. 9). Two hundred and thirty delegates from a wide range of voluntary associations would unanimously endorse a simplified version of the section, "Fundamental Principles," in the Special Committee's report—the CAAE Manifesto. Its primary author, Watson Thomson, commented on the meaning of the Manifesto for his *Food for Thought* audience: "In short, the Manifesto is a necessary declaration without which the CAAE could hardly dare to go to the citizens of Canada, regardless of race, class or creed. It testifies that, in this crisis, we offer men and women not only information, but something of vision and of faith. It testifies that, as for us, social change—radical social and economic change—is not something to be feared Neither is it something to be promoted from the standpoint of any sectional interest. It *is* something to be demanded and fought for in the interest of the fulfillment of the deepest principles and the highest hopes by which men of good will are sustained" (Thomson, 1943c, p. 11).

At London the CAAE had given itself a moral and ideological basis from which to act—"the beginning of a unified program of Adult Education in Canada" (Corbett, 1943, n.p.). To be worthy of the content and spirit of the declaration, Thomson observed, the CAAE and its allies had to make contacts with groups everywhere, in factories and on farms. The Farm Radio Forum had 1,200 listening-action groups with an average of 17,000 listeners in the 1942/43 season. The CAAE's new national campaign on the postwar world should have, he thought, five thousand groups in town and country. A challenging task, as future philosopher George Grant would later observe, the CAAE was hardly known in the industrial east. Throughout the summer months the planning committee for the proposed conference on Education for Reconstruction met. The committee felt that the emphasis should be placed not only on national and international problems, but also on community problems. The national program should indicate jobs that needed doing in the home community of the participants (public works, town planning, recreation, etc.). Groups would learn, they thought, more about vested interests by studying the particular problems of housing in a specific community than by academic discussion. National and local conditions had to be linked. Most important, they had to get "good people" at the conference. Representation from the people's organizations should be as broad as possible (Minutes of the Planning Committee, July 13, 1943).

The Education for Reconstruction conference opened on September 10, 1943, at Macdonald College in Quebec in a highly charged and expectant atmosphere. The Liberal government of Mackenzie King had, as Avison observed, postponed its reconstruction program, and was fearful of any "reconstruction program" outside their control. King's cabinet had responded to McGill professor Leonard Marsh's *Report on Social Security*, released to the public on March 17, with hostility. With the CCF gaining more support than ever before, and the CAAE and its allies in government agencies set to mobilize the Canadian people in a direction that might well go beyond mere welfare state amelioration, the moribund Liberals would be resurrected into action. But when the Education for Reconstruction conference began, the Liberals had not yet arrived at their "solution." Not until January 1944 would the Liberal cabinet even approve of three new departments: Reconstruction, Health and Welfare, Veterans Affairs (Granatstein, 1975). It was apparent that the Education for Reconstruction conference was the type of program many people had been waiting for—120 organizations represented by 165 delegates, many of whom had had no previous connection with the CAAE, were present. They were there to plan the campaign of public education, the groundwork of which had been laid in the summer months preceding the conference. Three Commissions—Curriculum, Methods, Organization—succeeded in clarifying, after some initial confusion, the responsibilities resting upon the individuals, local organizations, and national bodies such as the CBC. The onus of listening group organization would fall on regional or community committees. Where possible, committees were to be formed in all cities and towns to co-ordinate the listening groups with other associations. Manitoba did the latter very successfully.

The Citizens' Forum was, considering the lack of available resources, a very bold plan designed to build up in a short period a nation-wide organization to promote and carry out a study-action program. The organization of the Citizens' Forum was decidedly uneven. Some provinces were stronger than others; the four western provinces, excepting Alberta, had excellent organizations. In Ontario and Quebec the development of the Forum was marred by the absence of any permanent organization to carry out an effective program. In the Maritimes, Citizens' Forum programs were in the hands of overly busy Education Department officials. The Citizens' Forum failed to penetrate Canada's industrial heartland. Labour is partly to blame here. In February 1944 the Canadian Congress of Labour created an ineffectual Political Action Committee which siphoned off energy. Citizens' Forum Secretary George Grant wondered if the CAAE had erred in granting so much autonomy to regional organizations. But they had little choice, given the CAAE's perennial lack of finances and staff (Report to the Executive of the CAAE on the progress of the Citizens' Forums, 1943/1944).

In just under one year the CAAE Special Committee had succeeded in welding together over a hundred civil society organizations into a coherent force for organizing thousands of people for discussion and action on subjects of reconstruction. The educational visionaries proffered a conception of a democracy rooted in a dialogical process whereby policy would be formulated at the grassroots community level, with the government respond to the people's demands from below. Each group did, in fact, send the results of its deliberations to the appropriate department. Delegates at the conference were struck by the prevailing spirit of co-operation. "This spirit," according to Fletcher Peacock (1943), Director of Educational Services of New Brunswick's Department of Education and one of the CAAE's most ardent supporters, "prevailed to the very end. In fact, it increased in evidence as time passed. ... The idea of individual participation by citizens which seems to be the genius of the project is doubtless the right technique" (p. 19). For Eugene Forsey (1943), the implacable foe of Mackenzie King's Liberals, the Macdonald

College conference had outlined a program which "should be of great value to organized Labour." But he warned that staff shortage and preoccupation with self-preservation would "make it hard for the unions to play as large as part as they would like" (p. 19). The left-wing, increasingly Marxian-oriented FCSO, which had endorsed the Education for Reconstruction project at its national conference in July, saw in the integrated study-listening-action program of the Citizens' Forum a focal point for the organization of people in neighbourhoods for the discussion of vital issues and for democratic action. The FCSO suggesting forming groups among friends and neighbours, people in church congregations, people with special interests in reconstruction (in Toronto, the FCSO hoped to have a group relating each topic to Blacks) and among people in the community generally. And the FCSO would publish monthly bulletins related to the major questions involved in the topics to be covered. These bulletins, they thought, would "undoubtedly probe closer to the roots of the problems than the general broadcasts and study materials" ("Education for reconstruction," 1943, pp. 2-3). The educational visionaries who prepared the Special Report at Macdonald College early in 1942 could at least be satisfied that they had helped create, in Gregory Vlastos' (1943) poignant words, an "authentic instrument of the democratic process" (pp. 6-7). The basic idea of the Citizens' Forum challenged the existing capitalist political system which depended on mass apathy and rule by political elites in the interest of capital (Wolfe, 1977). Any mobilization of the people in liberal democracies is potentially threatening to the elite managers of the system, and King was no exception. The educational radicals who presided at London and Macdonald College in the spring and fall of 1943 wanted a dialogical society based on production for people and not profit. They wanted to examine thoroughly the meaning of democracy and advocate "co-operative movement, community planning, and collective action from below." The "passionate educators" (Faris' vivid depition [1975]) believed that the acquisition of "really useful knowledge" would in turn set Canadians free. They were determined to treat politics as a means of conducting genuine debate around the public interest (the commonwealth), not merely competitions between rival interest groups. The fact that so many Canadian civil society organizations joined in on this project indicates how deeply and widely these ideas had permeated the society—with adult educators of all stripe and colour playing creative roles. The great awakening in the four decades leading up the outbreak of the Depression had borne significant results—very much in the face of considerable obstacles.

A reading of the Citizens' Forum bulletins for 1943-45 reveals that, while they raised many pertinent questions about Canada's economic and political system, they did not always analyze problems in terms of class and power (Study bulletins, 1943-66). This fact lends some support to William Young's contention that the progressives in adult education "aimed at building up a middle-of-the-road consensus" (Young, 1978, p. 94). On the other hand, radical groups such as the FCSO recognized that the state sponsorship and financing placed constraints on the Citizens' Forum curriculum. But they fully supported the idea of creating a national forum for all Canadians to dialogue about their future. Nobody could impose the "correct view" from the top. Perhaps the educational radicals did the best they could in political and psychological reality of wartime, and pressure from the more conservative elements in the CAAE and the ruling Liberal party. They believed that people could be awakened through dialogue to create a better world. They concentrated on setting in motion a process of transforming the society's general will. By the 1950s, even a moderate Citizens' Forum would come under attack from business and government sources.

"Real Adult Education Springs from the Heart and Pains of the People:" The Antigonish Movement and the Impossible Dream

In late November 1927, a professor of education from St. Francis Xavier University in Antigonish, Nova Scotia, walked into the Halifax board room of the MacLean Commission inquiry into the crisis in the Maritime fishery, and sat down to testify. Although not particularly well known outside education circles and the troubled parish life of the Diocese of Antigonish, this man, plainly, was no ordinary presence. He stood six feet two and weighed over two hundred pounds. He had broad shoulders and a ruggedly handsome face, broad shoulders with piercing, coal-black eyes. He exuded toughness and self-confidence. Born in 1882 in the beautiful Margaree Valley of Cape Breton, Coady knew well the hardships and exertion needed to survive on a rural farm. Early photographs of this strapping, hard Irishman portray him standing on the back of a truck heaving bales of hay as if they were loaves of bread. His grand vision, that men and women could become "masters of their own destiny," was hewn out of his own and his family's struggle to be self-sufficient. His second cousin, Father Jimmy Tompkins, was mighty Moses' exact opposition: he was small, frail-looking, had a high-pitched voice and was insatiably restless of spirit. But he was in his own way brilliant and prophetic. Coady was no fool: but he was less cerebral and was mentored into his role as the leader and chief figurehead of the Antigonish Movement. Tompkins was an agitational presence in the Diocese of Antigonish, the one who spearheaded the reform movement and welded together a formidable network of priests, sisters, and community lay folk committed to breaking the people out of their culture of silence and oppression in feudal Nova Scotia. Tompkins' spirit and imagination was anarchic; Coady's tipped towards social engineering and blueprints for the co-operative society. This would lead to some conflict—particularly over the role of libraries in the intellectual and cultural life of the Movement and Nova Scotia itself.

Coady addressed the inquiry in a fiery manner. He told them that he was interested chiefly in the educational phase of the industry, insisting that the people, not just the fishing machinery, should receive attention. Times had changed and fishermen had been unable to adapt. Through scientific knowledge, he claimed, fishermen could take advantage of possibilities yet imagined. Maritimers had never been taught to think critically, Coady told the commissioners, and had overlooked the necessity of planning. Many small industries could be established in the small villages, if only plans were made in advance. Co-operation, in its broadest usage, was the way to progress, he said, pointing to the success of the Nova Scotia creameries as an example. Coady thought that while the common school could contribute a little to the solution of practical problems, the way forward really lay with community civic education. Adult education, he pointed out, is nothing more than an injection of ideas. Coady recommended that short, group courses be provided for the fishermen, and since the university had neglected to do anything, he urged the commission to have government institutions do the work. He concluded by arguing that unionism among fishermen could do much good and would keep them alive to all current questions. His ardent support for unionism had only emerged in the early 1920s, when Coady played a key role in organizing the Nova Scotia Teachers' Union. Like many other Catholic priests of his day, unions were often feared as both secular and red-tinged.

Nobody who heard Moses Coady's presentation before the Royal Commission in late 1927 could have imagined the trouble this forty-five-year-old priest would become to the vested interests over the next thirty years. Nor the extent to which they would hear this big man reiterate, tirelessly, in thousands of community halls, the themes of his commitment to the comments to the commissioners. The world was changing irrevocably. The educational institutions of the people had not prepared them to grapple with this changed world. People took precedence over money. People had the potential to think their way to new solutions. They had to co-operate to reach their full potential, as individuals, as communities, as a province. Who would show them the way? What direction should their economic action take?

In the face of rising bitterness about the failure of their own institution to respond to the plight of the primary producers and industrial workers of the scattered parishes of eastern Nova Scotia, reform-minded priests in Coady's Antigonish diocese had agitated unceasingly through the 1920s for an Extension Department at St. Francis Xavier University. With the MacLean Commission deliberating, the media in an uproar over mounting evidence of hunger, impoverishment, and destitution among fisher families, the coalfields in Cape Breton literally in flames, and priests and parishioners everywhere distressed and agitated, the board of governors officially approved the formation of St. Francis Xavier University Extension Department in November 1928. They asked Moses Coady to become its first director. Nobody could have imagined what would now unfold over the next thirty years.

In the fall of 1929 Coady and Angus Bernard (A. B.) MacDonald wondered where and how to begin, amid much controversy and behind-the-scenes lobbying. Coady was asked by the Canadian Department of Fisheries to organize the fishermen of eastern Canada. This would be the defining moment of his career. It would also become the basis for the myth of the "modern Moses" who sought to lead his people into the promised land of co-operation. For a variety of reasons, not everyone thought that Moses Coady was the right man for the onerous and treacherous task of organizing the notoriously individualistic fishermen. He faced opposition from several quarters. He had no previous experience with the fishery, and he was a vulnerable target. But he quickly proved his detractors wrong (some detractors were allied with the fish merchants and did not want any change to their exploitative marketing schemes). The in-shore fishermen were in a dreadful mess, largely unorganized and chained to the whims of merchants and middlemen. On September 28, 1929, Moses Coady began his "trying ten months" of organizing the fishermen at Canso. This was the appropriate place for the beginning. His cousin, Father Jimmy, the firebrand agitator and Coady's mentor for more than twenty years, was pastor at the Star of the Sea church in Canso, exiled there from his firmer position as vice-president of the St. Francis University in late 1922. Tompkins had initiated a series of adult education courses for local action initiatives in and around Canso. His agitation had sparked George Farquhar's series of articles in the *Halifax Chronicle* under the caption "Save our Fishermen" in June and July 1927, which helped press the government to create the epochal Maclean Commission. Ironically, perhaps, officials in the Department of Fisheries would be harbingers of a coming new day for fishermen in the Maritimes.

Working with remnants of the old Fishermen's Union (organized into stations), department officials aroused the countryside for Coady's visits. Coady blew into these communities like an Atlantic storm. Everywhere, hundreds came out to hear his gospel for organization—making his way systematically through all the fishing communities. Legendary stories emerge from this heroic venture. Organizing along the Eastern Shore was extremely arduous. Setting out in early December, Coady's large Buick (he loved these big cars) navigated along rutted, high-crowned roads veiled with ice, every mile a hazard. At times, the vehicle skidded out of control, coming near to plunging into the open water. Keeping schedule, he moved through the communities of Sheet Harbour, Spry Bay, Spry Harbour, and Tangier. Everywhere, fishermen waited eagerly for some direction. Just beyond Tangier, on a particularly nasty stretch of road in the wooded near Ship Harbour, the heavy car slid into a brook. Standing knee-deep in freezing water, Coady laboured to free his car until he broke the jack. When his shoulders also failed to lift the car, he walked the two miles back to Ship Harbour, where he obtained a pair of horses and a heavy wagon.

These efforts, too, proved useless, so he returned to Ship Harbour and phoned the nearby garage—eighteen miles away at Musquodobit Harbour. The wrecking truck was out of commission with a frozen block, but the garage man came to the rescue with a car and block and tackle, which eventually succeeded in pulling Coady's beloved Buick out of the brook. After staying with a friend (and drying out), he was up early and on the road again. And so it continued until Coady's triumphal moment in late June 1930 when the United Maritime Fishermen held its first convention in the Masonic hall in Halifax. Coady had emerged from his trial by fire and ice to lead his people out of their wilderness. He was a new and disturbing presence—a formidable foe for the vested interests of business, state, and church to reckon with. And it was only the beginning.

In the fall of 1930 the work of organizing the Extension Department at St. Francis Xavier University began in earnest. The director, Moses Coady, had to turn Extension into a dynamic educational mobilizing centre, but the university had few financial resources for this task. The department would have to find the money elsewhere. An Extension official needed to be furnished in order to meet the demands of hundreds of people in the diocese. Secretaries had to be hired to run the office. Books and literature had to be purchased. The Extension Department had only two full-time employees with whom to launch its project, but Coady had an ace up his sleeve. Coady's assistant director, A. B. MacDonald, was one of the most talented organizers and spell-binding platform speakers Canada would ever see (except perhaps, Violet McNaughton, the "mighty mite" of Saskatchewan). Like Coady, A. B. MacDonald was an impressive, big, dashing man. Always attired in a well-cut suit, MacDonald appeared to have emerged from a corporate board room. His appearance was very deceptive, as this elegant man was not on the side of business interests. He proclaimed that the only safe depository of the ultimate power of society was the people themselves. The common people loved his wit, humour, style, and passionate advocacy for a people's economy. He was also tough. One story tells of MacDonald's arriving at a raucous meeting hall, filled with rough lads ready to make trouble. Without missing a step, he broke a beer bottle on the edge of the table and proceeded to the platform. There was no trouble that night.

Like Coady, A. B. MacDonald had been hewn from strong timber and imbued with democratic ideals. He had enormous energy and panache, easily moving through four or five meetings a day. Moses Coady had enormous respect for his colleague. He saw him as a brilliant leader in a new profession, the profession of adult education for democratic action. Coady hailed him as Canada's greatest long distance organizer who was able, in a most spectacular way, to organize people from Cape North to Cape Sable, from Louisburg to Edmundston, and to do by some kind of sixth sense of telepathy. Father Jimmy had prodded him to forsake a lucrative job in the corporate sector for building an economic empire of the little people in Canada. Macdonald and Coady had to figure out how to proceed. They had to draft a plan, identify the agencies they could work with, discover the local leadership who could open up new vistas for the people, and find more staff to work in the field and office. In 1931, Coady asked Katherine Desjardins (née Thompson), a graduate of Mount St. Bernard College, Antigonish, and the Nova Scotia Teachers College, to return from New York to act as his general assistant for the Extension Department. She was a superb choice—a dedicated social reformer, excellent journalist, and skillful organizer. Other talented women, such as Zita O'Hearn (née Cameron) and Ida Gallant (née

Delaney) would follow Kay Desjardins into the cyclonic atmosphere of the Extension Department's early days. They would be joined by Sister Anselm (Irene Doyle), Sister Marie Michael, and Sister Francis Dolores, each highly intelligent and gifted. Coady and MacDonald would soon be men with suitcases, making their way from community to community, and meeting after meeting, to create study club nuclei as necessary preparation for social action. Though they stumbled initially by providing literature too complicated for some farmers, they gradually learned through their mistakes and began to discover how to proceed.

Coady and MacDonald had learned through trial and error that, first, one had to capture the interest of the adult learner, many of whom had minimal formal education. For Nova Scotians, the idea of studying together was a unique one, never before attempted among the primary producers and industrial workers. Would it work? What were the precise techniques to be used? Second, the learning process in the small clubs could not be academic or speculative. The primary producers had to see that their learning had a pay-off, that they were solving real problems. The adult educator had to prepare study material that struck the right note in accessible language. Thinking, Coady said, had to pay. The study clubs were the vehicle to organize the enlightenment process. Studying must channel learning into action. In the early stages of study club development, the clubs functioned largely as locally based self-help initiatives. People had to get their feet wet, try things out, experience the exhilaration of learning by doing and the joy of small beginnings. The Extension organizers had to nurture forms of action that were relatively easy to accomplish at the outset. By the 1930s Coady figured that he knew the secret of working with poor people. "We think now that the easiest beginning can be made in the field of money by establishing a credit union. This is non-controversial and teaches the technique of group action. Through this they move into the study of Rochdale principles, and when they are ready, into the field of marketing and producing and processing. The importance is to find something is safe and easy. This is very important in the case of very poor people" (Coady, 1938). Start safely, proceed easily. Only gradually would a coherent project for building a new economic and social order take shape in practice and imagination. Extension had to grow into a movement, and nothing was guaranteed in the fragility of the early moments.

Coady (1935) believed that adult education could mobilize "the spiritual and intellectual forces of the people for the purpose of attacking the problems confronting them. The intellectual awakening is brought about through the medium of the small study club, educational rallies, special courses for leadership, and general and regional conferences. The interests of the common people in such a program can only be aroused and sustained through appealing and energizing study material. It has been found that literature exposing the social and financial maladjustments of our times strikes the most responsible chord in the minds and hearts of the disinherited eighty per cent of the people" (n.p.). Coady wanted the primary producers and industrial workers to get their hands on the throttle of their own destinies. They needed to gain economic freedom: Coady knew well that this was more possible in the fishery and on the farms than the Sydney steel mills or coal mining towns (where battle between the communists and the Antigonish activists would soon be played out).

Coady's first organizational task was to organize study clubs in the fishing and farm communities. Extension workers would not enter the coalfields until the spring of 1932. A communication network, imperfect but adequate, was in place in the fishing communities. They had been organized into units of the United Maritime Fishermen in the fishing communities. Seasoned, committed, and competent leadership existed in most of the Nova Scotian fishing villages, particularly on the northwest coast of Cape Breton and along the Guysborough coastline and north shore of New Brunswick. In the agricultural communities, federal and provincial agricultural representatives ("ag reps") had been busy for over a decade, experimenting with buying clubs and other forms of co-operative activity. Reps like J. F. C. MacDonnell, S. J. MacKinnon, and R. J. MacSween were committed co-operators and passionate defenders of the interests of the primary producers. So were many of the priests in the farm communities. In the coalfields, the time was ripe for social action initiatives that might heal some wounds and solve some urgent problems. Extension had a few radical priests such as the taciturn M. J. MacKinnon and the pro-labour firebrand T. O'R. Boyle to assist. Social movement theorists inform us that for a social movement to flourish, the movement must have a communicative infrastructure—nodes of communication through which the message can circulate. It must have significant degrees of social solidarity and the lifeworld resources to respond to the call to learn and act collectively. Both the Roman Catholic Church (dominant in eastern Nova Scotia) and cultural heritage (primarily Scots and Irish) created the community integration. And the Church provided a meaningful, if contested, orientation to life (people were not nihilistic and completely bereft of hope). People had been forced to be self-reliant in

Moses Michael Coady with visitors from Indonesia. The Antigonish movement inspired people from all over the globe. (Credit: courtesy of Michael Welton)

their harsh environment. These were the cultural preconditions enabling the Antigonish leaders and activists to light a spark that would catch fire. The message had to resonate deeply in the cultural and spiritual lives of the people. Co-operativism could alleviate severe economic deprivation and enable the Catholic hierarchy to remain reasonably comfortable with the rumblings from below. In a sense, radicals like Coady, MacIntyre, and MacDonald were hemmed in by the Catholic social teaching framework. Still, the Catholic Church's strong emphasis on the importance of subsidiary associations between the state and economy was a powerful impetus to building co-operative institutions that did not uncouple the system and the lifeworld too drastically—as capitalist modernity certainly did.

Coady's role in the initial mass meeting was to stir the people into believing that they could do marvellous things. Accounts of his performances at these meetings indicate that Coady often appeared, in the first two or three minutes, to be inarticulate. His hands would paw the air awkwardly as he searched for the right word. Then the flow would come, and the rhythm of his speech would glide effortlessly over homespun and powerful metaphors designed to stoke the people into action. Adult education had to dynamite some cemented minds and crack open the ability to imagine living differently. The "good and abundant life" he spoke of so often began in the awakened imagination that had had its encrustation of old habits cracked. Coady's biggest challenge throughout the movement's most dynamic period was to place the scattered local initiatives within a coherent larger, interpretative framework. He had to show how the people's small actions contributed to the building of a better world for the primary producers and industrial workers. He had to show how little actions fit into the big picture. At the same time, he also had to attend to endless practical problems and the opposition that appeared quickly on the Nova Scotia scene. The prophet had to be both an organizer and a trouble-shooter. He had to be present at key decision-making rallies and meetings of people's organizations such as the UMF. He could not simply preach the beauty of the future kingdom; people had to see signposts, now, pointing the way. Between 1930 and 1935, the signposts began to appear, first among the lobster fishermen and the farmers, and slightly later in the industrial sector.

This was the Extension Department's greatest utopian phase, a time when tremendous creative energy was released into community life. By the end of 1931, 173 study clubs had been organized with 1,384 members. In 1933, the number doubled to 350 study clubs with 5,250 members; by 1935, 8,460 people in the communities would be participating in 940 clubs. In 1932, the first credit union—or people's bank—co-op stores and buying clubs, lobster factories and fish plants took their place on the Nova Scotian landscape. The February 1933 issue of *The Casket* captured the sentiments emerging from the communities. Dan Murray from New Waterford exclaimed: "We are all beginning to feel that our problems are not insurmountable at all." Mrs. D.O'C. Doyle of Melford felt that she had "developed a sense of appreciation as never before of the many possibilities for the future welfare of the districts we represent." Coady informed his cousin Chris J. Tompkins that "things are moving here at a great rate" (Coady, 1932, n.p.). This elated phrase peppered Coady's correspondence in the early 1930s.

For several reasons, the Antigonish Movement wanted to gain a foothold in industrial Cape Breton: the communists had a significant following in Glace Bay and surrounding coal towns and the Catholic Church was widely perceived to be hostile to unions and social change for a better world. They found Alex S. MacIntyre, a former left-wing trade union militant. MacIntyre had gone into the pits in Cape Breton around the turn of the century. Over the years, he had risen to prominence in the labour movement, and he had been a member of the ill-fated left wing in the convulsive 1920s. Blacklisted after the riots of 1925/6, MacIntyre had spent some years as a salesman to make ends meet. Converted to the co-operative movement in the early 1930s without ever divesting himself of his commitment to trade union struggles, MacIntyre had shocked the diocese with his vehement criticism of their outright neglect of the miners at a diocesan conference called by Bishop James Morrison to discuss whether the Extension Department should send its workers into the industrial towns of Cape Breton. For two hours, MacIntyre set the record straight in the blunt language of the working class. If the miners had left the Church, it was because the Church had turned its back on them in their times of distress. The miners had embraced communism because its followers were the only ones to offer help. Most of the men were not communists in their hearts, simply desperate workers fighting for a better life for themselves and their families. MacIntyre told the assembly of his own struggle, of his personal spiritual crisis when he had seen how he could remain faithful to his church and retain the confidence of the workers. The leaders of the Antigonish Movement realized that they had found their man in Cape Breton.

Antigonish-style co-operatives took hold in industrial Cape Breton in the early 1930s, and MacIntyre had much to do with this. Reports from the Sydney-Glace Bay area communities streamed in to the Extension offices. The first *Extension Bulletin* of November 7, 1933, told of thirty-seven self-help groups that had been organized. Composed of unemployed workers, these groups experimented with exchanging their labour for goods; several set up small cottage industries. They farmed vacant lots. These are just a few of hundreds of these small collective learning and action projects that sprang up in the earliest phase of study club organization. Indeed, the members of the study clubs were learning about an amazing diversity of economic activity. At Big Pond Centre on Cape Breton Island, members of one study club co-operated in cutting their winter's supply of firewood. They then planned to dig a bog for compost. The club members of the Glencoe District were learning about the tanning of leather, credit unions, ice storage, and budgeting of farm earnings and expenditures. Veteran activist Earnest Pelletier of the largely Acadian community of Larry's River informed Extension that his group intended to open a co-operative store in the early spring of 1934. In Cheticamp the men had studied co-operative canning and then proceeded to open a factory in 1934. They were now turning to the study of credit unions. Kay Desjardins, the secretary who became a philosopher, fielded the study clubs' endless questions on topics ranging from farm management to the growth of turnips.

Credit unions caught the imaginative of the debt-strapped communities. George Bennett of Dominion, a coal town that had seen many a battle, told Extension that their club had been named the "Keen" (after the Canadian co-operator George Keen, long-standing director of the

Canadian Co-operative Union). It had a large membership and was progressing rapidly. Its aim was to form a credit union in the town of Dominion. Ten clubs were now functioning, and Alex S. MacIntyre had recently addressed their club on credit unions. Initial steps had been taken to form a co-operative credit union society to serve New Waterford and the adjoining territory, known as district 20. Forty-six citizens had signed a petition addressed to the Registrar of Joint Stock Companies in Halifax to authorize "The New Waterford Credit Union." This gives us a taste of the learning energies that had been pent up for decades. The Movement was sweeping through Nova Scotia like a fire on parched heather.

Women poured into the study club movement. Some participated in clubs with the men; many others formed groups for women only. One energetic women's club in Brook River wrote that its members were getting more "interested all the time." They found the Department's literature on the washing and preparing of wool, as well as the soap recipes, very helpful. The Antigonish Movement actively promoted the development of crafts among women. Many of the women's clubs focused exclusively on handicrafts. In several districts, the art of weaving was revived, and the products of this would often be on sale (or displayed) at the co-op stores. The world was opening up for people in the small communities. They were hungry for knowledge. Tait Cameron of River Denys Station listed the topics their clubs were considering: ways and means of improving our community, fertilizers, and animal nutrition, the British marketing act, social re-constructionism, taxation, and price spreads. They were a particularly politically alert group of women. *The Bulletin* noted the innumerable number of problems pressing in upon women. But they believed that the problems related to the home would demand attention first. This meant studying proper diet for the family and how to build up healthy children.

The *Extension Bulletin's* "Woman's Page" constructed women's primary role as wife and mother. They had responsibility for care of the home, the spiritual aspects of home life, child rearing, the health and well-being of family members and education; all in all, a formidable, grinding task in poverty-stricken conditions (where some women had to sew flour sacks into dresses and other pieces of clothing). While acknowledging the busy role of women, *Bulletin* articles still encouraged them to get involved in the Movement in order to help maintain the unity of family life, serving as "man's help-mate." The *Bulletin* also recognized that women were the chief household managers, controlling household budgets, such as they were. Extension thought that women's participation in the study club movement was vital in order that they learn more about the economic benefits and the co-operative theory behind such things as the co-operative store. Ironically, women were not usually members of credit unions in those early days. The main reason was that women didn't have independent incomes, and families doubted the value of having two members pay the 25-cent dues. These were almost cash-less societies. Later, at Roy Bergengren's insistence, women would be allowed to join. In 1937, the first lady tellers were hired at the Coady Credit Union. Women gradually were allowed seats on board of co-ops, even though they often ran the day-to-day operations of a retail co-op store.

The women in the outports of Newfoundland were in similar dire straits to Nova Scotian women in the 1930s and 1940s. They were often illiterate, dependent, and poor. As part of its reconstructive efforts, Newfoundland created the Newfoundland Adult Education Association (NAEA) in 1929, financed with Carnegie funds. The NAEA initiated a culturally attuned adult education project for needy women called Opportunity Schools. Locally influential women like Elsie Farwell, Jessie Mifflen, and Sara Coady worked tirelessly (and dangerously in the winter months) teaching literacy and providing social and medical support in women's homes. The Opportunity School Method included a wide range of possible activities: but night schools and house visits served them best. English (2011) observes that "home visits to do group or individual teaching brought a new dimension to the work" (p. 29) of Newfoundland education. The teachers, like other women's organizations in the early twentieth century, focused on the usual fare of the lifeworld curriculum: "food preparation, child care, and mother's health, and formed clubs to learn skills like weaving" (p. 29). Although this form of lifeworld pedagogy did not challenge the paternalistic class and gender systems, the method of delivery was innovative and women could gain a measure of control over their lives. The teachers of these outport women in intimate situations discovered, as well, that teaching adults this way in Newfoundland was exciting and opened up career opportunities. English (2011) provides fascinating details on how Newfoundland women navigated in paternalistic waters.

The Antigonish Movement attracted powerful, smart young women to its staff. Evidence indicates that both Coady and Tompkins encouraged capable women to use all of their potential in the service of building a just learning society. They pressed the boundaries of the "two spheres ideology" without actually overturning it. Mary Elliot Arnold was one of the most intriguing characters who worked with Tompkins in Reserve

Mines from 1937 to 1939 to build the co-operative houses in what came to called Tompkinsville. Mary (and her lifelong companion Mabel Reed) was plain, manly, and tough: an outsider and interloper into clannish Nova Scotia (to this day outsiders can be labelled "come from away"). An American who knew architectural design, co-operative organization, and had once been an Indian agent in California, Mary had met the Movement leaders at one of the Co-operative League of the US tours that followed the famed Rural and Industrial Conference. Apparently captivated by Coady, her correspondence with him reveals deep affection. By the time she and Mabel arrived in Reserve Mines in the summer of 1937, Tompkins had already been conducting a study club on housing, but needed some further direction. She was invited to stay—Tompkins acquired a woman who was General Secretary of the Consumers Co-operative Services and board member and treasurer of the Co-operative League of America. Mary went into action to cut through the chaos of this project, gaining needed amendments to government acts, and taught these shooters, bottommers, and loaders about blueprinting and how to connect with legal and housing experts.

She also conducted a housing study group for women. "The great domestic revolution" had touched women's sensibilities as managers of the lifeworld; they wanted to have a say in how their kitchens and houses were designed. Mary opened this world up, and pressured the men to listen to their wives. They did, with women helping with shingling and other building activities. This did not turn out, however, to be quite enough for them to be co-signers on housing deeds. The men were sole deed-holders. Old habits die hard. By the spring of 1939, ten houses had been built. They are still standing: visiting Reserve Mines today, one sees rows of these plain-looking homes, proud icons of this self-help community project. Miners praised her, and the women staff at Extension didn't like her very much. She was odd and eccentric, not a "real woman," or at least one who fit the conventional categories. Coady made her head of the Movement's housing projects. But this miffed MacDonald, who had been overseeing this program. He was as strong-willed as Coady, and became increasingly unhappy with the low salary (and perhaps Coady's tendency in the post-1939 days to be away from the office, dreaming big dreams while attention to the grassroots organizations faltered). Arnold and Mabel left for the US, after a stint working in Newfoundland in 1940, for continued work with the co-operative movement. Rusty Neale (1998) observes that Arnold's presence in Nova Scotia in the 1930s, when the economic crisis was shoring up traditional gender norms, pressed against this invisible boundary. Tompkins pressed the boundaries as well: these outcasts obviously had much in common.

Sister Marie Michael of the Sisters of St. Martha joined the Extension Department in 1933 as director of the "Women and Work" program. Born in 1905, christened as Marie Sarah MacKinnon, she had been captivated by Father Michael Gillis of Boisdale, a long-time advocate of rural re-vitalization and co-operatives. In 1927 she was admitted into the Sisters of St. Martha and was immediately sent to study Home Economics at Macdonald College in Quebec. The Diocese of Antigonish had been considering a plan for instructing women in the household arts. She graduated from St. Francis Xavier in 1933 with her B.A. and joined the Extension staff of three. Typically, she had to design the program from scratch. In those early days she also ended up as a Jill-of-all-trades, assisting in the office run by Kay Desjardins with finesse (apparently mediating skillfully between Coady, the visionary, and Macdonald, the hard-nosed organizer).

> Women's study clubs, Marie Michael believed, were best suited for those topics that 'would not interest men,' topics like handicrafts, cooking, sewing, child care, homemaking and community improvement and handicrafts that used wool, hides, bark, roots, moss, lichens, rug making, dying, and the marketing of these crafts. Women's study clubs also discussed poultry raising, dairying (the production of butter and cheese), gardening, canning, curing meat, soap making, managing home conveniences, saving electricity, keeping financial records and marketing farm products (Neale, 1998, p. 149).

Tall, attractive, sociable, Sister Marie Michael argued forcefully before Extension staff conferences that women were integral to the social reform movement. Women had to protect the family, make the household beautiful, because the family was the base from which the full and abundant life would flow. She praised rural women's stalwart role in the reform movement, and doubted whether professional and business women had the general interest at heart. Women needed a broad-based education to assume various leadership roles. Her sociability made her the first-choice for guiding the tours that inevitably came to Antigonish. She also wrote articles for "Women's pages," gave speeches, and organized the Extension Department's library. Coady certainly encouraged women to participate in credit unions, co-operative stores, as well as in the Women and Work program of handicrafts, home economics, and consumer education. Marie Michael, Sister Anselm (Irene Doyle), and fieldworker Ida Gallant pushed the gender borders when they pressed the men to allow women to be on boards of directors, full members, and knowledgeable consumers.

But World War II proved disheartening for Marie Michael. The war had strained resources both of families and the Extension Department, and the "Women and Work" program was cancelled. Marie Michael had come up against the patriarchal wall: her call for women's full participation in the co-operatives and defence of her lifeworld project failed. Sexism existed in the Movement; it also existed in the Department of Agriculture, as it failed to hire female agricultural reps (Lotti Austin was the first one hired and worked in Hants County). Only six women attended the Congress of Nova Scotia Co-operative Societies, representing seventy-six consumer organizations in 1945. Ida Gallant and Sister Anselm were among those women present. Sister Marie Michael left Extension and prepared herself for librarianship. In 1946, she studied librarianship at the Catholic University and directed the Extension library from 1947 to 1956. Later, it was named after her.

Sister Francis Dolores Donnelly of the Sisters of Charity was the "smart young sister who had a degree" (Neale, 1998, p. 161). This brilliant, bookish, urbane woman had been missioned by her Superior, at Father Jimmy Tompkins' behest, to go to Reserve Mines to assist with his work. At first horrified at the thought of heading off to the backwoods (or work with groups), Sister Francis Dolores headed off dutifully to her new post. Born in 1914 in St. John's, Newfoundland, into a large Irish family of eight, this strong-willed and opinionated young woman loved books and was determined to become a scholar. She entered the Sisters of Charity, an order committed to education, to teach. When she arrived in Reserve Mines it had already begun its decline, with severe drops in coal production. It didn't take her long to see the connection between study and action for the community. She quickly re-organized Tompkins growing collection of books in the front room of the rectory. The Mother General of her order had assigned Sister Francis to be Father Jimmy Tompkins' personal assistant. Tompkins was known for his caustic judgments and irascible nature; this didn't bother her. In fact, she "loved" this man; it was platonic, but widely known in the Movement just how devoted she became to this old priest who, as legend has it, would ask his confessing youth only one question, "Can ya read, lad? Can ya read?"

Tompkins encouraged her to take various public speaking assignments. This was unheard of in those days: Catholic sisters were to be servants and submissive and quiet. Tompkins and Coady would have none of that. Sister Francis became remarkably adept. She shared their vision of the educative democracy: human labour had dignity before God, and men and women had to understand the necessity of developing their full cognitive, emotional, and spiritual capacities. Tompkins had often said that "ideas needed feet." Sister Francis, for her part, accentuated the need for better ideas. "This means contributing as far as we can to serving human rights for all, eliminating racial prejudice, safeguarding human development and in a word, taking an intelligent part in securing the region for social justice and charity" (Sister Francis Dolores, 1943, p. 5). Her deepest love, however, shared with Tompkins, was for libraries: books for the people. Both of these passionate adult educators wanted people to develop along their own chosen lines. They plunged into political action, pressing local and provincial authorities to create a library system. By 1944 the Cape Breton School Board became the first in the province to hire a full time librarian—Sister Francis Dolores. Guy Henson, who directed the new Division of Adult Education for the Nova Scotia government and Father Tompkins would get much credit for creating the provincial system. But Sister Francis Dolores and other sisters did the work in the trenches to see this big project to completion.

Sister Dolores stood by Tompkins in his dispute with Coady. Coady simply thought of the Extension library system playing an instrumental role in the co-operative movement: pamphlets and literature to the particular interests of the co-ops. Tompkins and Dolores dreamed differently. They imagined a "larger system of self-education" in which "It is up to everyone—adults and high schools and colleges as well—to prepare now to fight with the weapons of ideas" (Neale, 1998, pp. 173–74). This dispute signals that the Antigonish Movement was not homogenous: it had different tendencies. Tompkins and Sister Francis looked beyond the co-operatives' special interests. For this reason, it seems, neither of them liked Ida Gallant who they perceived as too identified with the Coady tendency within the Movement. By 1949, Father Jimmy was losing his mind. Stories are told of old Jimmy reciting mass, getting part way through, and starting again. He became increasingly irascible. Coady couldn't bear the sight of this withered, sick man: it broke his already broken heart. Delores had worked with Father Jimmy to finally achieve the Cape Breton Regional Library (she deserves honour for this; she is often forgotten). Her vision was that books and libraries be used to cultivate the capacity to build the new just, co-operative society. She went on to doctoral studies and was finally able to live the scholarly life this smart young sister had dreamed of.

Nora Bateson deserves far more attention in Canadian adult education history than she has received. These fiery, brilliant, and charismatic women who grew up in the old region of the early nineteenth Luddite rebellions, Westhoughton, England, also shared Tompkins' passion for books for the people. She established the Prince Edward Island regional library system in the early 1930s. In June 1935, while working in PEI, she visited Father Jimmy in Reserve Mines. Tompkins, Bateson, and Sister Delores believed that libraries were people's universities for the empowerment of the working poor. They were instruments of social progress and tools for adult educational formation. In fact, Bateson had learned from Dr. Helen Gordon Stewart, the legendary library builder, while working on the Fraser Valley Library Development Project in 1930, that one had to go to the people. Stewart worked tirelessly with community groups, promoting libraries as "the most potent agency amongst all educational institutions" (Morison, 1952, p. 49).

Bateson followed in her mentor's footsteps: in PEI she spoke to Women's Institutes, churches, service associations, and farmers' organizations. Father Jimmy captures the spirit of this radical woman (who ended up being fired by the Nova Scotian government for inappropriate critical comments): "Miss Bateson arrived here on Tuesday morning and will leave on the train this evening Friday from Sydney Mines after talked at Sydney Mines up to the moment of the train's departure. We had meetings at Reserve, Sisters at Glace Bay (to all the Sisters of around about), Glace Bay itself, New Waterford and twice at Sydney Mines … Now we have excogitated things revolutionary and she is wild and she has set me wild. … She is trying to get them standing on their hinds legs for reading" (Tompkins, 1935). Tompkins and Bateson carried this gospel to the Carnegie and Rockefeller Foundations and to various national and international conferences (Adams, 2009).

Tales of building a co-operative fishery require much space. But, gradually fishers in places like Judique, on the west coast of Cape Breton, learned that they were condemned to poverty and vulnerability when they left everything—from processing to financing—in private hands. They learned that, through applying co-operative business to their activities, they could regain control of the services need to produce wealth, finance their enterprises and supply consumer needs. In the spring of 1934, the fishermen of Judique organized and built a lobster factory. With thirty members, they were able to pay for the building and equipment of their factory. They improved the quality of the lobster pack and, with the UMF's help, began to regulate marketing of canned lobsters. A credit union soon followed in 1935, and a co-operative store in 1936. The people of Judique informed Extension that they were wealthier than they were a decade ago, both economically and spiritually, and had

gained significant confidence in managing their own affairs. In this utopian phase the people were mobilized for enlightenment and action. The
spaces had been available for co-operative action and the undermining
of age-old systems of exploiting fishermen. Large fish companies like
Robins, Jones, and Whitman had dominated every aspect of the lives
of fishermen and their families on the Gaspe coast and the west side of
Cape Breton. One even had to ask their permission to get married; the
company gave liberally to the Roman Catholic Church; the "liberation
theology" underpinning the Antigonish Movement intellectual's project
had to crack through this hegemonic control.

By the end of the 1930s, this Movement of the "little people" caught
the eye of the world. Journalists began to visit Antigonish to see the
"modern miracle." Stories were published in the *New York Times* and
many other journals. Popular books such as Bertram Fowler's *The
Lord Helps Those: How the People of Nova Scotia are Solving Their Problems
Through Co-Operation* (1938) exaggerated what was really happening in
this small, poor province of Canada. But something electrifying seemed
to be going on: perhaps a solution had been found that was neither
communist nor capitalist—a solution that actually empowered the little
people to become masters of their own destiny. The famous Rural and
Industrial Conferences of the late 1930s attracted considerable attention
from left-leaning Christians like Dorothy Day of the Catholic Worker
Movement, a pacifist, non-violent organization that worked with the
down and outs based in New York. The message of co-operation had
also been spread outside the Maritimes as Coady and other key organizers carried the Antigonish gospel throughout the land. The Movement
probably reached its peak in 1938/9. In 1938, the Movement received
official Papal approval. In its Annual Report for the year ending April
30, 1939, the Extension Department noted that staff totaled eleven full-
time members, several part-time, and thirty additional staff in the fishing
communities. A thousand people had attended the Rural and Industrial
Conference in August 1938. A co-operative institute held after the conference brought together two hundred educationalists, clergymen, social
workers, and others from thirty states in the Unites States and from every
province in Canada. It was easy to dream that the Movement was the
blueprint for humankind.

Moses Coady published his only book, *Masters of Their Own Destiny,*
in 1939 at the Movement's climactic moment. He had been very sick—
his heart was giving him trouble—before completing a manuscript that
was crushed out of his sickness. He sought help from his assistants—Ida

Gallant and A. S. MacIntyre in particular worried that they were not penetrating deeply enough into the communities—but found completion of
the manuscript tough slogging. The original manuscript was much longer and more complex than the version published by Harper and Row,
which was designed to be inspirational (Welton, 2001). The outbreak of
World War II in 1939 stopped the Movement from growing: just enough
progress and hope had been generated to seduce Moses Coady into
imagining that he had discovered the blueprint for humankind. The War
undermined the network of dynamic youthful leaders who were swept
up into the war to fight Hitler, the great enemy of democracy. It also
depleted people's reserve energies and the study club attendance dropped
severely. The Movement did, of course, continue, but one senses that
the Movement had reached its consolidation phase, as attention to the
grassroots became increasingly difficult. In its place, the Movement shifted
to leadership training and organizational maintenance. During the Cold
War era Coady began to preach an anti-communist gospel in Canada
and the United States. Mighty Moses also faced the return of corporate
capitalist confidence and bullying power. After World War II, the UMF
confronted a capitalist industry that introduced technologies that undermined the power of the in-shore fishers. The world can break your heart;
in Coady's case it may have. This great visionary activist couldn't bear to
see fishers turn away from the co-operative blueprint. He thought the
Church had sold out to the vested interests of big business. He thought
that Canadian democracy left most of us sitting in the bleachers twid-
dling our thumbs. He became, towards the end, a King Lear figure, raging
into the dying night.

Coady's core idea, self-reliance, was rooted in personal and communal experience homesteading in the Margaree Valley of Cape Breton.
He loved this land deeply, wondered often what lay beyond the mountains and took up the fate and struggles of the primary producers, from
whence he began, into his own body and soul. He also believed that God
had particularly favoured the Anglo-Celts in the world of races and ethnic groups. He cast his fate with the Anglo-Celtic primary producers of
the land. Coady could not help privileging the rural life over the urban,
and the organic community over the individual. Catholic social teaching
was steeped in the language of corporatism, and basically rejected pure
liberal individualism. Nor did he move fluidly into the brutal world of
industrial politics and militant trade unionism. Until he organized the
Nova Scotia Teachers' Union in the early 1920s Moses Coady had strong
anti-trade union sentiments. In *Masters,* Coady began his account of the

Antigonish Movement with an historical description of the economic plight of his people and the utter failure of formal educational systems to prepare them to understand and control their own worlds. Coady is an organic intellectual of the primary producers. He wanted to know why his people (they were poor Irish farmers) and his Anglo-Celtic ethnic group (they were mostly impoverished farmers, brutally exploited fishermen and miners) had lost control of their own destinies. He wanted to know how they might regain it. He was prepared to be their voice. Coady stands forever as a formidable presence against the oppression and exploitation of the earth's producing classes. He can also be resurrected as a tough populist proponent of syndicalism: that philosophy that posits that democracy—achieving the "good and abundant life"—is not really fully possible when workers do not control their own work and productive processes.

Coady's Roman Catholic Christian worldview profoundly shaped his cultural outlook on the fate of his people. He chose the priesthood in the early twentieth century, dedicating his life to its service by submitting his life to a supreme authority. He became part of the professional managerial elite, a network of priestly community leaders in the Diocese of Antigonish. This movement out of his class and into the professional elite introduced tension into Coady's relationship with his people (he was both one of them and their tutor). Like the medieval "Common Doctor," St. Thomas Aquinas, Coady believed that the world of nature and society were knowable through reason. He was certain that a blueprint for the right ordering of the human world existed, that it was discoverable through "scientific" thinking. Coady littered his speeches and writings with metaphors like "formula," "blueprint," and "science" over and over. "The ignorance that characterizes each level of society is due mainly to a lack of scientific thinking. His great secret of progress had been scientific thinking (Coady, 1939, p. 31): this is vintage Coady. The scientific way of doing things is set against ignorant ways of thinking and acting in the world. Coady's plain man's Thomism fuses Christian ideas with key elements from the Enlightenment tradition. The "natural law" tradition permeated Coady's thinking. But this permitted him to believe that a reasonable scientific understanding of society revealed the regulative principles for ordering the economic, political, and social worlds. He could, then, fuse "co-operativism" and "religion." Thus, "right education" could beam reason's light upon the world gone awry and irrational. He wanted to find the "one best way": in these days of pluralism and skepticism about any one best way, we may be inclined to think that his world outlook was too modernist. Yet he was right to argue about the irrationalities of capitalism and the necessity of economic democracy. We cannot forget either that Coady's war years' speeches were powerful indictments of capitalist militarism. They were dark, foreboding, melancholic thoughts. The suffering of his own class, ethnic group, Church and now the whole wide world were taken into his body and heart. He gradually fell apart, piece by piece.

Coady's fundamental belief was that there are more possibilities for human (and natural) development than are usually imagined and that life consisted of the realization of these possibilities. His developmental, humanist, Christian vision is one that withstands the ravages of time. Perhaps, when all is said and done, Coady's life at least from his late thirties until his death in 1959 embodied a central idea that we are in danger of losing. But one that Coady never let his beloved Nova Scotians and Maritimers forget: the world as it is, is not the way it has to be. We honour Moses Coady for his willingness to dream beyond the mountains and the will to bring it close to the ground. We honour the common people for believing that their lives could be better. They did get better, and in the end we are left standing in awe at the sheer audacity of "little Mosie from the Margaree." The historian as deep sea diver can offer the Antigonish Movement as a pearl, a liberating moment, for us in the dire circumstances of our twenty-first century world. There is powerful dynamite in adult learning and education. Our minds are also encrusted.

Adult Education and Union Education: Aspects of English-Canadian Cultural History in the Twentieth Century

Gerald Friesen's (1994) re-thinking of "adult and labour education" offers important insights into the Canadian labour movement as a vehicle for adult education between the 1930s and the 1970s. Adopting a comparative approach to understanding the ins and outs of labour education, Friesen observes that Canadian labour education, like its British and American counterparts, has always been ambiguous in aim and constituency. We have already noticed this ambiguity in our reflections on Mechanics' Institutes. Even in the early nineteenth century, a division between vocational and liberal education was evident (though rather mixed up or jumbled together). The ambiguity of aim and constituency, Friesen points out, was also manifest in the adult education movement from 1900 to the 1960s. Frontier College and the Workers' Educational Association are apt illustrations. Friesen thinks that the "two middle-class reformers, Alfred Fitzpatrick and Edmund Bradwin, can be easily described as an expression both of humane elite values and of worker-controlled education. Its primary goal was worker literacy and remains unchanged to this day" (1994, p. 169). Nonetheless, Friesen argues that we can detect a distinct "Canadian middle way" that sought to transcend class divisions by serving the whole community. In my view, however, the "middle way" does not adequately capture the radical theme of deliberation democracy that was powerfully present in Canadian adult education in the 1930s and 1940s.

The WEA under Drummond Wren's visionary leadership was our most significant workers' education association in Canada. Wren did not want to attach himself to any ideology or partisan form of politics. The goal of the WEA was "to teach people how to think, not what to think." But Wren didn't want to be misunderstood. This position did not imply an uncritical acceptance of the status quo. In its own way it was revolutionary: to teach how to think and how to apply critical judgment to existing social and economic wrongs, he thought, would eventually eliminate for our society all injustices. Workers' education was not for individual self-improvement; it was a form of collective learning for collective action to change the relations of production and the working conditions themselves. The WEA created a summer school at Port Hope. Its research bureau churned out pamphlets that were used by the Canadian Congress of Labour (which was aligned with the social democratic CCF). To reach more workers, it used film, radio, and other media to make its message more widely known. It was allied closely with the CAAE and its reconstruction projects. It aimed to be the educational arm of the Canadian working class movement. This was not to be. With the Cold War edging ever closer, and the CCF and the Communists battling it out for the leadership of Canadian trade unions and political allegiance—in the face of soon resurgent capitalism—the WEA would be caught in the squeeze.

The Vancouver WEA illustrates this destructive process well. The Vancouver branch, formed in 1942 under the leadership of Claude Donald, an industrial worker, who valiantly attempted to provide educational services by means of films and filmstrips, news bulletins, lectures, evening classes, open discussion, and summer conferences to the BC workers. The Vancouver WEA was only modestly successful in its endeavours to encourage active workers participation and to teach them to apply "critical judgment to existing social and economic wrongs" (Wren, 1945, n.p.). Any chance for the widespread acceptance of the WEA's activities was severely limited by the acrimonious Western labour movement. Claude

Donald simply expended too much energy just trying to keep the Vancouver affiliate afloat. After five and a half years of dogged effort to educate "intelligent, clear thinking workers," the Vancouver WEA would be destroyed by the internecine warfare between the social democratic CCF and the Communist Labour Progressive Party (LPP) for control of the union movement.

Accusations that the WEA's leadership was closely aligned to Communist sympathizers would plague both the Vancouver branch as well as its Toronto head office through the 1940s. Both Donald and his close friend Drummond Wren would be forced to resign their positions in the late 1940s despite vehement denials of Communist affiliation. Unable to achieve the necessary financial security to provide an extensive network of educational services, and lacking the full endorsement of the academic community and the wary BC labour bosses, the Vancouver WEA would not succeed in its goal of becoming a "militant workers' university" (Wren, 1945, n.p.). The Vancouver WEA tried to anchor its educational practices in the creation of a particular form of sociality that permitted open dialogue and debate, free of coercion. But the WEA as a social learning form was located within a social context not conducive to the development of critical judgment. The trade union leadership closed off debate and opted for authoritarian forms of pedagogy. The structural constraints on the development of a learner-centred, autonomous workers' education within the WEA were simply too much for it to bear. This argument is supported by the argument in a candid "Memorandum on Workers' Education for Local Charted Unions," published by the CCL in 1943 or 1944. The author, not named in the memorandum, was an insider to both the adult education and the workers' movement. The author argued that the WEA could not possibly be the educational arm for the CCL because, as a young organization, they needed to build up institutional loyalty. The WEA could not serve the locals, they would have to. They wanted their educational process to serve their political interests of supporting the CCF. The Congress had a more direct approach to the locals than the WEA could ever have. And the CCL could develop its own educational department ("Memorandum," c. 1943/44). The CCL wanted to mold its workers' minds and consciousness in a particular direction. The WEA in the late 1940s and 1950s ran into the "Red Scare." They were not alone.

In the 1930s when the International Ladies Garment Union (ILGWU) was organizing in the garments trades in Montreal, they faced Quebec Premier Maurice Duplessie's red squads who located and destroyed any printed material that seemed vaguely leftist. Lea Roback, who organized the ILGWU, worked with Jewish immigrant women from Russian and Poland to equip them with the critical capacity to understand how they were exploited (they were paid by the "quality" of their goods) and how to manage their threatened lifeworlds (they had language training, living well discussions, and created recreation programs) (Zinman, 1986). Roback managed to create solidarity among her workers, who had the courage to go on strike in the bitter year of 1937.

By 1952, the WEA would be moribund. Wren cannot be blamed for this development. The battle between the CCF and the LPP killed it. Tamed and domesticated, the Canadian union movement gained institutional power through its collective bargaining rights. In the 1950s and 60s, then, the union movement narrowed its focus, streamlining its courses and training programs to prepare stewards for work in the locals and training much needed leaders. Friesen (1994) observes that one text, "History and Function of Trade Unions in Canada," prepared in 1947 for trade union courses, still maintained a "militant, contestational, class-based approach so common in labour relations during the Second World War and with the expectation of an eventual socialist victory" (p. 177). By the 1960s, this militancy had disappeared from workers' education. The curriculum shifted to offering "tool courses," "technical training," and general courses such as how one might enrich his or her community. Now that the unions had a new role in the collective bargaining process, the Labour College of Canada was established in 1958 to enable unionists to acquire the technical skills necessary to engage in the bargaining process. The labour movement, like the adult education movement itself, was professionalizing and seeking legitimacy from the university sector (through taking courses for credits). The trade union movement turned inward to acculturate its members into their new community of practice. They tried to educate the public about the salience of unions in Canadian life. In the early years, their methods were on a small-scale. The Canadian Labour Congress, founded in 1956, encouraged locals to set up displays in schools and service clubs; nothing worked very effectively. The unions were losing their ability to counter the ceaseless propaganda extolling business and individual achievement—communicated through newspapers, journals, television, and movies. The "cultural hegemony" of the corporate elite had little to fear from a becalmed and technicized organized labour (and adult education associations).

Ed Finn, one of Canada's finest labour journalists and labour educators, observed that "education and communications" were "areas of

difficulty" for the unions (Friesen, 1994, p. 181). Public relations departments were established in many unions between 1950 and the 1980s.
But the big unions could simply not get a positive message out to the
Canadian public. Part of the reason for this, I believe, is the marked shift
away from creating critical capacity on workers' part to understand the
cultural, political, ethical, and economic worlds they now inhabited. Tool
courses and loss of contact with the base (which would have required
instituting procedures for participatory democracy) created elites within
both the labour movement and the co-operative movement. In 1946
the CCF had thought of setting up a network of weeklies to articulate
an alternative to the capitalist press. This never came about. As Friesen
(1994) expresses it, "The Canadian labour movement did not communicate an alternative vision of the social order to the rest of Canada, or even
to its members, between the 1940s and the 1970s" (p. 183). It couldn't
reach its own people, let alone the Canadian public itself. As Canada
was pulled inexorably into the neo-liberal globalizing capitalism period
(dated roughly from 1973 to the present), Canadian workers would suffer immensely because they lacked the critical tools to read the texts of
their changing and brutal world. "Canada's WEA aimed in the 1930s and
1940s to communicate 'knowledge essential to intelligent and effective
citizenship' and to enable workers 'to think for themselves and to express
their thoughts fluently and correctly' (Sandiford, as cited in Friesen, 1994,
p. 188). Wren's vision remains unfulfilled.

Intimations of the Just Learning Society: Guy Henson and Watson Thomson's State-Supported Projects

Watson Thomson had a unique vision of the role of adult education in
the world. He believed that revolutionary change in the external structures of oppression would be impossible without changes in individuals, masses could not bring about fundamental change. The co-personal
group had an absolutely crucial role to play here: individuals had to
choose freely to be initiators of a new revolution and had to learn in
face-to-face interaction with others, to break with egoistic individualism
and become personally allied with others in mutual love and care. One
had to both be and build the desired new world. He envisaged that economic and social life would be re-built around units small enough that
face-to-face relationships were never crushed. This belief in the primacy
of the co-personal group in social change would be one of Thomson's
distinctive contributions. Thomson was not a dogmatist (someone once
said he loved "pimps, prostitutes and Presbyterians"): his world outlook

enabled him to work in a wide variety of situations to put this vision into action. Before arriving in Saskatchewan in 1944—as we have already seen—Thomson had participated in a remarkable range of adult education and communitarian experiments. He founded chapters of the WEA in Calgary and Edmonton in 1937 and 1938, and played a leading role in the development of the Danish folk school-inspired Alberta School of Community Life and the University of Alberta's innovative outreach programs. As director of the University of Manitoba's Adult Education Office, he worked to revitalize rural Manitoban communities, often in dreadful conditions. He played an important role on the national scene: campaigning tirelessly for the Canadian National Refugee Committee. He provided vital philosophical direction at the high point of the CAAE's coordinating role: drafting the controversial "Manifesto." He broadcasted over the CBC on world affairs, and spoke out against those who were refusing to allow Jews into Canada during the war years.

In 1944, Thomson thought he could join Tommy Douglas' newly elected government and, for the first time, to link his transformative-communitarian educational theory to the social policy of the CCF governing party. The Saskatchewan government had swept the Liberal government party out of office, winning 47 of 52 seats. Although Douglas had won a decisive victory, he faced formidable problems in establishing a "beachhead of socialism on a continent of capitalism" (Thomas, 1982, p. 169). His political bureaucracy was ineffective; large numbers of farmers had not voted for him; and Saskatchewan Roman Catholics remained suspicious of the CCF. Douglas wanted not only to introduce legislation on health, collective bargaining, and education, as he had promised, but also to use a campaign of grassroots radical adult education—a massive campaign of study-action throughout the province—to begin the building of a humane socialist society. Watson Thomson thought he saw exciting vistas ahead. Woodrow Lloyd, the Minister of Education, imagined that a new Division of Adult Education should clarify the thinking of Saskatchewan citizens so that desirable social and economic concepts could prevail and provide adult education with immediate and tangible aims (co-operative farming, credit unions, health-improvement facilities, community centres, and leisure-time activities). Thomson's coherent vision of a just learning society is particularly remarkable.

Thomson moved quickly to establish government policy for adult education in Saskatchewan. His brief, "Adult Education Theory and Policy," (1944) outlined what he thought was the only possible attitude to adult education for a democratic socialist government to adopt. It was of the "utmost importance" (p. 1) that members of the government under-stand the educational theory and principles of the new Adult Education Division, both in itself and in relation to their own social philosophy. Education was not partial and socially neutral. In Saskatchewan, an adult education that would conform with the principle of the "social" theory had two primary concrete tasks: to support the people with relevant knowledge in their movement towards the new objectives for which the way had been opened up, whether they be cooperative farms, larger school units, or new public-health projects; and to awaken the people to a sense of the "central issues of the world crisis," so that there could be a clear way ahead for modern society. Thomson informed the cabinet that a socially minded education had to discover where a sense of social purpose was breaking through towards liberatory social change. Then that activation had to be fostered in every possible way and fed the mate-rial for its creative job of reshaping the environment. In the fall of 1944, Thomson wagered that a significant number of Saskatchewanites had opted to move towards a more participatory and self-reliant society. He saw his task as catalytic: helping people to clarify their goals and achieve their ends through critical dialogue.

The Adult Education Division did not want to convey knowledge for its own sake, rather for the sake of change nearer to the heart's desire of ordinary, decent people everywhere. Average people, Thomson believed, did not want to study the history of medicine in the abstract. But when they began to ask why they could not have a decent hospital in their own district and to get together with their neighbours to figure out some way of getting one, they were ready to learn some history of medicine. Aware that the trend in agriculture was towards increasingly mechanized, capital-intensive, large-scale units, Thomson urged farmers to bring their isolated farms together into single cooperative communities. He was convinced that the people could take the raw materials of a prairie vil-lage and create a new pattern worked out by the ordinary people from below. But one could not do that without study and cooperative action. "No study without consequent action. No action without previous study" (Welton, 1987, p. 156). This would be the banner of the division's study–action program.

The visionaries in the Division of Adult Education envisaged noth-ing less than a comprehensive adult education program for social prog-ress through which 500,000 men and women of the province would be encouraged to become active citizens and fully rounded personalities. This was bold, even utopian, thinking, made possible by the catastrophes of World War II, which fired people to imagine something other than the smouldering fires of the battlefield and incessant competition between, and within, nations. This was a most delicate, grand social pedagogical task: to enable people to imagine new possibilities without any form of coercion. Under the direction of William Harding, aided by district supervisors, the department began to proceed systematically to establish starting and growing points. A starting point, as Harding conceived it, consisted of one individual with an interest in a particular topic, and a growing point of four individuals interested in a common problem or issue. When ten units cohered around a common theme, a study group was formed. Three central issues were clear to Thomson and Harding. First, they understood that the Saskatchewan government had to demonstrate to the farmers, workers, and plan people that a democratic socialist government could affect tangible material improvements. Second, they knew that the mass of people must be mobilized and activated as rapidly as possible. Only by participating in the process of democratic deliberation and social change would people realize that "socialism is democracy extended" and that the bogey of "socialism as mere bureaucracy and regimentation" is ludicrous. Third, Thomson and Harding believed that the "political consciousness" of the mass of people must be so deepened that the foundations of prairie radicalism became unshakable (Thomson, 1944, n.p.).

The first task was one of legislation and administration, the second and third involved the consideration of matters in which adult education could play an important role. Study-action had been designed to meet the second need—mobilizing and activating the people at the grassroots level. It was essential, the study-action strategists contended, to begin with a broad approach to "communities as communities" (Thomson, 1944, n.p.) and to serve them in some appreciable way regarding their expressed needs. Study-action, citizens' conferences, and the Lighted School all aimed at serving communities in a non-partisan spirit. It was also educationally sound, they thought, to attempt to lead study-action groups from local and immediate concerns to the affairs of the province, nation, and, eventually, the world. *The Front Page*, edited by Eddie Parker, was created to that end; it turned out to be incredibly controversial. As people's awareness turned outward to the world, the issues discussed would inevitably take on a more political character, and groups would look to the Division of Adult Education for guidance. That guidance could then be given based on confidence earned through non-partisan services in the community-centred interests. Developing this political consciousness, though the most crucial task as far as the progressive movement was concerned, was also the most difficult.

The idea of the citizens' conferences was that ordinary citizens could come together with experts would could provide some analytical guidance, and government officers, who could provide some information regarding official policy. This may sound naïve to political realists, but Thomson explicitly rejected the notion that specialists were there to deliver their words, leaving the people to criticize or go home and pick the words to pieces. This was not the way to build a true democracy. Those who were not specialists had a right to have their say. Each conference (they were held around specific learning challenges facing the communities such as creating communities fit for the returning veterans, co-operative farming, health themes, and many more). Each conference utilized the familiar methods—speakers, films bearing on the conference themes, group discussion, panels, and strategy and action sessions. The heart of the citizens' conferences, from Thomson's viewpoint, lay not with the large assembly but in the small discussion groups. As issues emerged in the plenary sessions, clear and significant questions were then placed before these policy-making groups. Following the panel discussion, Thomson's role, a crucial one, was to intuit the audience's mood and address himself to the question "where do we go from here?" Action, as Thomson repeatedly pointed out, was of two orders: study and practical projects. Thomson was particularly enthusiastic about the reception in the Landis-Biggar area for co-operative farming.

During the month of February 1945, Thomson's main preoccupation had been with the training course for the field workers and staff. Morning sessions were taken up with educational theory and the practical problems facing field workers (problems of new Canadians and returned veterans, for example). In the afternoon, representatives from various government ministries addressed the students. In the evenings, field workers and staff saw demonstrations of film-forums, watched films critically, participated in panel discussions, and heard more talks from officials and representatives of community organizations. It was an exhaustingly thorough and exciting three weeks. And the excitement of the training school was no doubt intensified several days after the sessions ended. The staff opened the *Financial Post* of February 24 and read the headline—"Saskatchewan CCF Adult Education Program May Emerge as Straight Propaganda." Under this provocative headline, Gordon L. Smith malevolently linked Saskatchewan study-action with undemocratic education. "Nothing like it has ever been broached in Canada," he exclaimed. "One can only point to Germany or Russia or pre-war Italy for such a deliberately planed scheme of a mass education, perhaps more correctly described as mass propaganda." The anonymous author of the regular news column, "The Nation's Business," informed Canadians that if they wanted to know what would happen on the national level if the CCF came to power, they should look at Saskatchewan. "The evidence strongly indicates that they are in for a mass propaganda drive of the Goebells' [sic] variety, in which they are to be given that special set of facts and that special interpretation of those facts which suits the government in power." The author was quick to add that Watson Thomson was an exponent of "socialist and communist blueprints for utopia" who readily admitted that he felt "no obligation in educational work to present more than one side of the question."

This sort of "socialist-bashing" was, of course, nothing new to CCF, farm movements, and activist adult educators. Accusations that CCF was synonymous with totalitarian and regimentation had been hurled at Douglas throughout the bitter 1944 campaign. When farmers were establishing co-operatives in the 1920s, they were often labelled "communist." This was true also of Coady and his workers in Nova Scotia. What was new was the intensity of the anti-socialist propaganda engineered by people like B. A. Trestrail and supported by many business organizations (such as Eaton's). Through the spring of 1945 until the June federal election the CCF would experience its most vicious onslaught in in its twelve-year history. Despite the chicanery of the anti-socialist propaganda, the Trestrails and Smiths succeeded in undermining CCF support. This impairing was particularly effective in Ontario, less so in Saskatchewan where populism and co-operative traditions inoculated a good segment of the population against the diatribes of the bourgeois press. For his part, Watson Thomson thought the *Financial Post* comments were "pretty damning." But he still trusted that "all publicity was good publicity" (Thomson, 1945a). All he could do was to encourage his staff to "go ahead with your work quietly. Shrug off verbal opposition with a smile" (Thomson, 1945b).

If Thomson thought he lived in a "dangerous, fascinating, grandly terrible" world (Newsletter, 2, n.d), he was right. The first year of the study-action program went famously well. The grass roots were stirring. The province was alive; but so were those bitterly opposed to tinkering with the capitalist market economy and elite politics. The national CCF under M. J. Coldwell's leadership received reports from right-wing CCFers that Thomson had spoken with at a meeting for interracial co-operation that was allegedly associated with the communists. Watson was also blamed for disputes within the Manitoba CCF. The stirrings from below also unnerved the CCF leadership. In early March 1945 the original budget of $100,000 had been reduced to $60,000, possibly in part due to squabbles over the seed grain issue. The promised support from the government for Thomson and the Roslyn Road summer conference, "The Prairie School for Social Advance," were withdrawn, and an uneasy Thomson wrote his friends in Winnipeg that both Douglas and Lloyd were pulling back from previous commitments. The national leadership became increasingly suspicious that Thomson might be a communist who was boring from within. Though these accusations were false, they signal how paranoid the cultural atmosphere actually was: one had to choose sides, and any attempt to work for a more inclusive people's movement was doomed.

Bewildered, but still hopeful, Thomson (Corbett and other adult education leaders had praised their program) pressed on with the study-action program. He was overjoyed with the support he was receiving in Wynyard and Melfort for the citizens' conferences on "Community Meets Veteran," to be held in June. He now thought that Saskatchewan was the only place in Canada that was truly progressive. Lloyd and others were encouraging Thomson to play it safe, make sure *The Living Newspaper* gave no hint of trucking with the communists. Thomson did not think it was time to play it safe. The extension and consolidating of the widespread goodwill and citizens' conferences in the Division's usefulness and integrity, now being built through study-action, citizens' conferences, and, soon, the Lighted School (night schools for adult learners in schoolhouses), were immediate and urgent necessities. The plan was there, techniques known, a small but devoted staff at work as individuals and as a team. Opportunities far surpassed achievements because the Department needed more staff, research, writing, and field work. The time was ripe. The people, as the Division was finding them, were disposed to change and open to playing a dynamic role in local and regional affairs. But Thomson's days were numbered; he was dismissed in January 1946. Fitzpatrick had said that adult education was the "daydream of visionaries." Watson had big dreams, but perhaps Thomson's utopian fervour propelled him out beyond the average citizen. He wasn't playing ball with the communists, yet his inclusive radical democratic vision certainly attempted to break through the ideological sectarian fracturing of any coherent project of social reconstruction that has been so powerfully present in the "Education for Reconstruction" conference of 1943, which announced to all Canadians a humane vision of a common wealth.

Guy Henson was not as flamboyant as men like Corbett, Coady, or Thomson. A quiet man, Henson had a brilliant mind and superb administrative skills. He was the first Director of the Adult Education Division for Nova Scotia (1946-1956). Henson, a graduate of Acadia University, fell into the company of Moses Coady when he was a cub reporter, utterly captivated by his vision of the "good and abundant life." Henson had cut his teeth as an adult educator in Halifax in the 1930s, setting up a chapter of the WEA and fostering Antigonish-style credit unions in urban Halifax and Dartmouth. Returning from war service with the Canadian Legion Educational Service in Europe in the fall of 1945, Henson was asked to create a new Division of Adult Education. Dr. Henry Munro, Superintendent of Education, and former president of the CAAE, convinced both Henson and Premier Angus L. MacDonald, to create a Division of Adult Education primarily to respond to the plight of rural Nova Scotians. This support was much-needed: significant opposition to this new division was evident amongst MLAs in the government.

Henson spent many months collecting data on the discipline of adult education and other initiatives worldwide as part of his own learning process. His 1946 report *Provincial Support for Adult Education in Nova Scotia* became the guide for the work of the Division and, in itself, can claim an important place in the intellectual history of Canadian adult education. Like his counterpart in Saskatchewan, Henson thought that postwar changes in society were creating the possibility of creating an educative society. When he took on the task of setting up the new division in 1945, he viewed adult education as closely connected to his vision of associative democracy, which was that the very life of a democracy depends on the self-worth of the populace, intelligent and critical thinking individuals who would wrestle with controversial issues of the day and collectively organize and develop their communities. In the postwar world of Nova Scotia, Henson believed that adult education could play an axial role in revitalizing society and democracy. These themes had already been spread throughout the network of study clubs, credit unions, co-op retail stores, and consumer wholesale outlets in numerous fishing villages, mining towns, and farming towns.

Henson (1946) organized his famous report into three sections: "The Goals of Adult Education," "A Constructive Approach," and "Proposals for Action." It was plainly written, but brilliantly formulated, and Henson acknowledged that that formal schooling did not turn out the "finished product" and that "work activity" and the associative life of civil society had a deep "educational effect for the adult" (p. 9). "The newspaper, magazine and book, the radio, the film, the church, the political parties, occupational associations, social and fraternal groups form," he observed, "a complex of agencies which have the main part in transmitting knowledge and opinions to grown-up people" (p. 9). He then asked: "To what extent can the educational movement as such be strengthened so that an increasing body of people will turn to it for knowledge without bias, for skills efficiently taught, for attitudes towards life, and for the inspiration of the arts" (p. 9). Remarkably, Henson developed the first theoretical formulation in our history of the just learning society. For him, adult education offered by the Division was intervening in pre-existing learning domains (work, state, civil society) and that the learning process within these domains was not necessarily as deep, broad, or critical as it could be.

Like the formulators of the Special report (Special Committee on Education for Reconstruction, 1943) and the study-action plan, Henson (1946) did not focus primarily on the needs of the individual. Rather, he imaginatively drew the circle around the system and the lifeworld. Addressing the system domains of economy and polity, Henson argued that Nova Scotia's "economic circumstances call for more all-round intelligence and vocational skill on the part of the average citizen; for more alertness as to scientific progress, government policies, and business organizations, and as to what is going on elsewhere in our markets and competitive producing areas" (p. 11). This simple formulation anticipated the "learning economy" and "learning society" discourse of the late twentieth century information age. Turning to civil society, Henson insisted that "all the agencies of daily life which disseminate information, ideas and opinions, or teach skills, or give inspiration enter into the general framework of adult education" (p. 19). This included "institutions and activities" (p. 19) normally thought of as education, as well as the press, radio, film, churches, political organization, trade unions, social clubs, and enlightened conversation groups. In contemporary discourse, Henson understood well the role of voluntary associations and social movements as learning sites. He also grasped the central role played by media in the public sphere.

Henson's argument, still pertinent today, was that "educational planning" had to "concentrate on multiplying the means and the efficiency of continuing self-education of leaders and the average citizen" (p. 20). Education, then, within this holistic learning society framework, was an intentional intervention into pre-constituted learning domains whose purpose was to foster and a more just and self-conscious learning process. Henson was well aware that both the system and lifeworld domains contained miseducative tendencies and that the actually existing functioning domains excluded some and rewarded others (he was particularly concerned about the oppression and exclusion of Black Nova Scotians from the circle of the learning society). Henson believed that "democratic people want the means of self-education and help in making the best use of them. The task of educational leadership is to supply those means and that help, and to stimulate the individual and the group to realize their practical possibilities" (p. 23). Thus, civil society was the appropriate unit for continued education. Henson provided strenuous arguments for government interest in and provision for the continued education of young people who reach the age of citizenship and for men and women of all ages to have the best means of thinking and informing themselves about public affairs. In a sense, Henson's strong emphasis on the public sphere and active citizenship is a message almost forgotten by today's politicians. Henson grappled with the question of how, and to what extent, governments could stimulate and support the post-school learning activities of individuals, local groups, communities, and voluntary bodies of wide scope.

With this vision as guide, Henson (and field staff such as the remarkable Elizabeth Murray) created numerous projects. The Division created a folks school movement, patterned after the Danish model which sought to enlighten the rural population to farming, cultural, and broader social issues. These two-week residential schools, flourishing from 1948 to 1960, were intended to produce a new rural culture, one based on volunteer activity, projects benefiting entire communities, development of leadership from the rank and file community members, and civic awareness among the citizenry. Under Elizabeth Murray's inspired leadership, music (drawing on the folk songs collected by Helen Creighton [Harris, 1998; see McKay, 1994], the School of Community Arts and the Nova Scotia Festival of the Arts were established. Henson also encouraged popular artistic expression in rural communities, and initiated travelling art shows, which went from town to town, displaying the art work of ordinary people. In Ontario, Arthur Lismer, famed Group of Seven artist, held classes for unemployed workers in the 1930s and was a great supporter of the CAAE.

Henson also initiated historically important work among the African Nova Scotian community. He became a friend and colleague of Dr. William Oliver, a leading Black Baptist clergyman and social activist.

With Oliver, Henson and the work of the Division were readily invited into the Black community. Henson believed that the Blacks had been socially isolated and had suffered shamefully from the burden of racism and prejudice by the dominant white society. Oliver and Henson set about addressing this historical wrong by working with communities to set up educational and employment activities, social betterment schemes, and by organizing conferences and meetings leading to community improvement. Henson was a central figure in establishing a new school and teacherage in the community of New Road (North Preston). His leadership in no small way led to improvements in education and housing for many Black communities (Shand, 1961).

In 1956, Henson left the Division to take a position as director of the Institute for Public Affairs, located on the Dalhousie University campus. He summed up his earlier work with the Division. "It has been a hard, uphill, and often bitter struggle to secure and to keep support from a government, the majority of whose members until lately did not see the need or particularly believe it important. It is part of the evidence or facts for this purpose that at least three times I was able either to get action or retain support through offers from elsewhere which came at the right moment and once through offering my resignation if the work was not to be sufficiently supported" (Institute of Public Affairs, 1954-7).

Henson's educational philosophy, in sum, envisioned a mutually beneficial relationship between the state and civil society. His focus was giving the people the means to get the best from the state without state dominance or interference. To lessen the domination of the state and its corporate elites over the people, this took the form of volunteer agency and local leadership drawn from the people. Together, these volunteer leaders and the rank and file would change the inert mass into a conscious group of active citizens engaged in true democracy. This participatory form of democracy was meant to empower citizens to deal with local issues such as housing, unemployment, educational opportunity, and the arts as well as the broader social, political, and economic issues of the nation. Henson's ten-year tenure as Director of the Adult Education Division had helped to establish, even if tentatively, this interplay of state (governing systems) and a vibrant civil society.

These two projects—Henson and Thomson—contrast dramatically with the Newfoundland government's inability (or unwillingness) from the 1930s to the 1950s to imagine a coherent development plan for its people (services tended to be fragmented and field workers unreliable). McManus (2000)'s study of the tragic figure of Florence O'Neill (the first Canadian to receive a doctorate in adult education in 1944 from Columbia) documents both the difficulties this passionate educator had as a women and as one whose vision of adult education flowed in the community development stream (articulated by Columbia University professors like Edmund deS Brunner [1942]). Often treated badly and underpaid for her work, O'Neill tried to cut her way through the tangle of picky bureaucratic manoeuvres by her superiors. While at Columbia, she had devised a "plan" for the development of rural outport communities. But this plan ran aground when the government of Newfoundland shifted any commitment and sustained effort to holistically develop rural outports. Indeed, the government actually preferred adult education served up to individuals. By 1958—Florence had been Director of Adult Education from 1949 to 1958—Newfoundland educational policy shifted from adult education to preparing students for K-11 training. As well, the emergence of Memorial University's Extension Division in the 1950s siphoned off energy and ended the government's hesitant interest in adult education. O'Neill was shuffled off to a basement, more or less alone, overseeing leadership training.

Adult Education in a Chilly Climate: The Cold War Era

Since World War I, radical adult educators had been accused of being "communists" in order to undermine their educational and political projects and support the status quo. At the height of the Depression, the same accusations surfaced. In his first month in The Pas, Harry Avison was tugged pell-mell into the centre of national political controversy. Duplessis enacted the infamous Quebec Padlock Act against Quebec "communists" in 1938. In early January, the Quebec police raided the headquarters of the Canadian Labour Circle, and in late January, they had padlocked the Montreal Ukrainian Labour Farm Temple association after closing an alleged communist school on St. Lawrence Boulevard attended by fifty pupils (*Northern Mail*, January 27, 1938). Annie Buller, one of Canada's pioneering communists and seasoned political educators, spoke in a jittery voice in The Pas in early January to a general audience on "The War Danger" and to the ULFTA on the "The Road Ahead for the People of Manitoba."

The ULFTA protested Duplessis' Padlock Act and resolved that "Canada cease shipping nickel to Japan" (ibid.). In the midst of this controversy, radio and Associated Press reports hinted darkly that the "real purpose" of Harry Avison was to foment socialist revolution. The suspicion that he was a "communist" can be linked in part to his association with the ULFTA as well as his efforts to build a co-operative community. But it was Avison's work with youth that would touch a particularly sensitive nerve among some The Pas residents. A *Northern Mail* editorial (May 3, 1938) observed that Avison was receiving adverse comments, even though he had stimulated youth interest in recreational movements and citizenship. Right-wing anti-communists in The Pas really believed that when the Avisons encouraged youth to attend the Canadian Youth Conference national and provincial meetings that he was a red pied piper leading their children to their doom.

Although the Soviet Union was Canada's ally during World War II, the anti-communist theme was visibly present, as we have seen, in the trade unions, adult education movements, and political landscape. It is likely, however, that the mounting suspicion that Watson Thomson was not a trustworthy CCF government appointee was intensified when Igor Gouzenko, a cipher clerk with the Soviet Embassy, fled with one hundred or so files in hand. These files allegedly contained damning materials, claiming that some Canadians in government or political party positions, were disloyal and, in fact, spies for the Soviet Union. If the flame of anti-communism had been a mere flicker before this enormous event, it was now fanned into a bonfire. McCarthyism had arrived in Canada. Prime Minister Mackenzie King appointed on behalf of the government of Canada Supreme Court of Canada, Justice Robert Tascherau and Justice Roy Kellock. They were commissioned to "investigate the facts relating to the circumstances surrounding the communication by public officials and other persons in positions of trust, to agents of a foreign power." Popularly known as the Kellock-Tascherau Commission, it was commissioned on February 5, 1946 (Whitaker and Hewitt [2003] provide the historical context in their book *Canada and the Cold War*).

Twelve persons were charged with espionage, including Fred Rose, the Labour Progressive Party MLA. The Commission focused some special attention on the NFB. By the time of the interrogations, John Grierson had left his position as director. With tensions heightened, even to hysterical heights, the Commission could not pin the label "communist" on Grierson, whose name had been found in a Soviet Colonel's journal. One of Grierson's tasks was to make documentary films supporting Canada's war efforts. Now, they were scrutinized minutely for intimations of support for the Soviet Union. But the NFB under Grierson's charismatic direction had attracted a nest of left-wing and radical youth with bohemian dress and lifestyles. Many of them came under suspicion; some had their careers ruined. The red scare caused widespread anxiety and insecurity. The concern for finding perpetrators of internal subversion was easily stretched to include any persons whose views were critical of the economic, political, and cultural order. The RCMP busied itself investigating social clubs, left-wing groups, and rallies to tease out suspects. Men and women were arrested, and, under the *War Measures Act*, were held without charge and denied access to family.

Winston Churchill had announced in his historic speech delivered in Fulton, Missouri, on March 5, 1946, that an "iron curtain" had descended on the world. In a lesser, but still important, sense the descent of the iron curtain meant that dissent was forbidden and public spheres were closed off to authentic communicative action and open deliberation. Everything that the educational radicals had struggled so hard for had been stopped in its tracks. Thomson was fired, Wren muscled out of the WEA by CCF activists, and Grierson under suspicion (and thus the NFB's project of mobilizing community discussion and action). Stan Rands, Thomson's friend and director of the University of Manitoba Adult Education Office, was hounded out of his position in the spring of 1945 by the Manitoba Royal Commission on Adult Education, led by Harold Innis of the University of Toronto. All were accused of being propagandists and not objective educators. In 1949, the *Financial Post* accused the NFB of being a "leftist propaganda machine" infested with reds that needed surveillance and routing out. Thus, the icy finger of the red scare spread mistrust, fear, and anxiety throughout the culture. For adult educators, the cultural ethos was so corrupted, social capital so utterly depleted, that fostering any kind of open deliberation on urgent themes and issues facing Canadians became increasingly difficult, even treacherous, in the late 1940s and well into the 1950s.

By 1950, those who were searching for "leftists and their propaganda" under every bed and in every crevice of Canadian culture and political life, targeted the CBC and CAAE's Farm Radio and Citizens' Forums. A "Confidential Report," dated May 15, 1950, found its way on to the desk of J. Roby Kidd, then acting director of the CAAE. This group, which remained anonymous, had probably hired some persons to survey the forums and observe the live audience participation (only the Citizens' Forum was recorded in Toronto before a live audience). This report, then, appears to have been circulated to various business leaders, some of whom may have been contributors to the Association. Kidd thought the charges "seriously reflected on the intelligence and integrity of every member of the staff, executive and National Council" (Kidd, 1950a). Kidd's response, detailed and revealing, countered the Reports' accusations, point by point. He was alarmed that this Report had circulated on the underground, the names were not known—which made it difficult to know just how widespread these sentiments were.

Kidd (1950a) began his defence by arguing that the two national forums provided an "an opportunity for thousands of Canadians to listen to significant points of view regarding important national problems and to study and discuss their implications. Not only is there an opportunity for all significant points of view to find expression, a great deal of time and energy is spent to ensure that all such points of view are given an adequate presentation." The forums were the joint project of the CAAE, the CBC, and the Canadian Farm Association. The forums were governed by a National Council of prominent and respected Canadians. Topics for the Farm Forum were solicited from the listening groups across the country. The actual choice of speakers was made through extensive consultation with various persons and organizations. Proceeding carefully, Kidd stated that when a topic affected the government (a broadcast on income tax, for instance), government persons contributed. Similarly, if the theme under scrutiny affected business, a business representative was chosen. Kidd argued convincingly that those responsible for the forums knew they had to be perceived to be non-partisan. The "best argument" had to emerge from free and non-coerced communicative action among various chosen spokespersons articulating particular positions. Kidd (1950a) thought that a "great network of private individuals, local autonomous groups, provincial and national organizations, universities and departments of education are all collaborating in these projects of study and discussion. All are included in the determination of policy and the selection of topics. A series of regional and national conferences each year provide the opportunity for a regular review of all activities."

This scrupulous preparation of the broadcasts did not impress the right-wing businessmen behind the "Confidential Report." The forums were stirring up trouble on matters that might better be left alone. The CAAE's critics wanted to insulate Canadians from free interchange of ideas. Kidd identified five specific charges against the CAAE. The first—that the CBC was using the CAAE as a propaganda tool was easily dismissed through careful explanation of funding arrangements and how topics and speakers were actually selected. The second charge—that the CAAE and CBC conspired to attack "free enterprise" and successful businessmen—Kidd deemed "exceedingly serious." He thought this attack reflected on the intelligence and integrity of Corbett, the staff of the CAAE as well as several universities, departments of education, and national and provincial organizations. Kidd reminded the author of the Report that eight business persons had just been elected to the national council, and seven new members from business organizations elected to its Executive, including James Muir, president of the Royal Bank of Canada. Kidd observed that of 150 speakers on 44 broadcasts, only 7 speakers had criticized business. In fact, Kidd pointed out that some listeners charged that "labour" or "progressive" views were not being given a fair hearing.

The third charge of skewed selection of speakers got to the root of the matter. The Report complained that business' voice was omitted from a number of forums. Kidd countered with precise analysis of specific broadcasts. Business voice had been excluded from the topic, "Racial and religious intolerance," because, unlike the Canadian Labour Congress (who had a speaker), business did not have any organized committee for "combatting racial discrimination." If they had, they would have been invited. In fact, one speaker actually accused business of playing ethnic groups off against each other to lower wages and increase profits. This did not make the Report's author and adherents happy at all. The prickly topic, "Should industry provide employee pensions and insurance?" did not include a speaker from industrial management. Kidd stated that the CAAE had tried for one month to secure one, but business and industry in the Toronto, Hamilton, and St. Catharines area could not secure one. It was difficult, Kidd thought, to secure strong speakers representing business interests.

The Report accused the CAAE of deliberately organizing the panels with left-wing speakers. This wasn't actually the case, but many Canadians in this period were left-wing in sensibility and outlook. The grassroots movements did fear that Canada would move into the postwar era with governing elites and business interests returning to the old ways of dominating the society without much input from below. The "Confidential Report" reveals that this particular group did not believe that any criticism ought to be made of business practices or policies. If they thought that any critique of business practices could simply be labelled as left-wing propaganda, then some of the speakers were, indeed, left-wing. Business leaders like J. W. McConnell (1950), president of the *Montreal Star,* wanted the CAAE to stay clear of topics pertaining to politics and economics. He insisted that the CAAE could "not hold any position on political and economic matters"—they could not have a pre-determined ideology they were pushing. But as Watson Thomson and the educational radicals had articulated in 1943 and 1944, the CAAE had to take a stand on certain principles. Business, it seemed, feared that the crystal-lized opinion would challenge the way workers were treated and business conducted. They wanted to be insulated from criticism.

At the opening of Canada's "conservative decade" Kidd (1950b) had written: "Adult education in Canada could certainly not be considered very radical or very reaction, or even vary daring" (p. 23). This is a startling and revealing comment: the Canadian adult learning and education history is daring and radical. Kidd, it seems, was drawing his own iron curtain on adult education's radical past in order to survive in the Cold War ethos of the 1950s and re-fashion adult education as a professional practice. The Joint Planning Commission was Kidd's keystone response to the domesticated period into which he was emerging as a major leader. He and his staff developed co-operative relationships with voluntary organizations and government agencies active in some form of adult education. He laboured diligently and stealthily to maintain civil society's attention to common themes for deliberation. Kidd also kept the CAAE's commitment to the Farm and Citizens' Forums alive through this trying period. Kidd was certainly proving that he was an adept organization man: he could move through this "tangled multiplicity" (Thomas, 2001, p. 163) of voluntary organizations knowing just the right graceful touch to be non-threatening and gain support for the financially threadbare CAAE. Kidd's orientation was to awaken sensibility to individual learning pathways within large organizations. He was also laying the groundwork for the professionalization of the field (which required carving out a space within the university to create a base for this project). He would go on to play a major role in building OISE's Department of Adult Education in the late 1960s, and initiate the creation of the International Council of Adult Education in the mid-1970s.

The chilly atmosphere of the first phase of the Cold War did not stop the Saskatchewan government from launching an innovative experiment in participatory democracy in its third term in office. By 1952, the CCF had completed the tasks set out in its manifesto of 1944. Eight years of CCF governance had provided universal health care, auto insurance, farm security legislation, expanding transportation, education, and welfare services. But times were changing. Farms were mechanizing, consolidating and rural areas were de-populating as people moved into the urban cities of Saskatoon and Regina. The study of rural problems seemed urgent. In fact, the influential Saskatchewan Farmers Union (SFU) had requested that the government initiate a royal commission of investigation into rural life and problems. By the end of 1952, the CCF realized it had exhausted its urgent postwar political agenda and needed new ideas. The proposal for a commission was passed by the legislature unanimously in March 1952.

The government turned to W. B. ("Bill") Baker to head the Royal Commission on Agriculture and Rural Life. Bill Baker, born in 1919, had studied agriculture at the University of Saskatchewan, achieving his BSA in 1944. After a stint working as Dr. L. E. Kirk's assistant in the School of Agriculture, he became its director in 1947. An ardent promoter of the applied social sciences, Baker taught rural sociology for Emmanuel Theological College to theology students who were to work in rural areas. He was a radical proponent of participatory democracy. Baker and his staff used the methods that had been initiated by Watson Thomson in the mid-1940s. William Harding, the secretary of the Royal Commission, had worked closely with Thomson as his Study-Action director. Harding served as a bridge between the Study-Action projects and Citizen Conference structures of the 1940s and the Royal Commission's deliberative learning processes (Welton, 1981).

Baker selected his four commissioners from the four main blocs of constituencies: the SFU, the Saskatchewan Wheat Pool, the Co-operative movement, and Women. After a three month period of study (unheard of in the history of commissions), Baker knew that, given the scope of this project, he had to move beyond the traditional way of proceeding. Baker created a community forum structure: these forums would be held in communities all across Saskatchewan. They would use the small group form of learning, with reports to plenary, collective clarification, then returning to small groups to arrive at consensus on community concerns. The human relations dimension of decision-making was accentuated. By early 1953, ninety-five community forums had been held in all regions, with average attendance of eighty-six for a total of over eight thousand. Communities were also invited to submit briefs and sponsor "hearings" in their own communities (after seeding in 1953, fifty-seven were held, with 1,700 people in attendance).

The Commission also tapped into formal, organized sectors of Saskatchewan society: government, universities, professionals, co-operatives, agriculture, women, youth, business and commerce, health and welfare, education, religion, politics, and labour. Representations from over two hundred organizations attended two-day conferences, using the familiar methods used in the community forums. Briefs were also invited after the conferences were over. Provincial hearings were held during October 1953 over six days in Regina and five in Saskatoon as well as three days for agencies of the government to probe more deeply into the range of themes emerging from deliberative learning processes. Any gaps that remained required going directly to rural people for interviews and, in some cases, intensive social survey use. Baker wanted to move from "establishing the commission" to "communicate-study-act" by returning the core findings to the communities for their further reflection and input. But the government had run out of patience with Baker. The final report was a massive opus: it included fourteen separate reports, two hundred twenty-five recommendations totalling three thousand pages. At the heart of all the recommendations lay the cry of the community's heart: reduce our insecurity. Baker's inspiration and personal effort had engaged thousands of Saskatchewan citizens in an exemplary model of the Commission as social learning process. "For Bill Baker," Harding (1991) observes, "at least, probably the process of participatory democracy that he was attempting to build into the body politic was as important, even more important, than the recommendations for immediate action" (p. 61).

But William Harding (1991) thinks that nobody foresaw the extent of the mechanization of agriculture and rapid urbanization that would erode the co-operative and participatory ethos of Saskatchewan over the next decades. From 1957 until his untimely death in 1968, Bill Baker directed the Centre for Community Studies, which had been created as a way of continuing the assessment of social and economic changes in rural areas after the Royal Commission had ended its hearings. Baker had his big opportunity to put his applied social science vision into effect. The Centre was to have three central secretariats: technical to conduct careful statistical research; training of community leaders; and consultation to mediate social science knowledge to communities to enable problem-solving with a solid grounding. Baker, it seems, was initiating a movement to professionalize the process of working with community development programs.

Howard Baker (1991)'s reflections on the Centre reveal that Bill Baker and his Centre ran into considerable troubles. His relationship with the University of Saskatchewan was less than ideal. The University was miffed that it hadn't been properly consulted regarding the creation of an independent centre jointly sponsored by the university and provincial government, with an independent board. Some professors were also suspicious about the Centre's inter-disciplinary approach to their work. The opposition Liberal Party attacked the Centre for being the propaganda arm for the CCF (with social science being merely a code word for socialism). The Liberals had no time whatsoever for intellectual endeavours such as the Centre or any idea what a participatory democracy might look like. Everywhere Baker turned, he was under criticism, whether the media, the government, or his own staff (some thought he was too aggressive; others a poor administrator). When the Liberals took power, they cancelled its budget. Baker may well have been ahead of his time. He was offered financial support from an Ottawa body, but it was too late. Baker died at age forty-eight.

References

Adams, S. (2009). Our activist past: Nora Bateson, champion of regional libraries. *Partnership: the Canadian Journal of Library and Information Practice and Research*, 4(1).

Armstrong, D. P. (1968). Corbett's house: The origins of the Canadian association for adult education and its development during the directorship of E. A. Corbett. Unpublished M.A. thesis, University of Toronto.

Avison, H. (n.d). Harry Avison Papers. Public Archives of Canada. vol. 4, file 21.

Avison, H. (1944). Letter to E. A. Corbett, February 13. Harry Avison Papers. Public Archives of Ontario, vol. 40, file 24.

Avison, H. (1957). Letter to E. A. Corbett, November 2. CAAE Papers, Archives of Ontario.

Baker, H. R. (1991). The centre for community studies. In H. R. Baker, J. A. Draper, & B. Fairbairn (Eds.). *Dignity and growth: Citizen participation in social change.* Calgary (AB): Detselig Press.

Baker, W. B. (1957). Centre for community studies: Preliminary statement of organization and function. Presidential Papers, B Saskatoon (SK): University of Saskatchewan.

Brunner, E. (1942). *Community organization and adult education.* Chapel Hill (NC): University of North Carolina Press.

Cameron, D. C. (c. 1936-38). Adult education and the challenge of youth. Radio script. Donald Cameron Papers. Edmonton(AB): University of Alberta Archives.

Coady, M. (1932). Letter to C. J. Tompkins, May 7. St. Francis Xavier University Archives. Extension Papers. Personal correspondence.

Coady, M. (1935). Foreword. *How St. FX University educates for action.* New York: Co-operative League of the USA,

Coady, M. (1938). Letter to S. O. Bland, November 29. St. Francis Xavier University Archives. Extension Papers. Personal correspondence.

Coady, M. (1939). *Masters of their own destiny.* New York: Harpers and Row.

"Confidential Report: Canadian Association of Adult Education" (May 15, 1950). In J. Roby Kidd Papers, Ontario Provincial Archives.

Corbett, E. A. (1936). Annual Report, CAAE. CAAE Papers. Archives of Ontario.

Corbett, E. A. (October 5, 1938). *The Edmonton Journal.*

Corbett, E. A. (1939). The Canadians march. *Adult learning*, September-October.

Corbett, E.A. (1941). CAAE Annual Report, Archives of Ontario.

Corbett, E.A. (1943). CAAE Director's Report. CAAE Papers, Archives of Ontario.

Creighton, D. (1976). *The forked road.* Toronto: McClelland and Stewart.

Delores, Sister Francis. (1943). Address to the Sisters: The apostolate of education through good books, libraries and adult educators. *National Catholic Missionary Exhibition.* Toronto-Oct 15-18. MSVU Archives, Halifax, Sister Francis Dolores, Envelopes 1943.

Department of Adult Education. (1941-2). *Annual Report*, Winnipeg (MB): University of Manitoba Archives.

Dunlop, W. J. (1936). The movement in other countries: Canada. *Journal of Adult Education,* VIII, June.

Education for reconstruction. (1943). *Christian social action,* September-October.

English, L. (2011). Adult education on the Newfoundland coast: Adventure and opportunity for women in the 1930s and 1940s. *Newfoundland and Labrador Studies*, 26, 25–54.

Faris, R. (1975). *The passionate educators: Voluntary associations and the struggle for control of adult education in Canada, 1919–52.* Toronto: P. Martin.

Forsey, E. (1943). In my opinion. *Food for thought,* October.

Friesen, G. (1994). Adult education and union education: Aspects of English Canadian cultural history in the 20th century. *Labour/Le Travail*, 34, Autumn.

Granatstein, J. L. (1975). *Canada's war: The politics of the Mackenize King government.* Toronto: Oxford University Press.

Gray, D. (1973). *Movies for the people: The story of the NFB's unique distribution system.* Ottawa: NFB.

Grierson, J. (1944). Searchlight on democracy. *Food for thought,* April.

Grierson, J. (1966). Education for the new order. In F. Hardy (Ed). *Grierson on documentary.* Berkeley: University of California Press.

Harding, W. H. (1991). The Royal Commission on Agriculture and Rural Life. In H. R. Baker, J. A Draper, & B. Fairbairn (Eds.). *Dignity and growth: Citizen participation in social change.* Calgary (AB): Detselig Press.

Harris, C. (1998). *Sense of Themselves: Elizabeth Murray's leadership in school and community.* Halifax (NS): Fernwood Publishers.

Henson, G. (1946). Provincial support of adult education in Nova Scotia: A report by Guy Henson. Halifax (NS): King's Printer.

Institute of Public Affairs. (1954–57). Institute of Public Affairs Papers. Halifax (NS): Dalhousie University Archives

Kidd, J. R. (1950a). "The CAAE National Farm Radio Forum and the National Citizens' Forum." In J. Roby Kidd Papers, Ontario Provincial Archives.

Kidd, J. R. (1950b). *Adult education in Canada.* Toronto: CAAE.

Lotz, J. & Welton, M. (1987). "Knowledge for the people": The origins and development of the Antigonish Movement. In M. Welton. (ed.). *Knowledge for the people: The struggle for adult learning in English-speaking Canada, 1828–1973.* Toronto: OISE Press.

Lotz, J. & Welton, M. (1997). *Father Jimmy: Life and times of Jimmy Tompkins.* Sydney (NS): Breton Books.

McConnell, J. W. (1950). Letter to J. Roby Kidd, June 8. In J. Roby Kidd Papers. Ontario Provincial Archives.

McKay, I. (1994). *The quest of the folk: Antimodernism and cultural selection in twentieth-century Nova Scotia.* Montreal/Kingston: McGill-Queen's University Press.

McManus, K. (2000). Florence O'Neill, a Newfoundland adult educator: Alone in the wilderness. Unpublished Ph.D, Department of Educational Studies, UBC.

Memorandum on workers' education for local chartered unions. (c. 1943–1944). In my possession.

Minutes of the Planning Committee, July 13, 1943, Canadian Association for Adult Education Papers, D-I, Box 1, Adult Education Conferences, 1938-1967.

Morison, C. K. (1952). Helen Gordon Stewart. In Harriet Rouillard (ed.). *Pioneers of adult education in Canada.* Toronto: Thomas Nelson.

Munro, H. (1938). Adult education in Canada's national life: *Adult Learning,* March.

Neale, R. (1998). *Brotherhood economics: Women and co-operatives in Nova Scotia.* Sydney (NS): UCCB Press.

Peacock, F. (1943). In my opinion. *Food for thought,* October.

Pollard, J. (1987). Propaganda for democracy: John Grierson and adult education during the second world war. In M. Welton (Ed.). *Knowledge for the people: The struggle for adult learning in English-speaking Canada, 1828–1973* (pp. 129–50). Toronto: OISE Press.

Rands, S. (1942). Letter to Sidney Smith, May 8. Sidney Smith Papers, box 36, file 1.

Rands, S. (1946). Film forums and community action. *Film Forum Review,* Fall.

Report of the proceedings of a Special Programme Committee of the CAAE. (1942-43). Harry Avison Papers, vol. 5, file 25, Public Archives of Canada.

"Report to the Executive of the CAAE on the progress of the Citizens' Forum, 1943-1944." Canadian Association of Adult Education, B-I, Box 3, Citizens' Forum Records, Archives of Ontario.

Sandiford, P. (1935). *Adult education in Canada: A survey.* Toronto: Toronto University Press.

Souchotte, S. (1987). Dramatizing the great issues: workers' theatre in the thirties. In M. Welton. (Ed). *Knowledge for the people: The struggle for adult learning in English-speaking Canada, 1828–1973* (pp. 112–28). Toronto: OISE Press.

Smith, S. (1943). The President's address. *Food for thought,* June.

Study bulletins (1943-66). CAAE Papers, B-I, box 6, Citizens' Forum administration, Archives of Ontario.

Thomas, A. (2001). Roby Kidd—Intellectual voyager. In P. Jarvis (Ed.). *Twentieth century thinkers in adult and continuing education* (second edition). London: Kogan Page.

Thomas, L. (Ed.). (1982). *The making of a socialist: The recollections of T.C. Douglas.* Edmonton (AB): University of Alberta Press.

Thomson, W. (1943a). Letter to Sidney Smith, December 16. Sidney Smith Papers, box 61, file 6, University of Manitoba Archives.

Thomson, W. (1943b). Adult education and the crisis of democracy. *Public Affairs,* Spring.

Thomson, W. (1943c). The London Conference. *Food for thought,* June,

Thomson, W. (1944) *Adult education theory and policy.* William M. Harding papers (in author's possession).

Thomson, W. (1945a). Watson Thomson to Roslyn Road, February 27, 1945. Roslyn Road Papers (in my possession).

Thomson, W. (1945b). Adult Education Division Monthly Newsletter 1. April 2, 1945. William M. Harding Papers (in my possession).

Tompkins, J. (1935). Letter to Moses M. Coady. June 14. RG 30-2/1/4097. St. Frances Xavier University Archives, Antigonish, NS.

University Extension Programmes and Budgets (no author). (1937). Sidney Smith Papers, University of Manitoba Archives, Winnipeg, box 10, file 1.

Welton, M. (1981). Interview with William Harding, Regina, Saskatchewan.

Welton, M. (1983). "To be and build the glorious world": The educational thought and practice of Watson Thomson, 1899–1946. Unpublished Ph.D dissertation. Department of Educational Foundations, UBC.

Welton, M. (1986). "An authentic instrument of the democratic process": The intellectual origins of the Canadian Citizens' Forum. *Studies in the Education of Adults,* 18(1), 35–49.

Welton, M. (1987). A most insistent demand: The Pas experiment in community education, 1938–1940. *Canadian Journal for the Study of Adult Education,* 1(2), 1–22.

Welton, M. & Lecky, J. (1997). Volunteerism as the seedbed of democracy: The educational thought and practice of Guy Henson of Nova Scotia. *Studies in the Education of Adults,* 29(1), 25–38.

Welton, M. (2001). *Little Mosie from the Margaree: A biography of Michael Moses Coady.* Toronto: Thompson Educational Publishing.

Welton, M. (2003). Decoding Coady: *Masters of their own destiny* under critical scrutiny. *Studies in Continuing Education,* 23(1), 75–92.

Welton, M. (2006). Intimations of a just learning society: From the United Farmers of Alberta to Henson's provincial plan in Nova Scotia. In T. Fenwick, T. Nesbit & B. Spencer. (Eds.). *Contexts of adult education: Canadian perspectives.* Toronto: Thompson Educational Publishing.

Whitaker, R. (1977). Images of the state. In L. Panitch (Ed.). *The Canadian state: Political economy and political power.* Toronto: University of Toronto Press.

Whitaker, R. & Hewitt, S. (2003). Canada and the cold war. Toronto: James Lorimer and Company.

Wolfe, A. (1977). *The limits of legitimacy: Political contradictions of contemporary capitalism.* New York: The Free Press.

Wolfe, A. (1977). *The limits of legitimacy: Political contradictions of contemporary capitalism.* New York: The Free Press.

Wren, D. (1945). Typescript speech. Vancouver file. Drummond Wren Papers, Public Archives of Ontario.

Vlastos, G. (1943*). Education for morale.* Food for thought, *November.*

Young, W. (1978). "Making the truth graphic": The Canadian government's Home Front Information structure and programmes during World War II. Unpublished Ph.D dissertation, University of BC.

Zinman, R. (1986). Some education is better than none at all: The International Ladies' Garment Workers' Union of Montreal, 1936–1940. *CASAE History Bulletin.*

6

Adult Learning Under Siege in A Disorded World (1960-2012)

The great learning struggles of the Canadian people in civil society and various social movements from the onset of the Great Depression into the Cold War chilliness of the 1950s had led to a compromise: the welfare state. The agony and suffering of Canadians had been articulated in numerous study clubs, union and community halls, conferences, and stirring debates in the public sphere. The capitalist state in Canada and other liberal democracies, fearing collapse into another Depression and capture of the state by socialist parties, had to intervene in the lives of Canadians through the provision of various welfare goods. This Keynesian-solution resonated with the commitments of the participatory democrats who wanted to live in a society committed to the collective well-being of its citizenry. The emergence of the liberal social welfare state, however, was a mixed blessing. It provided Family Allowances in 1945, Old Age Security in 1951, Unemployment Insurance in 1956, Canadian and Quebec Pension Plan in 1965, Medicare in 1966, and the Guaranteed Annual Income Supplement (1967). But the social welfare-state created a new professional managerial class to regulate and manage various domains of the lifeworld.

From 1945 until the early 1970s a "highly encompassing liberal-democratic welfare state consensus" (Offe, 1985, p. 821) prevailed in Western Europe and North America. The catchwords of this political paradigm was economic growth, distribution, and security. Organized labour bought into this system in exchange for reasonable social security and elite management of the system. The sociological assumption underlying this tacit contract was that privatized "family, work, and consumption-centred patterns would absorb the energies and aspirations of most people, and that participation in and conflict over public policy would for that reason be of no more than marginal significance in the lives of most citizens" (Offe, 1985, p. 823). The energies of the political elite were directed to establish the social security conditions to enhance the dynamism of the political-economic system. In this period, the dominant collective actors were, one might say, created by the structural transformation of the capitalist system itself. Highly specialized "interest organizations and political parties" (Offe, 1985, p. 824) were the dominant collective actors of the time. Trade unions watched over their workers and represented their interests in institutionalized collective bargaining processes, and political parties acted as brokers in the limited sphere of electoral politics. Civic culture de-emphasized political participation. The emancipatory vision (economic democracy, active citizenship) so dear to the Canadian educational radicals' hearts was rendered "virtually insignificant" (Offe, 1985, p. 824) as the values of social mobility, private life, consumerism, authority, and order ruled the day.

The "organization man" became the dominant metaphor for the (middle-class) male, and "Rosie the Riveter," tossing her overalls aside, was transformed into cheery homemaker (even though more women would enter the labour force in the decades following World War II). But for this system to work, political elites had to insure that institutional spheres such as the family, work, science, and technology remained depoliticized. Too much democracy simply threatened the system. The division between the personal and the political had to be zealously maintained—the central animus of American neo-conservative politics (Huntington, 1968). But the welfare state had serious contradictions. This new form of society did provide much needed medical or unemployment security, but it could not provide the various, increasingly self-interested actors, with a collective identity. The Liberal party, coming to power under Lester B. Pearson in 1963, also recognized that initiating social welfare legislation did not begin to alleviate poverty in various parts of the country. In 1965, they declared a "war on poverty": the Liberal party under Pearson and Trudeau seemed to embrace the ideals of creating a just and participatory society. But they would determine what that meant and how the state could accomplish this. Our analysis of the Challenge for Change/Société Nouvelle programs launched in 1967 will provide a case study of the state's role in community development.

The social welfare state only met limited human needs and the enduring struggle for recognition. The 1960s themselves were a time of considerable rebellion and upheaval in Canadian and global society. Palmer (2009), claims that: "The country's long-standing self-image of itself as a settler dominion, an empire of the north, a British colony that marched progressively and valiantly to its particular version of nationhood, was dealt a series of decisive blows in this critical decade" (pp. 4-5). The struggles of the American civil rights movement spilled into Canada, helping to provoke anti-racist forms of struggle amongst African-Nova Scotians and indigenous peoples. "Black power" and "Red power" were added to the Canadian vocabulary of protest. Many harsh critiques of Canadian society appeared during this period from indigenous writers such as Harold Cardinal (*The Unjust Society,* 1969) and Harold Adams (*Prison of Grass: Canada from the Native Point of View,* 1975). These works signalled an intensely focused desire on the part of Native people to control their own education. Their hostility to Jean Chretien's White Paper of 1969, which had recommended the abolition of the reserve system, indicated that they had not forgotten the old strategies of the Canadian state. In Quebec, Pierre Vallières' vicious polemic, *White Niggers of America* (1968) shocked Anglo-Canadians who never imagined any Quebecer thought this way. Many English-Canadians were unaware of the separatist and radical fringe movements stirring in Quebec political backrooms, universities, and dingy streets of urban Montreal. Canadians were even more shocked when tanks appeared in the streets of Montreal in October 1970. Protest had moved out of cafés into the streets, provoking the state into abrogating citizens' rights under the *War Measures Act.* The liberal social welfare state, many thought, had revealed its true colours.

Throughout the 1960s, the US had been wracked by racial and civic strife as the Vietnam War devastated the lives of millions in south-east Asia and split American society into warring camps. On the global front, in June 1967 Israel occupied the Palestinian territory of the West Bank, East Jerusalem, and Gaza (the occupation still continues), demoralized the Arab world, and set the stage for endemic conflict in the Middle East. The Soviet Union invaded Czechoslovakia in 1968. The sounds of protest resounded throughout the major cities of Europe and North America from Paris to New York to San Francisco. With the Vietnam War casting its dark shadows over the United States and Canada, Canadian campuses began to see small groups of students carrying strange signs supporting SUPA (The Student Union for Peace Action) parading around, provoking curiosity and some debate. By the late 1960s in numerous Canadian universities, students gathered together in public spaces, inviting experts on global affairs and student spokespersons to address the students. The "teach-in" was born. These events were often stormy and tense. The origin of a male-led "New Left," which set itself against the dogmatisms of the old Communist left, introduced critical theoretical vocabularies into the formal settings of university classrooms. But their own male-centred analyses precipitated, in part, the emergence of the woman's liberation movement of the late 1960s. Women rebelled against their marginalization in protest movements. They also began to awaken to their own forms of oppression, propelled by the early feminist writings of

Simone de Beauvoir (*The Second Sex*, 1961) and Betty Friedan's best-selling text, *The Feminine Mystique* (1963), and several years later, firebrand Kate Millett's *Sexual Politics* (1970) and Germaine Greer's *The Female Eunuch* (1971). Soon, there was a burgeoning Canadian feminist literature and interest in women's experience and suffering. This intensity was reflected in the *Status of Women Report* of 1970. The Canadian male establishment and ordinary men were rocked to the core. The phrase "consciousness-raising" became popular as once again, women gathered in small study groups to share their experience and break through to common understandings. The feminist movement, never a single tendency, confronted serious learning challenges as they tried to articulate theoretical understandings that did not simply open the way for middle-class, white professional women to make it in universities, law firms, and hospitals. Where one stood on, and how strongly one advocated for, universal daycare for married women and single mothers was an index of either a professionalized or inclusive feminism. Rebellion also took cultural forms. Students were restive, and cultural forms of rebellion against the status quo were evident everywhere, from Toronto's Yorkville to the hippie enclave on Fourth Avenue in Vancouver's Kitsilano district. This was manifested, for a time, in the drug culture, the "flower power movement," and the anti-consumerist ethos of street life.

The 1960s was a time of optimism and hope. Many young people and university students thought they could bring in a creative, more humane, and peaceful world. The Canadian Liberal Party thought so as well. "Social problems," though evident, could be solved through state intervention by compassionate bureaucrats and social animators in disadvantaged communities. Between 1965 and 1969, government bureaucrats talked incessantly about community development and social action focused on the needs of the poor, urban renewal, and Native peoples. Prime Minister Lester B. Pearson's office launched the Company of Young Canadians (CYC) in April 1965, asking parliament to approve a project "through which the energies and talents of youth can be elicited in projects for economic and social development both in Canada and abroad." The CYC had rather contentions links with SUPA and some New Leftists feared contamination from the state bureaucracy. In Quebec, Michel Blondin was hired in 1963 as Canada's first social animator (though the animation process was deeply rooted in earlier forms of Canadian adult education practice). Based in the Social Development Council of Montreal, Blondin and co-workers created citizens' committees in various neighbourhoods as starting points for catalyzing local learning and action. Citizen participation, community development, and dialogue were very much the buzzwords of the day. OISE professor James Draper's edited collection, *Citizens Participation: A Book of Readings* (1971) captures the buoyant spirit of the day. The Challenge for Change project, then, can be linked to the creation of the CYC and the war on poverty.

Canada hosted Expo '67 in Montreal. The theme—"Man and His World"—reflected a deep belief on the part of Canada's elites that technology and social engineering could usher in a better world for Canadians. The IMAX screen was the biggest ever made, and people were dazzled by the innovative block housing project on the site. Two years later (July 1969), men landed on the moon, epitomizing what science and technology could accomplish. The computer was just edging its way into public consciousness. However, since the publication of Rachel Carson's *The Silent Spring* in 1962, science was also linked with environmental degradation. Popular works like Jacques Ellul's *The Technological Society* (1963), Herbert Marcuse's *One-Dimensional Man* (1968), and Jurgen Habermas' *Toward a Rational Society: Student Protest, Science and Politics* (1970) raised old fears of technological domination of nature and humankind. Other prophets of gloom (or toads in the garden) feared that capitalism was reaching its "limits of growth" (Meadows et al., 1974) and that the "population bomb was about to detonate" (Ehrlich, 1968). Educational elites and policy makers, manifesting the schizoid consciousness of the time (gloom punctuated with either a dream-like humanism that imagined that children could be liberated in soft, caring schools (*The Hall-Dennis Report* [1968]) or a belief in the emancipatory power of science and the new communications technology), were unsettling enough to criticize existing educational practices. Plainly, the formal educational systems were failing to either solve the big problems of the day, or prepare the youth for the changing complex world unfolding before their eyes. To prepare youth to grow and expand the economy, community colleges, and technical institutes were created in a frenzy of building in the late 1960s. This is one source of the vocationalization of adult education. Alan Thomas, the director of the CAAE, consciously adopted the "learning society" discourse in his writings and reports in the early 1960s. He would remain one of Canada's leading liberal exponents of humane "learning" against imposed "education" throughout the twentieth century (Thomas, 1991).

But the euphoria of the 1960s did not last as Canada and the world lurched through the economic recessions and wage freezes of the 1970s into the neo-liberal era associated with the Reagan and Thatcher governments in the US and Britain respectively. Elected Prime Minister in 1984, Brian Mulroney soon followed in their large shoes. From an adult education vantage point, the period from the Tokyo UNESCO gathering of 1972 (with "Learning To Be" its manifesto) to the Hamburg conference in 1997 had witnessed the radical re-configuration of the global geopolitical and economic order. During this period, a mere quarter of a century, the world had experienced the Lenin shipyards in Gdansk, Poland, festooned with posters of the Pope in August 1980. The rhetoric of civil society against the state now filled the intellectual air with new ideas and the return of some hopefulness. Even more startling to a world seemingly frozen into the Cold War bifurcated world (Soviet Union and client states against the United States and its clients), the Berlin Wall was breached on November 9, 1989. Vaclav Havel assumed the presidency of Czechoslovakia on December 29, 1989, heralding the "velvet revolution." In this miraculous year, we watched rulers lose their nerve and people gain strength to organize and assert themselves against the state. Two years later in 1991 the Soviet Union monolith disintegrated. The Cold War was over. After a brief moment of hope for a different society, the world entered a dangerous and disordered time that continues into our anguished present.

In these astounding twenty-five years the global economy was transformed into an integrated system, admittedly extremely unstable and inequitable, driven by the revolutions in telecommunications and giving rise to the new vocabularies of network society and the information age. This latest phase of globalization, initiated in the late fifteenth century and continuing its foreboding course into our day had drastic consequences for both the inhabitants of the rich North and the poor South. International monetary policies forced drastic curtailments of state spending on already besieged governments throughout the Third World. Everywhere in the Western liberal democracies, the social welfare state societies began to crumble as the governmental wisdom of the day cut spending on health, education, and general social welfare to facilitate economic profit-making. This neo-liberal phase of global capitalist evolution turned sharply away from the concern for the collective being of the citizens by releasing the restraints on capital by privatizing public enterprises and de-regulating government restrictions on investment. All educational systems were pressed into the service of economic growth and gaining competitive edge. The de-regulation of the financial sector in the US, initiated by Reagan and continued by the conservative Democrats Clinton and Obama, burst apart in the credit crisis of 2008, which tossed economies everywhere into dark pits. If we had trouble imagining the fall of the Berlin Wall and the Soviet Union, today we have even more difficulty imagining how it could be that Spain, Greece, Italy, or Portugal could be bankrupt, or that the standard of living of Britain could have fallen below that of 1980. Who could imagine that the US fights wars it cannot afford, and relies on Chinese loans and export of cheap goods to keep the country afloat? Who could have imagined the toppling of Arab dictators in the uprisings in the Middle East in 2011?

The 1990s were very dispiriting and disenchanting for those who imagined that new, and more democratic, world order would be able to emerge. The world was inactive and passive in the face of mass murder in Rwanda, Cambodia, and Iraq as well as Bosnia. We stood idle as 800,000 Tutsis and Hutus were massacred. Today, though the numbers are not as massive, the world stands paralyzed, or makes weak threats, as Syria murders its own citizens systematically under the nose of various observers. But the first decade of the twenty-first century has been even more distressing and tormented than the 1990s. On September 11, 2001, history took a perverse turn. It was not a good way to begin the new millennium. Like a lightning flash, the Al-Qaeda network struck the twin symbols of American pride, the World Trade Center and the Pentagon. Three thousand people died, mostly Americans but many from other lands too. It was an appalling and audacious pedagogical act. In the luminescent glow of the flames of the towers, the Islamic jihad imagined that evil westerners would see the truth of their corrupt regime. Osama bin Laden and others in this evil network aimed to goad the US into a reaction that would both inflame Muslim opinion and expose the decadent, autocratic rulers of some Islamic countries. The Bush government saw an opportunity to assert American power in the disordered world. They trumped up the case against Saddam Hussein for harbouring weapons of mass destruction and in March 2003 invaded Iraq for the second time in ten years. That country was devastated, turned into rubble and internal chaos, and Afghanistan was invaded as the search for Bin Laden pushed into the mountains bordering Pakistan. It, too, is an unholy mess.

In the US, the politics of fear now reigned supreme as Americans felt increasingly insecure, both economically and politically. This in turn exacerbated tensions between ethnic and religious groups. In Europe, commitment to a multicultural society became shaky and edgy. Canada, for its part, had a more regulated financial sector and weathered the crash of 2008 better than the US. Canada sent troops to Afghanistan, and the Harper government stealthily shifted its military into a more central place in the national psyche. Harper's Conservative government committed itself even more deeply to the neo-liberal agenda of focusing on economic growth at whatever cost to the environment or social fabric of the country in its budget of 2012 (they would prefer that social movements and other groups stay out of the entire process of getting oil and gas out to the west coast). This economistic focus occludes attention to actively building a multicultural (or cosmopolitan) society. Under Harper, who seems to prefer Chinese-styled capitalism, multiculturalism is simply assumed (not actively and creatively pursued). More worrisome, the Harper government has little respect for Canadian traditions of democratic deliberation. They have become more secretive and less willing to debate policy in open and proper ways. The chasm between civil society and government has grown wider over the past decade.

Throughout this period from 1960 to 2012, Canada's adult education community (of theorists and practitioners of every stripe) was under siege. The story that now follows narrates another of Canada's innovative adult education projects, the Challenge for Change use of media to animate communities, tells the tale of how the study of adult education as a discipline emerged at UBC in the late 1950s and into the 1980s, explores the crisis within academic theory and how the self-understanding of adult education theorists was created in response to neo-liberalism and theoretical developments in other disciplines, the centrality of civil society, social movements, and public spheres to our understanding of adult learning in the neo-liberal era, and, finally, how we have been propelled into the digital age and confront challenges not faced in previous Canadian history.

Media with the People: Challenge for Change/Societe Nouvelle

Challenge for Change/Société Nouvelle (CFC/SN), as Baker, Waugh, and Winton (2010) exclaim, was a "glittering chunk of the heritage of both Canadian arts and Canadian democracy" (p. 4). Imagined into existence at the euphoric apex of the Pearson liberal era in 1967, CFC/SN was an innovative (and ambitious) project bringing together government bureaucrats, documentary filmmakers, community activists, adult educators, and ordinary citizens. In the pre-welfare state era in Canadian adult learning and educational history in the 1940s, the NFB under Grierson's audacious leadership had pioneered in making films for the people. The local communities had little or no say in how they were made; in fact, Grierson insisted that his filmmakers frame a clear story and provide

John Grierson was a cinematic pioneer and is often considered the father of British and Canadian documentary film. (Credit: courtesy of Michael Welton)

answers to the problem for its audience. Now, with the state taking over the administration of domains of our lives previously left untouched, it wanted to find ways of understanding the needs and experience of its citizenry. In 1965, the Liberal throne speech had declared "war on poverty." This required active intervention in poverty-stricken communities in rural and urban environments. Both socially aware government bureaucrats and New Left activists breathed the same intellectual and cultural air of participatory forms of governance (which included dialogical communication from civil society to the state administrative systems). New Left filmmakers (like Colin Low, Peter Pearson, Bonnie Klein, George Stoney, Dorothy Henault, and Anne Poirier) believed that technology could be used to enhance democracy. Bill Nemtin's (1968) communiqué to the government (one of many from various persons) captures this historic moment. "The technology is here—it has been for some time. The society which incorporates in the fabric of its institutions a two-way dialogue and debate will counteract the tendency towards dehumanization that seems to go with ever-increasing size and complexity of our institutions. Democracy is based on participation and debate. The citizen must be brought back to the agora by the very technology that tends to screen him from the center of that vital discussion involving his survival and fulfillment on this planet" (n.p.). The CFC/SN was borne out of the complex interplay between idealistic government bureaucrats and incessant demands from activists and adult educators to give voice to the voiceless. Thus, government policy (what the state desired) and advocates of participatory democracy (what left-leaning filmmakers and disempowered communities desired) co-existed uneasily. Still, there was nothing else like this form of adult learning existing in the liberal democracies of the 1960s and 1970s. From the historian's eagle eye vantage point, this desire for active citizenship—to not be shut out of decisions having to do with our own life situations—was deeply rooted in our history.

From 1967 to 1977, CFC/SN produced over two hundred films and videos. One hundred and forty-five films and videos were made in English, and over sixty in French. Optimistic and enthusiastic filmmakers (and their crews) probed the shadowy places in Canadian society. Indian film crews, composed of CYC volunteers primarily, were amazed that the government might want to listen to their speech. They were used to being spoken to, and not speaking (eighteen films had been made about Indians). One film, taken at St. Regis Mohawk Reserve in Cornwall, Ontario, simply invited residents to use the camera to record their concerns and issues. There was no script. The CFC filmmakers soon learned that the process of putting the camera in the hands of ordinary people and then viewing the film with other community members created a more coherent and focused community. The SN filmmakers working in Quebec during a time of awakening nationalist consciousness wanted to create an alternative public sphere where Quebecers could imagine a "new and egalitarian way of living and interacting" (MacKenzie, 1996, p. 323). Quebec filmmakers accentuated the power of the image to transform cultural sensibilities. But they also worked in the same spirit as their English counterparts. Using the Urban Social Development Project's local committees of citizens in places like St. Jacques, Montreal, they provided videotape recorders to the residents so that they could record visually their common problems. This is a simple but powerful process: before this learning process began, the residents' self-understanding may have been fragmented and dispersed. Now, through this learning dynamic, their consciousness was pulled together as they developed a mutually satisfying collective sense of shared suffering. This was the starting-point, the cognitive grounding, for collective action. They had to acquire a collective viewpoint to speak to government. The image served as the basis for reflection: people cannot jump from their inchoate experience to a deep understanding of their plight or dilemmas. They need a mirror to reflect their experience in this visual (or codified) form. The necessary critical distance permits engagement in discussion and dialogue with others in order to break out of individualistic or idiosyncratic self and community understanding. This vision and methodology also shaped those CFC/SN filmmakers who worked with often angry citizens in Montreal, Toronto, and Halifax around their housing problems.

These films and videos were not simply reproductions of the NFB's work in the war years. They were bold experiments in "changing the world" with a camera. That idea—the filmmaker as teacher—excited Grierson enormously. Colin Low (1984), renowned for his work with the Fogo Islanders, claims that the CFC/SN filmmakers were "not only prepared to teach with film, they were also prepared to help ordinary people to make their own films" (p. 17). This was a step beyond Grierson. In fact, the NFB filmmakers began a small (and controversial) revolution in making films with the people. Over ten or more years, CFC/SN took on many issues: women's rights, housing, First Nations struggles, poverty, and agriculture. But the cornerstone of all of the CFC/SN projects was the work with the Fogo Islanders who were living in near destitute conditions about ten miles off the north-east coast of Newfoundland.

Colin Low had established himself at the NFB as one of its most artistic filmmakers. His *Circle of the Sun* (1960) was especially well known and lauded. In 1969, Low visited Fogo Island and began getting to know the people and their problems. This settlement of five thousand people was fraught with internal conflict and animosities. Their fishery had been undermined by the deep-sea factory fishing vessels leaving most of the Islanders without income. To make matters worse, they had no means to express their views: they were isolated and governed from the outside. They had little control over their life situation. Low had to shift his focus from placing artistry in the forefront of his approach to making documentaries. Early documentaries such as Flaherty's *Man of Aran* (1934) attempted to make an artistic statement; Low couldn't travel that route. He had to "provide a mirror for the islanders as they grappled with the difficult social and economic issues confronting them" (Wiesener, 1992, p. 83).

Fogo Island was a three-year project. It brought together Memorial University's innovative Extension Department under the leadership of Don Snowden with the NFB to begin a community development process. Snowden wanted to make a series of films that showed "real poverty in places like rural Newfoundland was the poverty of information, of isolation from decision-making, and of lack of organization" (Wiesener, 1992, p. 83). So, Low began with the mandate to make films on rural poverty in Newfoundland (on themes such as the effects of resettlement and urbanization on rural poverty). He discovered soon enough (with Extension worker Fred Earle's able assistance) that authority was vested in local merchants and clergy. They were the knowledge brokers and they made the decisions. Paternalistic elites in church, government, and commerce did not value the indigenous knowledge of the people on Fogo Island. 60% of the people were on public assistance. They were divided by religion and tradition. They had no local government, their homes lacked electricity, telephones, and reliable radio reception, they had no unions or co-ops, and 50% were illiterate. They were awaiting resettlement. But Low found that they did not want to be resettled. They wanted a revived fishery and much more.

Fred Earle, a native of the island and Extension educator, worked with the Development Committee to explore social and economic development before CFC arrived on the scene. To compete with the factory ships, the islanders needed longliners and an economically sound way of storing, processing, and shipping their catch. They also lacked organizational experience to engage government and outside business interests. Low and Earle had their work cut out for them. Their first task was to use film to create common understandings amongst the islanders. Low produced twenty-seven (or so) short "vertical" films (no inter-cutting) that simply depicted islanders talking about themselves (producer co-ops, ship building, education, resettlement, and the role of government and merchants in their lives). Films such as *Fishermen's Meeting* (fifteen minutes on fishing methods), *Thoughts on Fogo and Norway* (twelve minutes on comparing methods) or *Andrew Brett at Short Bay* (twenty minutes on the value of forming co-ops) were shown to islanders in schools, churches, and community meetings. Production and utilization were fused: films made in one community were watched in another with their reactions recorded on film and then fed back to the original community. This learning process broke islanders' isolation from each other as they talked about their own experience mediated to others living in scattered settlements across the island. Through this deceptively simple process, islanders found their own voice and melded into a more cohesive, authentic community of shared interests. Some of the NFB films (such as the *Cree Hunters of Mistassini* [1974]) were filmed from the outside looking in. In the Fogo project, the filmmaker and community residents were both inside, with residents involved in editing decisions. And, unlike films made for the general public, the emphasis was on stimulating dialogue and problem-solving.

But dialogue and collective problem-solving does not come easily in conflict-ridden communities such as Fogo Island. People must at least be willing to try mediation through film, institutions with power must be open to listening to community articulation of need and concern, and both parties (state and community) must be willing to trust the NFB. Wiesner (1992) observes: "The films helped them to recognize common problems and differences by showing them removed from every day interaction. The playback on these expressions in the community could reveal the contradictions in individual and also in group attitudes. It could be a beginning in the modifying of attitudes, achieved not through dissemination of information or propaganda but through a real participation that had the potential of creativity"(p. 87). This process, Low emphasized, permitted islanders to break through their "culture of silence" and raise issues that could not be faced directly. Paulo Freire (1972) called this "naming the world."

What was the impact of the Fogo process? Although no formal, quantitative measurements exist, Fred Earle claimed that "no tradition of debate in our communities, people would avoid it [debate]. But now, as the new films show, many people are prepared to stand up and express their opinion" (Gywn, 1972, p. 7). Other outcomes of community deliberations were the establishment of a fishing co-op and a central school. Some critics of the Fogo process have wondered just what role film actually played in the community development process. Tony Williamson (1988), a Memorial extension educator, commented: "It is tempting to say that the films, in themselves, fostered all of these things and to draw linear relationships between the films and subsequent action and development, but it would be incorrect to do so. The Fogo Process … was critically linked to a sustained program of community development efforts of the university and government. Although the attention Fogo Island received (the 'Hawthorne Effect') for the filming and screening undoubtedly helped to accelerate developments on the Island, a passive viewing of the films in isolation from any constructive discussion and follow-up planning meetings would have created no more than a passing moment of excitement and interest at best" (p. 7). The Fogo films were, then, an integral part of communicative action: ripped out of context, they lose their significance.

The Fogo Island process was a delicate one. Filmmakers themselves struggled with the ethical dilemma of permitting subjects to represent themselves. In the end, they couldn't overcome the separation of process from product, leading to the CFC/SN's demise by the early 1980s. However, as Jerry White (2006) has concluded, "The Fogo Island series offered an aesthetically open-minded, socially engaged vision for Canadian cinema at a crucial time in Canadian history. That Canadian cinema as a whole basically decided not to follow its path does not make it any less important" (p. 79).

The Emergence of Academic Study of Adult Learning and Education

UBC launched Canada's first degree program in adult education in the late 1950s. This would turn out to be a perilous and ill-fated journey. In fact, the movement activists of pre-war Canada—Alex Laidlaw (1970) called them "amateurs out to change the world"—were deeply suspicious that something fundamental could be lost when adult education "professionalizes" itself. Fitzpatrick (c.1930) accused the universities of distorting the mind "out of all proportion to … hand and heart" (n.p.). Fitzpatrick (1923) excoriated the philanthropists who endowed universities and ignored the Campmen—"neglected citizens"—who lived in appalling and degrading conditions. "What is needed by these men of the camps, buried socially, intellectually, and morally, is not charity, but more social justice" (pp. 36-37)—ringing words from *The University in Overalls.*

Pioneering animator Father Jimmy Tompkins (cited in Boyle, 1953), himself banished from the academy to a desolate parish in eastern Nova Scotia, identified with the poor and voiceless. "It is not Christianity that is the opiate of the people. … It is fossilized education that is the opiate of the people. … It is the duty of Adult Education to make the mute vocal, and to make the blind see. … Our experience in the Antigonish Movement is that there is more real Adult Education at the pit heads, down in the mines, out among the fishermen's shacks, along the wharves, and whenever the farmers gather to sit and talk in the evenings, than you get from one hundred thousand dollars' worth of fossilized formal courses. It springs from the heart and pains of the people" (pp. 228-29). Coady believed in training for those active in the co-operative movement; he worried about loss of vision and depletion of spiritual energy if adult education became an object of study. So, too, did Corbett, who asked Kidd in the late 1940s (who was teaching a course at the Ontario College of Education) if there was enough material for a university-level course on adult education.

Indeed, the pioneering amateurs out to change the world had good reason to be suspicious. As Gordon Selman (1988) observed, the "history of the field … is increasingly, becoming two histories, that of institutionalized, professionalized adult education as it emerged … over the past thirty years particularly, and a popular education movement which is of the people and an instrument of spiritual, cultural, social and political change" (p. 43). But in the late 1950s, with the movement's leaders off the scene and the fires of social change barely aflame, professors with interest in adult education were deliberating under the auspices of the American Commission of Professors. In Canada, the postwar expansion of the welfare state looked promising for a university-based program to prepare the professional adult educator. At the 1957 meeting, Abbott Kaplan, an American professor of adult education, posed the key question at this epochal gathering of mainly American (including Coolie Verner, Cyril Houle, and Malcolm Knowles) and a few Canadian professors (Roby Kidd and Alan Thomas) to discuss how the discipline of adult education ought to be constructed. "What," he asked, "is the content, the essential ingredient of adult education, that marks it off from other fields or disciplines" (Knowles Papers, 1957, p. 16). This innocent-sounding question turned out to spark much controversy over the next five decades.

Reading the transcript of this meeting permits us to be flies on the wall as the professors fumbled and struggled with Abbott's question. They were uncertain about many things; they were certain, though, that they had to mark out an area within the wider disciplinary territory that clearly distinguished it from others. Students of adult education had to be studying something unique. The behavioural psychologists had claimed "learning" and pedagogues had colonized the educational domain. The professors of adult education could try to differentiate adult from child learning (this would be called "andragogy": a term first used in the early nineteenth century in Europe and popularized by Knowles. I use this term to characterize the move to create a special, professional field of practice). Other social sciences could certainly contribute pieces, but then their identity would be as sociologists or political scientists specializing in a particular region of the delineated field. They were profoundly aware that if they couldn't identify the "differentiated element" then they were out of work in the academy. But they also knew that the academy had a long history of professional studies, with medicine being the premier exemplar. The transcript reveals the powerful pull of medicine as model for their imagined new profession.

Professional knowledge cannot be understood as disciplinary knowledge as such. Rather, professional forms of knowing are cued to social practices that have evolved over time, ways of thinking, codes of practice, and technical and methodological procedures. A "particular set of problems," once identified, then propels the professional actors to search various disciplines for the scientific knowledge to legitimate the practice. Medicine as a complex set of practices (distributed to various specialties) grounds its practice in scientifically tested experimentation. The prestige of this premier profession resides in its anchoring in the natural sciences, which are able to cumulate knowledge and enable medicine to continually modify sets of practices in every specialized domain. This monopoly of competence (which includes esoteric knowledge little understood by ordinary people) entitles only them to do medical work (as physicians, surgeons, radiologists, and so on). The state legitimates their right to practice medicine, and credentialing bodies determine who can and cannot practice medicine.

Unlike adult education scholarship, medicine is not forever re-inventing the wheel. There are many internal debates and discussions pertaining to the understanding of different diseases and their treatment. But one always knows where the debate rests, and how authoritative the recommended intervention may be. One can observe the professors leaning towards building the academic study of adult education around the problems pertaining to the practice of teaching adults. But for adult education to become a bona fide profession, the state would have to designate a domain of practice that required university-training in adult education. The "essential ingredient" that marked off the academic study would have to align with a designated domain of practice that only professional adult educators could enter.

As one Commission of Professors professor expressed it, you start with job analysis or the crucial knowledge ingredient. In order to construct a solid professional identity, one must have a powerful means of signifying that one has arrived. Students must know that they are nurses not social workers, lawyers not architects, adult educators and not educators of children. Status accrues, historians of professionalization (Larson, 1977; Gidney and Millar, 1994) inform us, to those professions that can monopolize competence. The process of monopolizing competence necessarily means that some knowledge-claims will be rejected (or overturned) by professions staking out their claim. In the history of medicine, for instance, scientific medicine gradually undermined the claims of folk medicine or homeopathy. Professors of adult education sought to discover and monopolize the set of competencies required to do the work of the adult educator. In other words, adult educators needed to know things that their relatives teaching children did not need to know.

For these mid-twentieth century post–World War II men and women, adult educators had to know the characteristics of the adult learner and the appropriate methods for teaching them. Positivistic psychology, they believed, could inform them about how adults learned; their own scientific study of instructional design could identify the specific methods for specific contexts. Thus, the professionalizing ethos prevalent in the mid-1950s pressed the discipline-builders towards a technical, instrumental, rational approach to the individual learner. The vast, effulgent, and colourful landscape of adult learning was screened out. To accomplish their project, the professionalizers had to figure out how to gain social and cultural credibility so that only professionally trained "adult educators" would be able to teach other adults (akin to nurses who are the only ones authorized to do nurse work). This latter task consumed much of Coolie Verner's energy as director of UBC's Department of Adult Education. This impossible dream would not be fulfilled.

But the stars seemed aligned for those who wanted to create a "professional community' of adult educators" (Damer, 2000a, p. 1) at UBC. John Friesen, born in 1912 into a Manitoba Mennonite community, was the main protagonist for this new Department of Adult Education. Highly accomplished as an administrator and adult educator, with a doctorate from Columbia, he had accepted the invitation to direct UBC's growing Extension Division in 1954. Like Roby Kidd and Alan Thomas, he, too, wanted to forge a new direction for Canadian adult education—from movement to profession. This required university-legitimated knowledge and methodology particular to teaching adults. Fortunately for Friesen, UBC's president Norman ("Larry") MacKenzie was a friend of the CAAE (he was the president in 1957). As a young political science professor, he had participated with Watson Thomson and others at the University of Alberta's Extension Department's folk school held at Olds, Alberta, in the fateful summer of 1939. He had known Friesen since 1949; and this personable, liberal-minded man was receptive to both Friesen's proposal and the applied direction the social sciences at UBC were taking. He knew how important adult learning was to creating a vital democracy. So, apparently, did MacKenzie's Dean of Education, Neville Scarfe, who fancied himself as an avant-garde educator willing to take risks.

UBC was keen to play an active role in promoting the social and economic development of the province. During the heyday of human capital theory (the 1950s and 1960s)—under the free-wheeling W. A. C. Bennett-free enterprise government—education was perceived to be the key determinant of economic development and social progress. Scarfe was initiating new degree programs in education (the Faculty of Education was shifting away from its old normal school practices), and he was convinced that qualified educators of adults could increase human capital's potential to build a better BC. Kidd, who knew Friesen, MacKenzie, and Geoff Andrew (MacKenzie's assistant and great advocate of the arts and liberal education) well, taught the first summer course, "Administration of Adult Education," in 1956. This demonstrated that the demand for adult education was there. Alan Thomas arrived at UBC in September to begin laying the groundwork for the new department. He was MacKenzie's nephew, and they shared common interest in Canadian nationalism and the usefulness of the social sciences. Thomas' upper middle class background (his father, Alan Thomas Sr. was vice-president of Copp Clark publishing house), it was imagined, would enable him to provide intellectual status to the emergent profession.

Thomas' main task was to gain broad support from UBC academics and the "helping professions" (social work, health, and business). Friesen already had connections with two prominent anthropologists Harry Hawthorn and Cyril Belshaw as well as Leonard Marsh (Policy Studies) through the Social Science Research Institute at UBC. They were all proponents of applying social science research to improve society. Belshaw worked for various UN projects, and taught courses in social change and applied anthropology. Hawthorn's survey of *Indians of BC: A Study of Contemporary Social Adjustment* (1958-1960) is still read today. Marsh was widely recognized for his Report on Social Security in the 1940s. UBC's fondness for "applied research" was scorned by prominent political economist Harold Innis of the University of Toronto who loathed applied research and couldn't imagine "adult education as an academic discipline." Damer (2000a) thinks that: "The academic status of adult education rested on it being a sort of applied sociology, and this was acceptable to several scholars at UBC" (p. 17).

In 1945 UBC offered its first social work degree. By the 1950s social work was anchored in government welfare policy: they had clients galore and social workers had a delineated domain for practice. Those committed to professionalizing adult education desperately needed the state to designate such a domain for their exclusive practice. If they could, they would have secure status and place in the academy. Students could enter this territory and acquire a strong identity as professional adult educators. During his directorship of the CAAE, Kidd had worked assiduously to cultivate links with social work and nursing. They had status; adult education as a professional field of practice had almost none. Gaining support or sympathy from social work and nursing (both of which had significant pedagogical elements) was one thing; creating an autonomous adult education domain in the academy another. Damer (2000a) argues that social work and nursing set the stage for adult education to take a place in the academy. The mental health movement was interested in adult educators who could educate the public in good mental hygiene. The Faculty of Agriculture was still offering a degree in agricultural extension. They were supportive of the project to create an adult education department. Even the Faculty of Commerce supported adult education: economic growth and industrialization required high skills, and this meant that adult educators had work in training workers in various sectors of the economy.

So the situation seemed promising for those adult educators desiring to carve out their own space and get busy preparing adult educators for work in a multiplicity of institutional contexts in the emergent welfare state. The old amateurs out to change the world were fading from memory. Adult education now appeared becalmed and technicized. The main purpose for adult education in the conservative decade of the 1950s was to maintain the status quo and manage the learning process so that it would not disrupt or challenge the existing power structure. The CAAE had cut its ties with the labour movement and now identified strongly with business interests. Laidlaw (1970) worried that once "you have succeeded in making Adult Education a distinct academic discipline you have robbed it of its spirit and destroyed half its value for society." He was not off-target about loss of spirit; he was wrong that Adult Education would be able to establish itself as a distinct academic discipline.

The youthful Thomas found that the university insiders and enough academics across the campus supported the idea of creating a Department of Adult Education. Thomas thought he saw a market for freshly trained adult educators. Many institutions appeared to need specially trained adult educators: the BC Penitentiary; school boards; libraries; the provincial Department of Agriculture, Labour, Education, and Community programs; co-operatives and credit unions; the Federal Department of Indian Affairs; various health organizations; and the Canadian Mental Health Association (to name a few). In 1957 UBC announced "A New Graduate Program in Adult Education." Damer (2000a) comments: "The UBC program would benefit by attracting students from a wide variety of settings. For the first time in Canada, people would earn a degree in Adult Education. The task now was to secure the various resources that would ensure a long and stable life for the Adult Education program" (p. 30).

Norman MacKenzie's university worked through personal acquaintances. When Coolie Verner arrived on campus from Florida State

University as a visiting professor in the winter of 1959 to teach, the program was being offered full-time (with very few students). From 1957 until Verner arrived, Thomas had taught a single course in winter, with one or two offered during the summer. Both Friesen and Thomas had encouraged Verner to come to UBC. But he was an unknown quantity to MacKenzie and Scarfe. A dynamic and bristly character, Verner's background was in rural sociology (which made him attractive to the Faculty of Agriculture). Verner's main strategy after arriving on campus was to establish a network of supporters in order to gain legitimacy for the department and to hire professors of adult education. He also loved cartography and old books. This energetic, enigmatic, and gay man met with faculties of nursing, social work, sociology, agriculture, and education. He gained the confidence of Hawthorn and Belshaw, and taught rural sociology in the Anthropology and Sociology department. He promoted himself relentlessly: to the YMCA, Nursing Association, to School Boards, and the BC Council of Adult Education. He hammered away on his big theme: those working as adult educators needed university training. Adult education was "something specific, something useful, and something that required special study" (Damer, 2000a, p. 34).

Thomas, Scarfe, and Friesen were convinced that Verner was the right man to be first professor of adult education at UBC. The offer of full professorship at a salary of $12,000 per annum came, and he was appointed to begin his work on July 1, 1961. He was also cross-appointed to the Department of Agricultural Economics. To gain support for adult education through networking is one thing, but professors and administrators come and go. Their replacements may not be at all friendly to adult education as a field of study. Verner had to answer Kaplan's question—what is the essential ingredient that distinguishes adult education from other disciplines—by constructing the curriculum. The territory had to be mapped, original research published, grants obtained. Professional adult educators needed "special knowledge generated by university academics working on the 'discipline' of adult education, vaguely defined as either a form of scientific study, a body of systematic knowledge founded in theory and research, or a more precise inquiry founded on methodological canons" (Damer, 2000a, p. 93). Verner (1964) defined adult education as the teaching of adults by a professionally trained adult educator. This rigorous tautological view was not shared by Thomas, who had, Damer suggests, "oriented his first courses to social philosophy" (Damer, 2000a, p. 94). Like other American adult education professors of the day, Verner de-emphasized social philosophy and emphasized scientifically validated methods and instructional design.

The postwar academy—from 1945 to around 1970—was dominated by positivism and functionalist models of social science. As a graduate of Columbia University, Verner imbibed the regnant formidable ideas that social inquiry had to be value-neutral: its task was to discover facts through experimental processes and generate laws about the working of social systems (including education). Research had to be quantifiable; social surveys were the chosen vehicle for gaining scientific data. UBC's approach to the social sciences was dominated by American pragmatism and empiricism. Verner, then, acted as a "conduit for the dominant American intellectual tradition" (p. 96). At Columbia, Willard Hallenbeck and Edmund deS. Brunner taught Coolie Verner that adult education was a "tool to move people from role to role (even class to class) in order to maintain stability and harmony" (p. 96). This conservative functionalism would disintegrate in the 1970s and 1980s. But in the 1950s and 1960s, the belief that the social sciences had to emulate the methods of the natural sciences was simply taken for granted. To buttress his understanding of learning, Verner looked to the behaviourist work of his old colleague at Florida State, Robert Gagné (1975, 1992), and Ralph Tyler's (1949) influential rational-instrumental approach to program planning. A scientific view of education could enable, it was thought, educators to use the right techniques and methods to achieve particular ends.

Damer (2000a) states that Verner actually "wrote very little about the specific ends to which adult education should be put" (p. 98). The pattern in Canadian history, however, is quite the reverse: the vision of the "good and abundant life" articulated by Moses Coady and many others dominated the thinking of our great adult educators. Vision found the methods. Verner's conceptual schemes were not particularly well-received, though other adult education departments in North America did not deviate too far from empiricism and preoccupation with methods and instructional design. Verner's core course—"Methods of Adult Education"—replaced Alan Thomas' on "Adult learning": this course remained on the books until 1984. His "Introduction to Adult Education" was based on his labyrinthine conceptual schemes, and replaced Thomas' course. Verner's approach, his logic, his choice of course content, was guided by his fierce, perhaps obsessive, commitment to building a profession of adult education (to qualify as a "profession," it must be grounded in the natural sciences). Theory had to guide practice: in the same way as medical practice and procedures are anchored in scientific discovery and experimental research. True to this vision, Verner's students wrote theses in the 1960s that used hypothetic-deductive methodology and statistical data analysis. Doctoral students of the 1970s were required to work within the scientific paradigm and know the latest methods of statistical analysis. The authoritarian Verner made sure they did: he supervised all twenty-one of the doctoral dissertations in the early 1970s.

By the end of the 1960s, professors of adult education such as Robert Carlson (who spent most of his career at the University of Saskatchewan) were criticizing Verner for having an excessively narrow view of adult education research. In fact, other models—interpretive and critical—were available (Fay, 1975). Verner brushed aside this critique. John Niemi, who worked in the adult education department from 1966 to 1974, did not go along with Verner. He was interested primarily in media studies. Verner prohibited Niemi from doctoral supervision (he was on only two doctoral committees from 1970 to 1974). The first Canadian hired, Gary Dickinson, however, shared Verner's passion for survey-based research. One study, conducted by Verner, Dickinson, and Niemi, surveyed the "educational participation of underprivileged people and left virtually unanswered the question of what should be done and why" (Damer, 2000a, p. 114). This disconnect between theory and practice lent support to Laidlaw's (1970) caustic criticism of adult education in the academy. "Adult education has become a conversation piece for professionals and subject matter for the classroom." For Verner and his students, the scientific approach to adult learning was used so that the educator could "select the instructional techniques (and devices) deemed most effective for certain people" (p. 115).

Recruited by Verner, Roger Boshier arrived from New Zealand in 1974. He focused his considerable energy on doing statistical studies of adult participation in education. Gordon Selman, the second Canadian hired in the first two decades of the Department's existence, had been working with the Extension Division. Widely respected locally and internationally, with a Master's degree in history, Selman was not attracted to the Verner project. Over the years, he would produce numerous historical studies, mainly chronicling BC's adult education and learning histories (Selman, 1988, 1991, 1995). He also collaborated with Kidd (1978) to put together collections of readings to serve emergent departments of adult education. Dan Pratt, a graduate of the University of Washington, was an expert on the "psychology of communications" working in the Faculty of Education. Although he was not trained in adult education, he transferred to the Department of Adult Education in the mid-1970s.

Pratt settled in to determining the essential ingredients involved in effective teaching. In the 1970s, Verner, Dickinson, Boshier, and Pratt flowed in the scientistic current of scholarship.

By the mid-1970s, with the Verner era grinding to its end, the Department of Adult Education had created its own subculture. They were isolated from the rest of the faculty, geographically and intellectually. Their research had not made much of an impact in the university or larger culture. The "old boys" network that had protected Coolie Verner's department was no longer in place. As Damer (2000a) puts it, "If adult education faculty had only modest support from the Faculty of Education administration, they also had little academic support from the professoriate" (p. 71). And Coolie Verner came under fire for "administrative improprieties" and "student overload." He had given up the chair in 1973, but stayed around, mainly out of sight, until his resignation in 1977. This is a somewhat forlorn and sad story. A nervous Faculty of Graduate Studies chose Alan Thomas, now at OISE, and an eminent American adult education scholar, Alan Knox, to review the program. They concluded that the "Department was isolated, lacked cohesive goals and expectations, and suffered from various student, curricular, and research problems" (Damer, 2000a, p. 72). They were under considerable pressure to integrate their Department into the Faculty of Education. They finally did become the Department of Administration, Higher and Adult Education in the early 1980s (though they stayed in their Toronto Road building on the edge of the campus). The situation for the Department of Adult Education was rather bleak as the 1970s drew to its end. Although it had been able through the Verner era to serve other faculties (like nursing and agriculture) by providing instruction in teaching methodologies and instructional design, as well as catering to students, mainly women, by offering courses later in the day, the dream of creating a high-status profession failed. Even those adult educators who were employed in hospitals, colleges, universities, government, and other public institutions identified with their own particular sites and routes up the hierarchical ladders rather than affirming (or claiming) a strong professional adult education identity. It almost seemed as if adult education was a self-effacing labour of love, serving those who needed it and receiving little reward for doing so. But Verner had, however one viewed his project, opened up some space on the margins of the academy for students to consider the power and significance of adult learning in society. And maverick students, ill at ease in other departments of the university, found solace on Toronto Road.

William Griffith, an American professor of adult education, arrived from the prestigious University of Chicago in 1977 to begin re-shaping a department in shambles. Griffith had wide-ranging and diverse interests—literacy, corrections, family planning, and agriculture. His academic background melded empirical science (his MSC was in agricultural science) with professional adult education (his Ph.D obtained from the University of Chicago in 1963 under Cyril Houle). He was also passionate about training for professionals working in these diverse areas. During his time at UBC, he assisted professional organizations such as the Canadian Society of Extension; however, Griffith took little interest in CASAE. In fact, like most of the UBC adult education faculty his gaze was southward. This combative man was a thoroughly conservative American intellectual who came of age in the ethos of anti-communism in the 1950s. He was one of the first of the professional adult education professors to critique Paulo Freire when his ideas filtered into university circles (Griffith, 1972). He accused Freire of being the kind of person who would prevent others' freedom as soon as he and his vanguard achieved theirs. In the mid-1970s, as Budd Hall (2012) tells the story, he and Ted Jackson and Deborah Barndt had been promoting the idea and practice of Participatory Research in space opened up by the ICAE. Griffith attacked their intellectual project for violating the canon of positivistic research; he even accused them of hubris. This man who pulled no punches decried the lack of serious scholarship in adult education. He didn't like the research produced by the Department of Adult Education at UBC, either, and put considerable effort into improving Adult Education's research status. The rather perfunctory survey-research in vogue during the Verner era was dismissed. After Kjell Rubenson spent time as "visiting professor" from Linkopping, Sweden, in 1979/1980, Griffith expressed his preference for his empiricist and sociological orientation. Rubenson was hired as full professor in 1982 (two other Americans, Tom Sork and Peter Cookson, were hired in 1981 and 1979 respectively). Paz Buttedahl—an enthusiastic proponent of social movements and Paulo Freire—was hired in 1982 as a research associate, and then as assistant professor (she left the Department in 1986).

By the early 1980s, the old scientist paradigm had collapsed and the field opened itself up to a variety of critical perspectives. With the professionalizing project exhausted—neither Kaplan's question of the "essential ingredient" nor the state designation of exclusive sites where only authorized adult educators could teach had been answered—the study of adult education entered into a prolonged crisis of identity. The Adult

Education Department at UBC was also plagued by interpersonal conflict. Several key players in the Department succeeded in ousting Griffith from the chair in 1983. Griffith was as prickly in personal relationships as he was feisty in intellectual combat. The Department was also unable to offer a coherent vision of adult education as a discipline of academic study. Rubenson continued with his sociological and policy studies. His seminal paper on mapping the territory of adult education (written in 1982) charted some new directions for the discipline, but they were not pursued with any seriousness by his colleagues. Boshier, Sork, and Pratt engaged some of the new critical currents (like phenomenology or Foucault) in their work in the 1980s and 1990s, opening up some previously closed dimensions of program planning, teaching, and lifelong learning (Damer, 2000b). But none developed thorough research programs within a critical theoretical framework.

The Canadian Association for the Study of Adult Education (CASAE) was born in 1981 in this time of crisis of academic adult education's identity and future. At the Montreal meeting held with the Learned Societies in May 1985 considerable unease within the professoriate of adult education was evident. OISE had just had its Ph.D revoked, allegedly on the grounds that professional publications were not "academically respectable." The Adult Education Department at UBC, now warily nestled within the Department of Administrative, Adult, and Higher Education, appeared to be in danger of dissolving into the muddy sea of the Faculty of Education, itself in chaos. And the third major centre of graduate adult education, the University of Montreal, was also in danger of losing its autonomy. Were adult education professors failed academics? How should we educate adult educators? Did the educators need educating? Did we need radically new paradigms of graduate training? These questions nipped at our heels through the meeting and a "circle the wagons" mentality prevailed.

The Montreal meeting only reflected the questioning and debates within CASAE from its inception as well as the long-standing uneasy relationship between practitioner and theorizing in the Canadian adult education tradition. In mid-January 1984, Kjell Rubenson wrote to James Draper, president of CASAE and professor at OISE.

> There is too much emphasis on practice and too little on the creation of knowledge. In order to create some equity we need to concentrate for a while on the knowledge development. This can and should be done by mapping out some broader issues to be treated in more depth and to invite scholars from other disciplines to participate in this process....The undue emphasis on practice is just an excuse and a way of legitimating

the anti-intellectual behaviour of academics in Adult Education. The people that we want to serve deserve something better.

In the August 1984 CASAE Newsletter Rubenson elaborated on his critique of the view that CASAE ought to be "more practice-oriented." Rubenson argued forcefully that the present crisis in the study of adult education was based on a misconception about the relationship between theory and practice, and the state of the art of discipline of adult education. The basic purpose of research was to "understand and explain phenomenon not to address the solution of day-to-day problems in adult education. The purpose of research is to develop and test theories and thus lays the necessary foundation for applied research." Roger Boshier (1980) also believed that "graduate programs in adult education were producing scholars who had skills in programme planning and instruction, but few understood the social contexts for or foundations of adult education" (p. 272).

Critical theory's movement into CASAE was rocky and tumultuous. To permit personal observations, at the Montreal meeting, after a panel discussion on "New perspectives on the history of adult education," one professor spoke to me. He said: "I know what you are. You're a communist." That was a little unsettling. At other meetings, the New Zealander Michael Law thundered out in defence of Marxist orientations to adult learning. At the 1992 meeting held in Saskatoon, a panel discussion on the new "black book" edited by Peter Jarvis and John Peters (1991) was basically shouted down as members of the audience railed against those who had excluded women and Blacks from the text. Several panel participants never returned to another Adult Education Research Conference (AERC) or CASAE meeting. Similar explosions were also evident at the Syracuse Symposium on workers' education sponsored by the Kellogg Foundation and the critical theory working group within the American Association for Adult and Continuing Education (AAACE). In July 1995, Michael Collins and his associates at the University of Saskatchewan called a major emergency conference in Canmore, Alberta, to examine the question of the future of adult education as a field of study and practice. Prominent scholars came from Britain, Australia, New Zealand, the United States, and Canada. The mood was ever more morose and contentious than ten years earlier. Many were pronouncing the end—Budd Hall and Kathy Rockhill spoke of upheavals and chaos at OISE, and Michael Welton of the collapse of the School of Education at Dalhousie.

These anecdotes reflect the struggle and tension within an academic organization that had functioned tacitly within a broad andragogical consensus framework and commitment to professionalized forms of practice. Like an invader from another tribal enclave, various forms of critical theory challenged the major assumptions, categories, and motifs of andragogy. The new categories, motifs, and vocabulary certainly reflected upheaval within the existing paradigm—which always occurs when the old one no longer adequately explains the messy world of reality. The 1991 special issue of *The Canadian Journal for the Study of Adult Education* on critical theory crystallized some of the thinking that had begun to circulate within CASAE. The appearance of the writings on the new social movements by Matthias Finger (1989) and Budd Hall (1979), and Michael Law and Sue Collard's (1989) critique of Jack Mezirow methodological individualism in the late 1980s, signalled new theoretical developments in the study of adult learning. In the early 1990s, flashy University of Alberta graduate students Donovan Plumb and Derek Briton (1993a, 1993b) introduced exciting new postmodern theorists (Jacques Derrida, Jacques Lacan, Michel Foucault, Vaclav Havel) to CASAE. Feminist theories had been circulating for some time outside adult education, but seeped into the discipline of adult education primarily through Mechthild Hart's (1985, 1990a, 1990b) brilliant writings. Michael Collins (1991) introduced us to the vocational consequences of the radical paradigm and to the enduring worth of Ivan Illich and socialist theorists like Rosa Luxemburg as the dreadful decade of the 1990s dawned. As well, the recovery of the radical workers' movements of early and present day by Bruce Spencer (1995) provided us with a sense of solidity and confidence that a new paradigm could both account for learning occurring in the system and lifeworld domains. We also believed that new theory could engender new ways of how adults learn and how teaching actually occurs in life situations.

The contributors (Welton, Plumb, Hart, Mezirow, Collins, and Hart) to *In Defense of the Lifeworld: Critical Perspectives on Adult Learning* (1995) all reflected the dialogues and debates occurring in CASAE and other international adult education arenas. Habermas was one of our worthy dialogue partners. However, it needs to be stated clearly that the Canadian and international adult education network of professors and researchers contained many exemplary critical voices, speaking with different tonalities and accents as the scholarly world moved into an unnerving postmodern formation. The CASAE texts—produced in 1998 and 2006—indicate the range of perspectives now available. But the irony of the appearance of the new paradigm simultaneously with the collapse of the old CAAE and the arrival of the tsunami of neo-liberal pressure to harness all forms of learning from child to elder to the Money-code—to radically vocationalize all learning and education—has led to deep confusion within the ever-fragile university departments of adult education. The old andragogical paradigm, symbolized in the houses that Kidd and Verner built, had been dismantled. A new paradigm was ready to provide some orientation and passion, but, alas, it was forced into exile, destined to be homeless. The old guard was dismayed and the new critically oriented educators without a secure place to lay their heads. The remaining larger departments of adult education, such as OISE and UBC, were fractured and lacked commitment to lay an adequate foundation to a distinctly Canadian tradition and practice.

In Defence of Civil Society: Canadian Adult Education in Neo-Liberal Times

In 1983 the Catholic Bishops of Canada precipitated a major debate with their statement "Ethical reflections on the economic crisis." The statement termed unemployment a "moral disaster" and called for alternative, people-oriented and social policies. In particular, it urged government not to fight inflation at the cost of high unemployment. In 1993, the Canadian Conference of Bishops issued another pastoral letter, "Widespread Unemployment: a call to mobilize the social forces of the nation." In this document they declared that unemployment was worse than it had been ten years previously. Estimating the unemployed and underemployed at one quarter of the labour force, the Bishops observed that "widespread and sustained unemployment generated a continuing social crisis," with increases in social pathologies like spousal and child abuse.

Through this period, which coincides with the neo-liberal regime of Brian Mulroney (1984-1993), the Canadian welfare state began to shake and tremble as the neo-liberals laid siege to what Canadians had fought so hard to achieve through the struggle years of the 1900s through the 1950s. But it was not only our economic and welfare state that was trembling. The very existence of the Canadian nation-state seemed more fragile than ever in this improbable bi-national country. The October 1995 referendum on Quebec separatism was bitterly contested and the outcome indecisive. The increasingly angry showdown between Quebec separatists and the rest of Canada deepened the uneasiness and uncertainty felt by many Canadians inside and outside of Quebec. We did not know if our country would be fractured irrevocably, with a new Quebec wedged between the historically impoverished and economically underdeveloped Atlantic region to the east and the wealthier Ontario, with First Nations peoples carving out an ambiguous relationship with English Canada and the new Quebec. Canadian liberal democracy was in serious crisis. But the epoch had the salutary effect of shaking us out of our complacency, opening up possibilities for a radical re-thinking of the purpose of socially responsible adult education and the meaning of democracy in our post-1989 world.

One might argue that democratic theory had reached an impasse by the early 1970s, with the utopian potential of the welfare state gradually exhausting itself. Social democracy in Canada had run out of steam—it had generated nothing of intellectual interest or excitement in the past two decades (with the exception, perhaps, of the left-nationalist Waffle movement). In power (in the provinces) it acted like a neo-liberal government; out of power, a pall of silence fell over its national leader, Alexa McDonough. In 1997, the New Democratic Party lost its official party status, garnering about 6% of the popular vote and winning only nine seats. The Canadian national political scene had been radically reconfigured with the separatist Bloc Quebecois in opposition; the pseudo-populist Reform Party was just two seats behind. The right now appeared to speak for the common people, addressing their fears that communities were unravelling, families falling apart, and meaning eroding in the jungle of mass consumerism. They had convinced the ordinary Canadian, or least quite a few of them, that the welfare state bred clientelism and dependency, and that curbing the deficit would invigorate a sluggish economy and revitalize morale.

Our social nation-state was under assault; our social legacy and emancipatory adult learning traditions, forged in the bitter fires of the late nineteenth and early twentieth century movements, depression and war years and hammered into shape in the 1950s and 1960s, were in danger of being undermined. Canadian economists Errol Black and Robert Chernomas (1996) believed that the neo-liberals were trying to transform Canadian society from a "form of social or communitarian capitalism to a miniature replica of the US form of individualistic capitalism" (p. 23). By the mid-1970s the Western world had entered a period of profound change, both economically and ideologically. Global ruling elites, with the transnational corporations as their power base, began a complex process of dismantling social forms of capitalism in order to liberate market constraints or regulations. All forms of learning, from school to higher education institutions, were harnessed to the Money-code (Welton, 2005). By now, in 2012, we are familiar with the brutal consequences of global elite "development" policies: World Bank and International Monetary Fund structured adjustment programs pushed southern (and northern) economies into the dirt, wreaking havoc with welfare policies and general human well-being. Capital had been wrestling itself free of tutelage from either the state or civil society. In fact, it was now going to teach civil society a thing to two.

Taking his cues from his idols Reagan and Thatcher, Mulroney fashioned his "Agenda for Change." Restraint was the keyword: he would reduce the deficit to deal with the fiscal crisis, and would rely on a "free" market to foster economic growth. Deregulate transportation, communication, finance; privatize crown corporations; reduce spending on social welfare programs: this was the neo-liberal agenda. This agenda, McBride and Shields (1993) observed, was a "natural" response to the irresistible demands of globalization. To forgo tax revenues from corporations and to keep interest rates high were choices selected from a range of possibilities. Neo-liberalism is heavily imbued with ideology.

The regressivity of the tax system, changes to unemployment insurance, and the introduction of workfare divide the collectivity, setting up an insidious dichotomy between haves and have-nots. Indeed one notices that, increasingly, the rich and well-off live within a "culture of contentment" (John Galbraith's barbed phrase). Those within this culture have withdrawn compassion from the less fortunate, who are now held accountable for being out of work or simply out of their minds. The commonwealth was now rent apart by neo-liberal policies, making one wonder what they were conserving and leading one to despise what they thought was new. A neo-fascist odour lingered over the mean policies of Ontario's right-wing Premier Mike Harris (1995-2002) (drastic cuts to poor mums, abolition of anti-scab labour legislation, and reduction in daycare facilities, etc.). We should take note, too, of the anti-union policies of the Harris government. Neo-conservatism did not tolerate oppositional learning sites. Here we simply observe that the federal neo-liberal withdrew funding from numerous popular groups including the CAAE and about one hundred international educational centres across the country, and radically reduced funding for labour education. These developments sent shivers down the spines of adult educational professors in the mid-1990s. They were a shocking betrayal of our emancipatory adult learning and education traditions.

The crisis of the welfare state and the weakening of civil society threw Canadian adult education into disarray and conflict in the last three decades of the twentieth century. We were in the midst of a struggle for the heart and soul of adult education. Adult education has always been pulled between serving two masters: the system or the lifeworld. As the market—discourse and logic—became ascendant in the 1990s, adult education coupled its caboose to the corporate training and development model. This model largely instrumentalizes adult education for the purpose of corporate development and growth. For neo-liberal federal government bureaucrats in charge of our training policy initiatives, life-long learning is a signifier for lifelong adaptation to the "needs" of the "new" global economy. No doubt about it, there has been a major shift in discourse in Western countries from education to learning. But this concept of learning most assuredly meant the adaptation of isolated, individual learners to the corporate-determined status quo. Professionalized Canadian adult education had jumped aboard the "learning for earning" bandwagon of the 1990s.

But rebellious forms of oppositional learning persisted in all parts of Canada. In the late 1980s, Prime Minister Mulroney tried to constrain and muzzle public learning processes within civil society regarding the North American Free Trade Agreement. He failed to do this, and numerous groups (but particularly Labour and the Action-Canada Network) entered into civil space to make their arguments and identify problems with the agreement. For months, public learning processes were vibrant as hundreds of thousands of Canadians were drawn into the discussion. Although the agreement was passed, forms of solidarity were fostered. A similar learning process occurred during the contentious debates following the 1992 Charlottetown Accord (basically an attempt to finesse Quebec into the federation without really addressing their major concerns). Widely denounced by ordinary people as an elite ("men in suits") attempt to manipulate Canadians into an agreement with Quebec, the Accord was soundly defeated. One of the by-products of the public learning process regarding the future of our nation-state were the Citizens' Forums, initiated by the Tories (led by Keith Spicer), that sprang up everywhere to permit Canadians to speak about their own desires for the country's future. While many Canadians might not have understood that the idea of a citizens' forum had originated with adult educators in the 1940s, these gatherings were deeply rooted in our public tradition of creating communicative spaces for reflection and action. That they were despised by neo-liberal journalists is no surprise, either. The

Keith Spicer and Prime Minister Brian Mulroney are seen here in Ottawa, June 27, 1991, where Spicer released the final report of the Citizens' Forum on Canada's future. (Credit: CP PHOTO/Chuck Mitchell)

contemporary CBC's use of various kinds of panels for discussion about domestic issues of the day has its roots in the early experiments in linking listening-study groups-action in the 1940s. Peter Mansbridge is a newscaster and adult educator.

The concept of civil society (which is now global) was the great gain, or discovery, of critically oriented adult education theorists in response to neo-liberal policies in the western liberal democracies and the global upheavals in Europe (Poland, Hungary, Czechoslovakia, Romania, Romania, and East Germany). Civil society is a very nuanced, contested, and multi-layered concept. Habermas (1996) maintains that the "sphere of civil society has been rediscovered … in wholly new historical constellations" (p. 366). It cannot be identified with the bourgeois society of the liberal tradition, which Hegel identified with the market system involving social labour and commodity exchange. Most theorists of civil society argue that the concept no longer includes the economy. For example, Habermas claims its institutional core is the non-governmental and non-economic connections and voluntary associations that "anchor the communication structures of the public sphere in the social component of the lifeworld" (p. 367). Habermas explains:

> Civil society is composed of those more less spontaneously emergent associations, organizations, and movements that, attuned to how societal problems resonate in the private life sphere, distill and transmit such reactions in amplified form to the public sphere. The core of civil society comprises a network of associations that institutionalizes problem-solving discourses on questions of general interest inside the framework

of organized public spheres. The 'discursive designs' have an egalitarian, open form or organization that mirrors essential features of the kind of communication around which they crystallize and to which they lend continuity and permanence (p. 367).

The idea of civil society was rediscovered in the 1970s by Eastern Europeans, particularly the Polish Solidarity movement, who created all kinds of independent, self-governing associations and publications alongside the official party and state apparatus. They discovered that genuine civic mindedness emerges less from traditional forms of party politics than from the hidden spaces and islands of freedom to be found in civil society (learning spaces). They discovered that a vital civil society fosters and develops the capacity of ordinary citizens to exercise responsible public leadership. These associations, movements, and publics function as schools of citizenship. They create communicative spaces conducive to reasoned reflection where citizens can deliberate about public problems (some extraordinarily serious, like those faced by those in midst of overthrowing Middle Eastern dictators). Since the heady days of "civil society versus the state" struggles in Eastern Europe, many activists and learning theorists have begun to speak about a global civil society. This concept strives to capture something new and exciting that is percolating in many countries of the globe. One could cite innumerable examples of networks of wonderful variety that create communicative spaces across national boundaries. Women's organizations have proliferated since the UN International Women's Year of 1975. Think of WAND (Women and Development in the Caribbean), CAFR (Caribbean Association for Research and Action), Indigenous Women's Network, Commonwealth Women's Network, the International Women and Health Network, the Women's Global Network on Reproductive Rights, and hundreds more (Miles, 1996). These networks and others like them, besides enabling reflective learning in their own networks, participated in the great gatherings of civil society in the 1990s: Beijing (women), Rio de Janeiro (environment), Copenhagen (social welfare), and Hamburg (adult learning). Now that we are being forced together by the contradictory impulses of economic globalization, we understand that civil society is the key social space for democratic learning processes as well as personal and collective need articulation. But the great French sociologist, Pierre Bourdieu (1998), counsels us that these forces of civil society, at present, "lack a genuine international organization of the forces capable of countering the new conservative revolution" (p. 59).

The "critical turn" in adult education theory in Canada was propelled by three forces: first, the crisis of identity of university-based adult

education; secondly, the emergence of the power of civil society to overturn governments; and thirdly, by new developments within critical theory itself. The "new" language permitted theorists and activists alike to
make sense of attempts to reform Soviet-style state socialism without
armed resistance. It also helped them to understand the complex learning dynamics of the struggle against bureaucratic authoritarianism in the
south and the emergence of the new social movements in the West. This
new, hopeful political discourse didn't take long emigrating into aca-
demia. During the 1980s the vocabulary of civil society pervaded the
social science literature. By the 1990s, the discipline of adult education
had begun to host this conceptual stranger, working its emergent understanding of social learning in terms of the new orientation to understanding the dynamics of social life.

During the twentieth century, critical theorists began to break with
Marx's economistic reductionism. Gradually, thinkers associated with the
Frankfurt School such as Theodor Adorno (1903–1969) and Max Hork-
heimer (1895–1973), and the Italian Antonio Gramsci (1891–1937),
developed ideas that enabled civil society to be uncoupled from both
state and economy. Puzzling over the question of why the European
masses weren't revolutionary, both Gramsci and the Frankfurt intellectuals turned to the cultural sphere for answers. They discovered that the
network of institutions comprising the modern civil society (churches,
schools, clubs, associations, social movements, public spheres) was used
instrumentally by the dominant classes to establish their hegemony over
the lower orders. The family was also included in civil society's domain
because it was an institution central to shaping the character and political
disposition of its members. This cultural turn within critical theory made
ideas (about self, others, the world) less the economy's prisoner, more
an actor on their own terms. Today civil society is understood as the
sphere of identity formation, social integration, and cultural reproduction (Chambers, 2002). Scholars face the task of unveiling the cognitive
grounding and pedagogical processes inherent in these three axial processes of building a society.

The stage was set for Jurgen Habermas, the inheritor of the Frankfurt
mantle, to wed his communication theory to the discourse of civil society. Habermas' now famous argument that Marx had reduced the evolution of the human species to its remaking of the natural world through
labour and had not taken account of how inner and sociocultural worlds
are made through symbolic interaction, burst into the social sciences.
Unlike liberal thinkers, Habermas postulated communicative autonomy

as the defining feature of civil society. The system realm—dominated by money and power—operated differently from that of the lifeworld system. Administrative systems coordinated action through coercion, and the economy pursued profit, efficiency, and instrumental success. In contrast, civil society (the lifeworld expressed in institutions) required communicative interaction oriented to understanding for its reproduction. Habermas' decisive argument was that relationships within civil society were not governed by instrumental logic. One could now consider how the system realm could colonize the lifeworld realm, introducing distorting dynamics into the communication process (Chambers, 2002).

Over the last decade or so, propelled by a desire to develop a social learning theory that could provide the needed frame for the discipline, Canadian adult education scholars have increasingly found a home in the evolving discourse of civil society. The core value structure of adult education (evident in our history and thinking)—our affirmation that the lifeworld is the foundation of meaning, social solidarity, and stable personality, our commitment to the enlightened, autonomous, and reflective learner and to the centrality of social learning processes to the formation of the active citizen, and to the fostering of discussion, debate, and dialogue among divergent views—leads us straight to the civil society camp. This, I have argued in this book (and other places), is our natural home, implicit in our voluntarist, social movement, and personal growth traditions (Welton, 1997a, 1997b, 1998, 2001, 2005, 2011). When Habermas executed his famous transformation of critical social theory into a critical communications theory, this move was fortuitous for the discipline of adult learning and education, enabling adult educators to link communicative and learning theory. The act of communication creates the possibility of interactions that open the dialogue partners to new ways of thinking and acting in the world. Where communication is distorted or silenced, the deeply inter-subjective learning process is thwarted. One can imagine, then, that the putting in place of a civil society over time can be re-conceptualized as the building of society's learning infrastructure. The struggle to build a democratic civil learning infrastructure is closely allied, in western countries, to modernization processes, to the historical unfolding of Canadian society from colonialism to the information age.

To be sure, important learning dynamics occur within the spheres of economy and polity. But civil society is the privileged domain for non-instrumental learning processes. It is here, within the network of family, school, associational movement, and public life, that citizens are able to raise issues or topics requiring public attention and system-action. Here, for example, associations like trade unions (which bridge the lifeworld and the system) can raise pertinent issues pertaining to exploitation and oppression within the workplace, on the shop floor. Left to their own logic and devices, neither economic nor administrative systems are hospitable to learning new ways of seeing and being. Economic and political complacency must be ruptured; new forms of learning must break through into public space. The risks of genetic engineering, ecological threats, global warming, feminism's plethora of themes, the rights of gays, lesbians, and transsexuals, skyrocketing impoverishment of the Third World, radical inequality between rich and poor, indigenous peoples' movements, the HIV/AIDS epidemic in Africa—these issues (and many more) swirl out of learning conversations of radical intellectuals, ordinary suffering citizens, and citizen advocates and organizations. When these learning conversations crystallize into publicly persuasive formulations, these demands can migrate into the system realms for attention and action. Thus, there must be fluid learning gateways constructed between civil society, the economy, and the state. When the state clamps down on these freewheeling conversations and demands articulation, citizens are forced into various forms of dramatic public learning: protesting and occupation initiatives. Until recently, in the Middle East (and elsewhere) the very idea of a gateway from civil society to the state decision-makers was unimaginable. In the liberal democracies, all now ruled by neo-liberal governing parties; the idea of the gateway is imaginable, but increasingly blocked.

Several axioms pertinent to adult education theory and practice emerge through our engagement with the discourse (and practices) within civil society. We have already suggested that, filtered through the learning lens, civil society can be revisioned as society's essential learning infrastructure. From here, we can then make the following four observations. First, it is within the realm of civil society that social capital is produced. Concepts like physical and human capital are well known, social capital less so. Social capital refers to the way the dynamics of associational life produce norms of reciprocity and trustworthiness. We form connections to benefit our own interests (networking or jobs). But social capital also affects the wide community—a well-connected community permits individuals to accrue benefits. Social capital is clearly both a "private good" and a "public good." Service clubs, for instance, produce friendships and business connections while mobilizing resources to fight disease. Social capital is vital to the learning climate of the civil infrastructure. If relations of trust and reciprocity are damaged or only thinly present, persons will not be open to each other. Indeed, they may look out for number one and exclude any willingness to walk down a conversational road.

Second, the scope and vitality of a society's associational life is a prerequisite for building a deliberative democracy. We learn to be citizens not be participating in politics first, but in the "free spaces" of school, church, 4-H club, and YWCA. Associations carry considerable potential to create opportunities for people to learn to respect and trust others, fulfill social obligations, and how to press one's claims communicatively. Tyrannical and oppressive states understand the potential of civil society associations and informal chats in coffee shops. They will inevitably move to create elaborate surveillance mechanisms to spy on citizens and prevent learning from crystallizing into outright opposition. Canadian adult educators (in various stripe, colour, and name) have been acutely aware that citizens needed to have associational and institutional opportunities to deliberate with one another across time and space. The study group and citizens' conference are an enduring illustration of Canadian commitment to the vitality of civil society as a means to creating democracy and fulfilling human needs (of all kinds). Early in our past, tribal wilderness learning cultures of native peoples (Iroquois and Huron) had these listening spaces built into their tribal procedures. The contemporary public sphere emerged gradually out of eighteenth century enlightenment struggles to create conversational space between the grand state and the market activities in western societies. It is a core conceptual category for the discipline of adult education's struggle to renew itself in the 1980s and 1990s; it most surely is a coveted concept for our work for the future.

Third, the new social movements are an integral, if disruptive, part of the civil society learning infrastructure of our day. They are social revolutionary learning sites (Welton, 1993); the discovery of the new social movement as learning site is one of the discipline of adult education's most luminous discoveries (Finger, 1989; Spencer, 1995; Holford, 1995; Hall, 2006). It permitted us to look back into our history and discover previous hidden secrets about how Canadian men and women actually did acquire knowledge, skill, attitudes, and dispositions to survive and build lives of meaning and beauty. New social movements (to distinguish them from the older movements of the working class and socialist parties) are not perfect places; they are flawed, human, and contentious; they are not trying to transform the entire society. The new social movement's tasks are to produce a broad shift in public opinion; to alter the parameters of organized will-formation, and to exert pressure on parliaments, courts, and administrations in favour of specific policies. Movements educate themselves (through a variety of pedagogical forms) and they educate the public. The women's awakening and creation of numerous associations from the late nineteenth century to the present speaks profoundly of the dialectic of inward-turned learning processes and the outward-turned variety of pedagogical forms selected to educate the public. Clearly, a key factor in all new social movement action is the pedagogical attempt to gain attention to themes and issues of significant importance that the state administrative and parliamentary system neglect. The struggle for recognition in our contemporary period of gays, lesbians, and transsexuals speaks out of great pain, humiliation, and suffering to a society that had turned its head away and gazed downward. It also has links with the all struggles for recognition—an elemental form of learning—in our history from the Natives Cartier first met (recall that he thought they were inferior and strange) to the Muslims and Sikhs that now populate previous Anglo-Saxon, Christian space (cultural and geographical) in Canada.

Movements may also act defensively to maintain the existing structure of associations and public influence. Certainly there are social movements—like religious fundamentalism—that occupy the terrain of civil society and compete to undermine other's conceptions of the good life or vital democracy. And we know that, after 9/11, new and bitter forms of intolerance have appeared in Europe and throughout the world. Churches burned and bombed; the Qur'an burned; head-scarves of Muslim girls banned for school wear; special surveillance of Muslims; virulent intellectual attacks on Christianity: the unacceptable other keeps appearing in human history. Here, the state's role is to ensure that rules of tolerance and respect for the other's viewpoint are adhered to (Maclure and Taylor, 2011) and religious practices "reasonably accommodated" (Bouchard and Taylor, 2008). In contrast to fundamentalist movements, the new social movements (such as the women's, peace, ecology, human rights movements) are salient learning spaces within modern societies. They have placed fundamental themes on society's learning agenda (from schools to post-secondary seminars, from the streets to government decision-makers): the degradation of the ecological substructure; the militarization of our minds and society; the rendering inferior of one class, religion, race, gender over another, and the urgent need to learn how to speak out of difference to each other; and the unceasing demands for recognition from every corner of society.

The fourth general affirmation about the new direction for adult learning research indicates that the creation and maintenance of exuberant public spheres is central to civil societarian adult education. Certainly, the new social movements often serve as public spaces creating learning opportunities (through forums, innovative actions such as occupying city spaces, etc.). But in post-modern societies, the public sphere is substantively differentiated. Following Habermas (1996, 2006) we can talk of popular science and literary publics, religious and artistic publics, feminist and "alternative" publics, and specialized publics concerned with health-care issues, social welfare, or environmental policy. We can also differentiate publics in terms of the density of communication, organizational complexity and the special range. The media—the complex of information-processors and image creators—play an enormously powerful role in influencing how we see and act with each other in the world. To be sure, most adult educators insist that the mass media be committed normatively to creating an enlightened public who are perceived to have a capacity to learn and to be criticized.

However, globalization brings both an avalanche of information and the transformation of corporate-dominated media into instruments for powerful, special interests. Critical adult educators have the task, where appropriate, of guiding students and sister-learners to alternative learning sites. Al Jazeera news is only one example of a powerful "alternative" to Fox News; it played an essential role in the Arab Spring uprisings that shocked the world in January 2011. The Internet continues to offer endless blogs and websites teeming with information. This has created often exciting new forms of self-directed learning and study. However, the question of whether the Internet actually creates publics is a debatable proposition. Millions of sites—Wikipedia is a prime example—present themselves usually without any sense of authority. Why should I accept this view? With traditional publics—say the literary public sphere—writers who know their sources and material—crystallize considered viewpoints for debate and discussion. The debate has some chance of going somewhere, of arriving at consensus with good reason. This is not the case at all with the Internet. But the newest form of media—the social media—has taken the world by storm in the last five years. Facebook, YouTube, and Twitter have connected millions of people in the whole world in remarkable (and disturbing) ways.

In fact, many social movement activists, particularly among the youth, make startling claims that the social media was the prime cause of the Arab Uprising and Occupy Movement. They did enable organizers to mobilize people and act strategically on the ground in the midst of confrontation. Cellphone videos of mayhem, violence, and death in the streets of Cairo or Damascus certainly fuelled awareness. Still, the social media in themselves do not create necessary face-to-face forms of solidarity in the society. Communities require physical proximity, shared concerns, and common responsibilities. The social media do not necessarily create coherent thinking, either. That comes from patient and careful work with texts with knowledgeable others who desire to reach consensus on how one translates the desire for dignity, respect, and voice into the practical realities of a state-dominated media and a society still ruled by the military. The discourse on civil society and the public sphere in the contemporary social sciences and humanities is richly suggestive for adult learning theorists and practicing adult educators who are designing pedagogical strategies for a just and honest learning society (Dean, 2003).

Pioneers of the Learning Age

Today, the notion of the "learning society"—and its cognates, the "learning organization," and the "learning city"—has made its way into corporate boardrooms and the policy dens of governing elites. We have become increasingly self-conscious that we are some sort of learning society; that a learning organization is a hopeful kind of enterprise, that something good might happen if we think of our cities as learning cities. What is it that our troubled global society is trying to name, to discover, to accomplish? Is the learning age rhetoric just one more desperate gasp at breathing life and hope into our world of terrorism, financial meltdown, global pandemics, celebrities, and mayhem? Some skeptics and cynics might think so. But I think differently. Humankind's consciousness has advanced to the point where we now recognize the centrality of learning processes and pedagogical procedures in all domains of existence. This acute learning sensibility represents a significant shift in education discourse in the last fifty years. When adult education was trying to carve out a space in the academy it did so by imagining that it could conceptualize "adult education" as the activity of professionally prepared adult educators. They called it "andragogy" to differentiate the fledgling discipline from pedagogy.

This attempt to draw a circle around a thing called "adult education" fell apart in the late twentieth century. It disintegrated because things were moving so fast, things were so fluid and speedy, that our inherited scripts could no longer guide us through the night and rough seas. Zygmunt Bauman (2000) and Ulrich Beck (1992) speak of our time as an age of insecurity and risk. This naming of the world may, however, obscure the fact that, since the industrial revolution in the mid-eighteenth century (launching the "Age of Improvement"), the transformational trajectory of industrial learning societies has been constant and unsettling change with times of some stability nestled uneasily between great thresholds of transformation. Capitalism has moved inexorably from its early crude factory phase in the mid-to-late eighteenth and early nineteenth century to the golden age of the welfare state in Europe and North America. From 1973 until the present, the global capitalist system has pushed beyond previous boundaries into something startlingly new. With the arrival of the new forms of electronic communication, globalization was able to transact its business at dizzying new speeds. Essentially, life *is* busier and faster-paced. Our historical study has shown that new ways of producing goods and knowledge feed new problems (or learning challenges) into the lifeworld of citizens. Today, we have become conscious of ourselves as persons who were constantly adapting to new learning challenges—in our bodies, minds, and spirits, at work, in civil society's many domains, in cultural expression and play. The absence of solidity and permanence stripped us down to a core or elemental understanding that learning was our most precious resource, symbolizing hope that if we can only find the right pedagogical procedures and suitable organizational modalities, we would be able to confront the many problems before us in our ever-shrinking world. We can learn our way out. We are not without hope.

Economic globalization in our neo-liberal era has fundamentally transformed the way the work of producing goods and services gets done. Everything is made in China these days; manufacturing in Canada is not what it used to be (GM in Oshawa has dropped from 40,000 jobs in the 1990s to 8,000 in 2012). Post–World War II forms of permanent employment (based on tradition and customs) assumed that employers would pay a decent family wage, pay benefits, and provide paid sick leave and a pension. Employers provided training, fostered work-life balance, and social activities. Strong socially oriented unions provided two different forms of workers' education: to raise consciousness and equip workers with needed knowledge and skills to participate in the work place. But this "standard employment relationship" has been abandoned in more and more work places in Canada. Neo-liberal norms and values (privatization over the public good and de-regulation over planning) have shredded those sustaining this classic form of permanent employment. Now, a large (and growing) number of Canadian workers work in precarious forms of labour. Less permanent forms of work are "growing faster than overall employment" (Lewchuk, Clarke, and de Wolff, 2011, p. 3).

One quarter of all Canadians work in precarious forms of employment. Workers now simply expect to find short-term employment that is insecure and without benefits. The absence of solidarity (or social capital) in the contemporary work place is astounding. Employers make few commitments; they pay only salaries. Precarious work is usually temporary without benefits. Even those claiming to be self-employed usually work without benefits and for low wages. Precarious employment impacts negatively on worker personal health and that of their households. It also cripples the motivation to participate in the community. Lewchuk, Clarke, and de Wolff's (2011) study, *Working Without Commitments: The Health Effects of Precarious Employment* is an important study for adult learning theorists. Our theoretical affirmation that work is a curricular structure in itself (Welton, 1991) and our normative assertion that we advocate the creation of just learning organizations (Welton, 2005) is under serious assault in these neo-liberal times. In fact, a blanket of silence has fallen over the workplace. Work and learning is a troubled domain (Spencer, 2010)

In *In the Age of the Smart Machine*, Shoshana Zuboff (1988) argues that the new world of "information technology"—computer-mediated work—"brings about radical change as it alters the intrinsic character of work—the way millions of people experience daily life on the job" (p. 11). She postulates that the informating capacity of the new technologies (not only do they automate, they render visible the production process itself) has undermined the "historical role of the body in both industrial and white-collar work and depicts the emerging demand for intellective skills, that frequently supplant the body as a primary source of know-how" (p. 16). This material and symbolic transformation within the domain of production sends strong signals that the "knowledge society" as an alternative social imaginary has been hatched inside the very space that, earlier in its history, had tried to block the developmental potential of the workplace for most human beings forced to work for wages. Zuboff's provocative idea challenges adult learning theorists to search for ways that technological developments disclose possibility for more cognitively complex (and satisfying) work. However, the big picture in the global economy, it appears, is that of only a small segment of the world's work using intellective knowledge and skills (and being rewarded handsomely). In fact, one might argue that Harry Braverman's (1974) influential argument in *Labor and Monopoly Capital: The Degradation of Work in the Twentieth Century* that capitalist work design dissolved the unity of thought and action, conception and execution, hand and mind embodied in pre-industrial craft (in New France, for instance) is true for most workers of the world. Does Zuboff's insistence that capitalism's latest transition to a knowledge-based cyberspace mode of production carry the potential to subvert the old Taylorist logic? I have my doubts.

Learning which is lifelong, lifewide, and just, has many forces aligned against its realization. Powerful people and organizations in our world (in economic, political, and cultural systems) skew learning processes and substance in particular directions. Corporate leaders can use the learning organization rhetoric to mobilize learning resources to learn how to dominate marketplaces, and not how to create well-being in their own organizations. The lovely language of empowerment may mask practices that do the opposite. Governments scheme and connive to maintain their power. They choose not to mobilize energy to create the suitable forms for participatory democracy, even when they have the technological capacities to make new ways of learning citizenship possible. The mainstream media fosters an in your face, win at all cost, anti-intellectual culture of cruelty. It also is evident that our scientific and technological acumen is not matched by our moral and ethical advancements. Our knowledge does not always translate into wisdom. One British film-maker has even suggested that when future citizens look back at our time they will all call it "The Age of Stupid" (Armstrong, 2008). Thus, the complacent idea that we have been propelled into a shiny, new, bright learning society and that "it's all good" must be challenged. In our time human learning in the service of the Money-code has captured the lion's share of human motivational resources, intelligence, and energy. But our adult learning traditions suggest that Canadian men and women will not permit elites to determine their fate or receive mere crumbs from the tables of the best-off. They desire to live in a society that distributes knowledge equitably. They insist that their voices be heard in the great debates of the day. They will create the pedagogical forms to enact these goals.

The beautiful dreams of the Learning Age promise us many great and wondrous things. Techno-utopians insist that the "computer revolution" will guarantee a perpetually dynamic economy, creating unimagined wealth for many and making life better for just about everyone. This dream has crashed in 2012. Street demonstrations everywhere in the world rage against the neo-liberal program of austerity and high unemployment (Spain, to give one European example, has a 25% unemployment rate) imposed on people without any form of democratic deliberation. In the hands of the information society ideologues, the market has been transformed into the arbiter of democracy, a kind of "market populism" that eliminates the need for political deliberation of the citizenry. The market gives the people what they want, and Bill Gates becomes a man of the people. Like father of old, the market knows best. Information society ideologues also promised vastly streamlined access to information essential to one's well-being. Ordinary citizens can get expert advice about their health from a website. They can do their banking without waiting in line for a teller. They can purchase goods through the Net. Choices appear to be endlessly widening: information technology is offered as the great social equalizer. Every domain of human interaction and learning is under fantastic pressure on get on board the train travelling down the information highway. We are told in no uncertain terms that there is only set of tracks; they lead to cyberspace and they all worship at the market's altar, all others lead down dead ends. Citizens are told that computer-mediated "town meetings" can replace the old-fashioned face-to-face meetings initiated by adult educators of by-gone days. No matter that scarcely anyone has ever participated in such a computer-mediated deliberation (though cyber-democracy does contain significant potential to enhance deliberative processes). Consumers are encouraged to sit at home, avoid Main Street, twitter and tweet on Facebook, purchase on the Net, enjoy life, and leave governing to the elites seemingly barricaded behind parliamentary walls. But now citizens are no longer sitting at home. They are out in the streets demanding to be heard. They are even banging pots and pans in the Quebec demonstrations of 2012 against increased tuition for students, widespread corruption, limited work opportunities, and an exhausted Liberal government.

The age of information is not "good news for postmodern man." Being deluged by information does not mean we are more knowledgeable and wise. The United States invaded Iraq, and a National Geographic Education Foundation (2006) study revealed that 63% of American youth could not locate Iraq on a map! Many theorists of our postmodern time of discontent have pointed out that we live more and more in virtual, simulated worlds that seduce us with endless entertainment and propaganda for commodities. Sherry Turkle, author of *Alone Together: Why We Expect More from Technology and Less from Each Other* (2011) and expert on robotics and social networking, says that we now live in a "culture of distraction." Paradoxically, the more we connect, the less we converse, and the more we connect, the lonelier we are. Turkle thinks that "something important" has been lost when Twitter or Facebook connections are substituted for conversation that shows "we're alive to each other, empathetic with each other, listening to each other" (Nolan, 2012, p. 56). She also thinks that in the "cascade of communication"—some young people send 10,000 text messages a month—we lose our "capacity for solitude, the kind that refreshes and restores. The kind that allows us to reach out to another person" (Nolan, 2012, p. 56).

Pedagogical Advice for Perilous Times

We have to be courageous pioneers of the new learning age. If we are going to be able to enable our students to acquire the knowledge, skill, sensibility, and attitudes to hold their heads high and speak with clear voices in our confusing and anguished world of too much information and too little wisdom, we have to be courageous pioneers of the new learning age. Our early pioneers were nimbly resourceful—travelling down muddy roadways in isolated, rural countryside—to carry knowledge to the people. In our time, we are deluged with information at the click of a key. Knowledge for our pioneers was power—to exercise mastery over their life situations. This challenge confronts us all; but let me offer some insights on the specific problems university students face in the information age—if they are to achieve critical consciousness.

First, our world on speed encourages us to surf, skip lightly, bounce distractedly, and lose concentration. Winifred Gallagher, in her recent book, *Rapt: Attention and the Focused Life* (2009), suggests that we may be experiencing a new moral panic. Professors report that their students are often tired, insanely busy, distracted, and unfocused. "Paying attention"—the mind's cognitive currency—is a diminishing resource. Students seem rushed, almost breathless sometimes, as they scamper to complete assignments. The ethos of surfing, inability to live with silence and constant battering by aggressive media (social and other) makes it difficult for students to concentrate, and to really dig into topics. Far too many students make assertions without evidence, accept conventional, media-imposed and politically correct narratives, and have little sense of what it means to sustain an argument. Few have acquired the composition skills of respectful dialogue with other writers. Few seem to want to probe deeply into a subject, to read and think widely, to arrive at the "best argument." Even fewer pay attention to the proper citation of sources.

Thus, our task as university educators is not just about making knowledge resources, packaged in lovely self-directed modules, accessible to men and women. We are inducting them into a "community of practice" that contradicts the frenetic worlds of social and conventional media. University study ought to slow us all down and teach us to concentrate.

Students should be nurtured to read widely and slowly, to never settle for any easy answers. We ought to build a "culture of critical discourse." a phrase used by the late maverick sociologist, Alvin Gouldner (1979). The university as a "community of practice" ought to counterpoint the restless, monkey mind that is fermented by our information age. We need to figure out how to encourage our students to focus their minds for extended periods of time. This means switching off other inputs; it means being absorbed in our work of discovery and articulation.

Second, in an age of info glut and instant information, we educators must help our students to not only slow down, but also acquire the interpretive frameworks for making sense of the world. They need to learn the skill of discernment, how to assess the authority of the countless sources presented to us. A quick glance at a Wikipedia entry on Locke's philosophy just won't do. Universities can be islands of clear, rigorous, deep thinking in a glossy sea of information and propaganda. But we will have to teach courageously for this to happen. The art of discernment, I believe, is intimately linked to understanding the reasons why we think the way we do and how we justify our actions in the world. These culturally formed knowledge and deliberative skills then feed into the civil society domains enabling respectful dialogue to occur. In his recent polemical book, *Empire of Illusion: The End of Literacy and the Triumph of the Spectacle* (2009), Chris Hedges stated bluntly, "To train someone to manage an account for Goldman Sachs is to educate him or her in a skill. To train them to debate stoic, existential, theological and humanist ways of grappling with reality is to educate them in values and morals. A culture that does not grasp the vital interplay between morality and power, which mistakes management techniques for wisdom, not its speed or ability to consume, condemns itself to death" (p. 103). Antonio Gramsci (1916), the Italian revolutionary who rotted to death in Mussolini's prison, believed that the educational system ought not "to become incubators of little monsters, aridly trained for a job, with no general ideas, no general culture, no intellectual stimulation, but only an infallible eye and a firm hand" (n.p.). Gramsci and Hedges underscore the fact that learning must be directed by a strong moral and ethical framework. We must know why we are doing what we are doing. We cannot become, as Richard Hoggart said, "blinkered ponies" (as cited in Hedges, 2009, p. 105).

Third, the profound realization that "all of society is a vast school" (Gramsci, 1971) as Gramsci once said, enables the small band of adult educators in universities to bear prophetic witness for all citizens to become aware of the nature of the learning that is occurring in their workplaces, civil society domains, and public spheres. The intellectual breakthroughs accomplished by critical learning theorists have made it possible to see how societies actually work as learning societies. This means, for one thing, that adult education visionaries can enable people who are actually teaching other adults to become aware that they are actually doing so. For another, this means that we must bear testimony to the way learning is structured and organized to either block or open up possibilities for human cognitive, moral, ethical, and spiritual development in the interest of well-being for all creatures. Our task, then, is to play the role of midwife; to make the ambiguous (and often exploitative) learning society aware of itself as a learning society in the first place, and then to press it beyond its present form toward a just learning society. This, it seems to me, is to reimagine the role of the adult educator in the twenty-first century that keeps faith with our emancipatory traditions, fought so hard for by hundreds and hundreds of McNaughton's and Coadys. What a journey this will be!

References

Armstrong, F. (Director). (2008). *The age of stupid.* [Motion picture]. United Kingdom: Spanner Films.

Baker, M., Waugh, T. & Winton, E. (2010). Introduction: Forty years later…a space for Challenge for change/Société nouvelle. In T. Waugh, M. Baker & E. Winton (Eds). *Challenge for change: Activist documentary at the National Film Board of Canada* (pp. 3–14). Montreal/Kingston: McGill-Queen's University Press.

Bauman, Z. (2000). *Liquid modernity.* Cambridge: Polity Press.

Beck, U. (1992). *Risk society: Towards a new modernity.* London: Sage Publications.

Black, E. & Chernomas, R. (1996) What kind of capitalism? The revival of class struggle in Canada. *Monthly Review,* 48(1), 23.

Boshier, R. (Ed.). (1980). *Toward a learning society.* Vancouver: Learning Press.

Bourdieu, P. (1998). *Acts of resistance: against the tyranny of the market.* New York: The New Press.

Boyle, G. (1953). *Father Tompkins of Nova Scotia.* New York: P.J. Kenedy and Sons.

Bouchard G. & C. Taylor. (2008). *Building the future: A time for reconciliation.* Final report of the Consultation Commission on Accommodation Practices related to cultural differences. Quebec: CCPARDC.

Briton, D. & Plumb, D. (1993a). Recommodification of adult education. Proceedings of the Adult Education Research Conference. University Park (PA): Pennsylvania State University.

Briton, D. & Plumb, D. (1993b). Remapping adult education: Posthegemonic possibilities. Proceedings of the 12th Annual Conference of the Canadians Association for the Study of Adult Education. Ottawa (ON): University of Ottawa.

Chambers, S. (2002). A critical theory of civil society. In S. Chambers & W. Kymlicka (Eds.). *Alternative conceptions of civil society.* Princeton: Princeton University Press.

Collins, M. (1991). *Adult education as vocation: A critical role for the adult educator.* London: Routledge.

Damer, E. (2000a). *The study of adult education at UBC, 1957–85.* Unpublished Ph.D dissertation, UBC.

Damer, E. (2000b). The rise and fall of a science of adult education at the University of British Columbia, 1957–85. *Historical Studies in Education* 12(1-2), 29–53.

Dean, J. (2003). Why the net is not a public sphere. *Constellations.* 10(1), 95–112.

Draper, J. (1971). (Ed.). *Citizen participation—A book of readings.* Toronto: New Press.

Ehrlich, P. (1968). *The population bomb.* New York: Ballantine Books.

Fay, B. (1975). *Social theory and political practice.* London: Allen and Unwin.

Finger, M. (1989). New social movements and their implications. *Adult Education Quarterly,* 40(1), 15–22.

Fitzpatrick, A. (1923). *The university in overalls.* Toronto: Frontier College Press.

Freire, P. (1972). *Pedagogy of the oppressed.* New York: Herder and Herder.

Gagné, R. (1977). *Conditions of learning.* New York: Holt, Rinehart and Winston.

Gagné, R. (1979). *Principles of instructional design.* New York: Holt, Rinehart and Winston.

Gallagher, W. (2009). *Rapt: Attention and the focused life.* New York: Penguin Press.

Gidney, R. D. and Millar, P. J. (1994). *Professional gentlemen: The professions in nineteenth-century Ontario.* Toronto: University of Toronto Press.

Gouldner, A. W. (1979). *The future of intellectuals and the rise of the new class.* New York: Seabury Press.

Gramsci, A. (1916). Unsigned, Piedmont Edition of *Avanti!*, 24 December, under the banner "Socialists and Education."

Gramsci, A. (1971). *The prison notebooks.* New York: International Publications.

Griffith, W. G. (1972). Paulo Freire: Utopian perspectives on literacy education for revolution. In S. Grabowski. (Ed.). *Paulo Freire: A revolutionary dilemma for adult educators.* Syracuse: Syracuse University Publications in Continuing Education.

Gywn, S. (1972). Film, videotape and social change: a report on the seminar organized by the Extension Service. March 13-14, St. John's, Newfoundland: MUN Extension Service.

Habermas, J. (1996). *Between facts and norms.* Cambridge, Ma.: MIT Press.

Habermas, J. (2006). Political communication in media society: Does democracy still enjoy an epistemic dimension? The impact of normative theory on empirical research. *Communication Theory,* 16.

Hall, B. (1974). Participatory research: Breaking the monopoly of knowledge. In John Niemi. (Ed.). *Viewpoints on adult education research.* Columbus (OH): ERIC Clearing House.

Hall, B. (2006). Social movement learning: Theorizing a Canadian tradition. In T. Fenwick, T. Nesbit & B. Spencer. (Eds.). *Contexts of adult learning: Canadian perspectives.* Toronto: Thompson Educational Publishing.

Hall, B. (2012, May 20). Correspondence with M. Welton.

Hart, M. (1985). Thematization of power, the search for common inerests, and self-reflection: towards a comprehensive conception of emancipation. *International Journal of Lifelong Education,* 4(2), 119–34.

Hart, M. (1990a). Critical theory and beyond: Further perspectives on emancipatory education. *Adult Education Quarterly,* 40(3), 125–38.

Hart, M. (1990b). Liberation through consciousness raising. In J. Mezirow. (Ed). *Fostering critical reflection in adulthood.* San Francisco: Jossey-Bass.

Hedges, C. (2009). *Empire of illusion: the end of literacy and the triumph of spectacle.* New York: Nation Books.

Holford, J. (1995). Why social movements matter: adult education theory, cognitive praxis and the creation of knowledge. *Adult Education Quarterly,* 45(2), 95–111.

Huntington, S. (1968). *Political order in changing societies.* New Haven: Yale University Press.

Jarvis, P. & Peters, J. (1991). *Adult education: evolution and achievements in a developing field.* San Francisco: Jossey-Bass.

Kidd, J. R. & Selman, G. (1978). (Eds.). *Coming of age: Canadian adult education in the 1960s.* Toronto: CAAE.

Knowles, M. (1957). Malcolm Knowles Papers, box 18, October. Syracuse: Syracuse University Archives.

Laidlaw, A. (1970). Return of a native. Alexander Laidlaw Papers, vol. 10, file 62, Public Archives of Canada.

Larson, M. S. (1977). *The rise of professionalism: a sociological analysis.* California: University of California Press.

Law, M. & Collard, S. (1989). The limits of perspective transformation: a critique of Mezirow's theory. *Adult Education Quarterly, 39,* 99–107.

Lewchuk, W., Clarke, M. & A. de Wolff (Eds.). (2011). *Working without commitments: The health effects of precarious employment.* Toronto: McGill-Queen's University Press.

Low, C. (1984). Grierson and Challenge for Change. In T. Waugh, M. Baker & E. Winton (Eds.). (2012). *Challenge for change: Activist documentary at the National Film Board of Canada.* Montreal/Kingston: McGill-Queen's University Press.

MacKenzie, S. (1996). Société nouvelle: The Challenge for change in the alternative public sphere. In T. Waugh, B. Baker & E. Winton (Eds.). (2010). *Challenge for change: Activist documentary at the National Film Board of Canada.* Montreal/Kingston: McGill-Queen's University Press.

Maclure, J. & C. Taylor (2011). *Secularism and freedom of conscience.* Cambridge (MA): Harvard University Press

McBride, S. & Shields, J. (1993). *Dismantling a nation: Canada and the new world order.* Halifax (NS): Fernwood Publishers.

Meadows, D. et al. (1974). *The limits to growth: A report for the Club of Rome's project on the predicament of mankind.* New York: Universe Books.

Miles, A. (1996). *Integrative feminisms: Building global visions 1960s–1990s.* New York: Routledge.

National Geographic Education Foundation (2006). *National Geographic-Roper Public Affairs 2006 geographic literacy study.* Retrieved from http://www.nationalgeographic.com/roper2006pdf/FINALReport2006GeoLitsurvey.pdf

Nemtin, B. (1968). Report on Fogo Process (3 October). Fogo Island Production file. NFB Archives, Montreal.

Nolan, J. (2012). A conversation with Sherry Turkle. *The Hedgehog Review.* Spring.

Offe, C. (1985). New social movements: challenging the boundaries of institutional politics. *Social research, 52*(4), 817–68.

Palmer, B. (2009). *Canada's 1960s: The ironies of identity in a rebellious era.* Toronto: University of Toronto Press.

Selman, G. (1988). *Invisible giant: a history of adult education in BC.* Vancouver (BC): Centre for Continuing Education, the University of BC.

Selman, G. (1991). *Foundations of adult education in Canada.* Toronto: Thompson Educational Publishing.

Selman, G. (1995). *Adult education in Canada: Historical essays.* Toronto: Thompson Educational Publishing.

Spencer, B. (1995). Old and new social movements as learning sites: Greening labour unions and unionizing the greens. *Adult Education Quarterly, 46*(1), 31–42.

Spencer, B. (2010). Workers education. In C. Kasworm, A. Rose & J. Ross-Gordon (Eds.). *Handbook of adult and continuing education: 2010 edition.* Los Angeles: Sage Publishers.

Thomas, A. (1991). *Beyond education: A new perspective on society's management of learning.* San Francisco: Jossey-Bass.

Turkle, S. (2011). *Alone together: Why we expect more from technology and less from each other.* New York: Basic Books.

Tyler, R. (1949). *Basic principles of curriculum and instruction.* Chicago: University of Chicago Press.

Verner, C. (1964). Definitions of terms. In G. Jensen, A. A. Liveright and W. Hallenbeck (Eds.). *Adult education: Outline of an emerging field of study.* Washington DC: Adult Education Association.

Welton, M. (1991). *Toward development work: The workplace as a learning environment.* Geelong, Victoria: Deakin University Press.

Welton, M. (1993). Social revolutionary learning: The new social movements as learning sites. *Adult Education Quarterly,* 40 (3), Spring, 152–164.

Welton, M. (1995). (Ed.). *In defense of the lifeworld: Critical perspectives on adult learning.* Albany, NY: State University of New York Press.

Welton, M. (1997a). Civil society as theory and project: Adult education and the renewal of citizenship. In D. Wildemeersch, M. Finger & T. Jansen (Eds.). *Adult education and social responsibility: Reconciling the irreconcilable.* Peter Lang: Europaiser Verlag der Wissenshaften.

Welton, M. (1997b). In defence of civil society: Canadian adult education in neo-conservative times. In S. Walters (Ed.). *Globalization, adult education and training: Impacts and issues.* London and New York: Zed Books.

Welton, M. (1998). Educating for a deliberative democracy. In S. Scott, B. Spencer & A. Thomas (Eds.). *Learning for life: Canadian readings in adult education.* Toronto: Thompson Educational Publishing.

Welton, M. (2001). Navigating in the new world disorder: Global adult education faces the 21st century. *The Canadian Journal for the Study of Adult Education,* 15(1), 47–63.

Welton, M. (2003). "No escape from the hard things of the world": Learning the lessons of empire. *International Journal of Lifelong Education,* 22(6), 635–51.

Welton, M. (2005a). *Designing the just learning society: A critical inquiry.* Leicester: NIACE Publishers.

Welton, M. (2005b). Civil society. In L. English. (Ed.). *International encyclopedia of adult education.* New York: Palgrave Macmillan.

Welton, M. (2011a). Pioneers of the learning age. *Explorations in Adult Higher Education. Our Work Today.* SUNY State College of New York: Occasional Paper Series, Summer (1), 3–10.

Welton, M. (2011b). Falling into the company of adult educators: Travels with CASAE. *The Canadian Journal for the Study of Adult Education.* Vol. 23(2), 1–10.

Whitaker, R. & Hewitt, S. (2003). *Canada and the cold war.* Toronto: James Lorimer and Company.

White, J. (2006). Les filles du roy. In T. Waugh, M. Baker, & T. Winton (Eds.). (2010). *Challenge for change: Activist documentary at the National Film Board of Canada.* Montreal/Kingston: McGill-Queen's University Press.

Wiesener, P. (1992). Media for the people: The Canadian experiments with film and video in community development. In T. Waugh, M. Baker, & E. Winton (Eds.). (2010). *Challenge for change: Activist documentary at the National Film Board of Canada.* Montreal: McGill-Queen's University Press.

Williamson, T. (1988). *The Fogo Process.* St. John's, Newfoundland: Snowden Centre for Development Support Communications, Memorial University.

Zuboff, S. (1988). *In the age of the smart machine: The future of work and power.* New York: Basic Books.